DEC 21 2001

P9-DHK-687

WITHDRAWN

VERNON CAN READ!

VERNON CAN READ!

———— *a memoir*

Vernon E. Jordan, Jr.

WITH Annette Gordon-Reed

PublicAffairs
New York

Published in the United States by PublicAffairs™, a member of the Perseus Books Group.
All rights reserved.

Printed in the United States of America.

Library of Congress Cataloging-in-Publication Data
Jordan, Vernon E. (Vernon Eulion), 1935–
Vernon can read!: a memoir / by Vernon E. Jordan with Annette Gordon-Reed.
Includes index.
ISBN 1-891620-69-X
Jordan, Vernon E. (Vernon Eulion), 1935– 2. African Americans—Biography.
3. African American political activists—Biography. 4. African American lawyers—
Biography. 5. African American civil rights workers—Biography. 6. African Americans—
Civil rights—History—20th century. 7. Civil rights movements—United States—History—
20th century. 8. National Urban League—Biography. 9. Atlanta (Ga.)—Biography.
I. Gordon-Reed, Annette.
E185.97.J78 A3 2001
323.´092—dc21
[B]
2001041867

Book Design by Jane Raese

FIRST EDITION

10 9 8 7 6 5 4 3 2 1

TO THE MEMORY OF

MY MOTHER AND FATHER,

WHO TAUGHT ME SO MUCH

AND TO MY GRANDCHILDREN,

WHOM I HOPE WILL BE INSTRUCTED

AND INSPIRED BY THIS EFFORT

CONTENTS

INTRODUCTION

IN THE SUMMER OF 1955, at the end of my sophomore year in college, I worked as a chauffeur in my hometown of Atlanta, Georgia. It had not been my first choice of jobs. I was originally supposed to work as a salesman for the Continental Insurance Company, which had made me an offer during a campus interview at my school, DePauw University. When the interviewer said there was an opening for me in the company's Atlanta office, I jumped at the chance. It was the perfect arrangement for me. I would have a job in the place where I most wanted to be—at home in Atlanta. At the end of the term, brimming with the confidence of a young man with two years of college behind me, I packed my bags and headed south thinking everything was in place.

After a few days settling in with my family, I put on my best suit and headed downtown to the Fulton National Bank Building, where Continental had its offices. I went up to the receptionist's desk to present myself.

"My name is Vernon Jordan," I said. "I'm a student at DePauw University, and I'm here to begin my summer internship."

The receptionist seemed in need of a translator to help clarify what I had just said. She was, at that moment, like a machine whose gears had ground to a halt and was struggling to get restarted. When she finally realized she'd heard what she thought she'd heard, she called for the man in charge of summer workers. "You won't believe this," she told him, "but there's a colored boy out here who says he's a summer intern."

The supervisor, a tall fellow who looked to be in his mid-thirties, came out. I introduced myself.

"I'm Vernon Jordan. I was hired to be a summer intern in your office."

His reaction was not unlike the receptionist's. But he quickly composed himself and took me inside his office. An awkward moment passed before he said, "They didn't tell us."

"They didn't tell you what?" I asked, even though I suspected where he was heading.

"They didn't tell us you were colored," he replied. At that time in history, we had not yet become "black."

He went on. "You know, you can't work here. It's just impossible. You just can't."

Of course, segregation was still very much a fact of life in Georgia in the summer of 1955. I was well aware of that, and of the rules that were still propping up the system. But I had thought—hoped— during those months after my interview that I had somehow made my way around them. It was my policy then, and it remains the same today, never to expect defeat before making an honest effort. Also, by then I'd come to think of Jim Crow as a lame horse that was about to be put down. The feeling was in the air. And I wanted to do whatever I could to help speed the process along. But it wouldn't happen on that day at the Continental Insurance Company.

Although I was disappointed, I knew there was nothing to be done about the situation at that particular moment. As I got up to go, my never-to-be-supervisor, not wanting to leave things as they stood, said, "I'll tell you what I'll do. I'm going to call J. L. Wolfe Realty. We do business with them sometimes, and we can see if they can give you an office."

While Continental was willing to honor its commitment to hire me, under no circumstances could I sit in its offices as an employee. J. L. Wolfe Realty, a black-owned real estate and insurance business on Auburn Avenue—"Sweet Auburn," the heart of Atlanta's black business district—was the proposed solution.

The Continental representative called Wolfe Realty and explained the situation. The head of the company agreed to give me an office out of which I sold Continental's income-protection insurance policies to black businesses employing five or more people. On occasion, my white supervisor came down to my office to make calls.

It was absurd. As a black person, I could not sell the policies of a white company to black businesses while sitting in the white company's office. Yet my white supervisor could come in to the black business office and sell the white company's policies to black firms. This was a prime example of the craziness, the backwardness, the inefficiency of Southern life.

The job was also very boring. Although I managed to sell some individual policies (mainly to my mother's friends), I couldn't muster even a minimal interest in my work. My lack of enthusiasm certainly didn't help when it came time to sell policies to people who were not friends of the family.

When I could stand it no longer, my mother, who knew I was deeply unhappy, suggested an alternative. The summer was passing, and the opportunities for other office jobs had dwindled. I wanted to work. So why not, she asked, work the balance of the time using other skills I had? I was a good driver and, like many young men in the 1950s, I was in love with cars. My mother ran a catering business, which meant she had contacts within most, if not all, the prominent white households in Atlanta.

That is how I became a chauffeur for Robert F. Maddox.

Robert Maddox was one of the leading figures in Atlanta's white elite for most of the early part of the twentieth century. He was mayor of the city in 1910, and before that he had been active in the civic and social affairs of the town. A man of finance, he was the president of the First National Bank of Atlanta and president of the American Banking Association. Maddox's interests and influence were wide-ranging. He had a fabulous garden on his grounds and was, for a time, the president of the Garden Clubs of America.

In many ways Maddox was a symbol of the New South—open to

business and economic development and devoted to progress, as long as it was within certain boundaries. When Booker T. Washington gave his famous Atlanta Exposition address (sometimes called the Atlanta Compromise), Maddox had been among the dignitaries on the platform, listening while the "wizard of Tuskegee" assured whites that blacks would make no immediate press for social equality.

Maddox was very proud of having built the first very large home in Buckhead, one of Atlanta's most exclusive neighborhoods. When I encountered him, he was well into his eighties, a widower living alone in that spectacular house, attended by a small group of servants: Joe, the chauffeur and butler, whose place I took for the month of August, when he was away; Lizzie, the cook, a middle-aged woman who played the piano at the Mount Zion Baptist Church; and Troy, the yardman.

Every morning I picked up Lizzie and brought her to work. If needed, I would then press one of Maddox's Palm Beach suits as Lizzie fixed his breakfast. When she finished doing that, she would take the meal up to Maddox and then return to prepare my breakfast, which I ate in the butler's pantry. Lizzie also made breakfast for Troy. But Troy worked in the yard and, according to age-old protocol, was not allowed to eat inside the house. His meal was handed out to him by Lizzie, and he sat on the back porch of that huge Southern house and had his breakfast.

My routine varied little. Maddox, in his old age, was a creature of habit. He would come downstairs, get his hat, and select one of his many walking canes. We'd go out to the car, a four-door blue Cadillac. In a bid for independence, Maddox usually insisted upon opening the passenger door himself, although he could have used my help. I would drive him from the back of the house around to the front and stop near the rose garden. At that moment, Troy, cued by the idling of the car's engine, would appear from the garden with a single rose—sometimes red, sometimes white or yellow—for Maddox's lapel. Then our day's journey began.

At Maddox's insistence, we took the same route each day: down West Paces Ferry Road, right on Habersham, down to Peachtree Battle, left on Peachtree Street, and down to the First National Bank

Building, where Maddox kept an office. He would go up and stay sometimes ten minutes, sometimes two hours—I never knew what to expect. But I knew that whenever he finished, our next destination would be the Capital City Club, where Maddox, and sometimes a companion we might pick up along the way, went to have a drink and lunch. Then it was back home for Maddox's afternoon nap. So, by 1:30 at the latest, my duties as chauffeur were over. I had nothing to do until six o'clock, when I took on the mantle of butler and served dinner.

Maddox had a wonderful library that soon became a place of refuge for me during the dead hours of the afternoon. Shakespeare, Thoreau, Emerson—it had everything. What I read most eagerly, however, were the various books of speeches in his collection. There are few things I enjoy more than a good speech and good preaching. I've tried my hand at doing both. The experience of saying aloud what needs to be said in front of a group of willing listeners is intoxicating. The good speaker or preacher is apart from the audience but always with them in some fundamental way—rising when they rise, falling when they fall, directing them but being directed as well. When a speaker has a talent for doing this, there is nothing more exciting to watch. This is all better as live theater, but the power of a truly well-written speech can come through even when read silently.

One book in Maddox's library contained Booker T. Washington's Atlanta Exposition address. Maddox was deeply impressed with Washington, as the well-thumbed pages of that part of the book showed. Maddox had vigorously underlined one particular passage, to the point of damaging the page, where Washington had said of the races, "In all things purely social we can be as separate as the fingers yet one as the hand in all things essential to mutual progress." This was Maddox's credo, but, obviously, not mine. I was, after all, sitting in his private library.

I sat there day after day, drinking in the atmosphere of the place—the smell of the books, the feel of them, the easy chairs. The way of life that the library symbolized—the commitment to knowledge and the leisure to pursue it—struck a chord in me that still resonates. I wanted all this for myself and my family. This was what going to college was for, to become a part of a community that appreciated and had access to a place like this. I knew I belonged there.

Lizzie, on the other hand, did not think so. Whenever she saw me headed in the direction of my sanctuary, she would remind me that the place was off-limits to servants. Although I had never heard Maddox himself say so, it seemed likely that this was true. I was sure of one thing, however: This was not really any of Lizzie's business. And I would tell her gently, but firmly, to mind her own. She continued to bother me about it until I decided to play hardball.

Lizzie, it turned out, had her own little secret. She had an operation going on with the local grocer. He would overcharge Maddox, and Lizzie would look the other way in return for provisions—hams, turkeys, and the like—that she would take to Mount Zion for after-church dinners. I suppose she thought it was all somehow in service of the Lord. But I don't think even He would have been able to help her if Maddox's family had found out about this. After I casually suggested this to her, I heard no more carping about servants in the Maddox library.

One afternoon, as I sat reading, Maddox walked in on me. He had awakened early from his afternoon nap and had come down in his underwear, with a bottle of Southern Comfort in one hand and a glass in the other. He was clearly startled to see me there.

"What are you doing in the library, Vernon?"

"I'm reading, Mr. Maddox."

"Reading? I've never had a nigger work for me who could read," he said.

"Mr. Maddox, I can read. I go to college."

"You do what?" he asked.

"I go to college."

"You go to college over there at those colored schools?"

"No, sir. I go to DePauw University in Greencastle, Indiana."

He pondered this for a moment.

"White children go to that school."

"Yes, sir."

Then the inevitable.

"White *girls* go to that school."

"Yes, sir."

"What are you studying to be, a preacher or a teacher?"

"Actually, I'm going to be a lawyer, Mr. Maddox."

"Niggers aren't supposed to be lawyers."

"I'm going to be a lawyer, Mr. Maddox."

"Hmmm. Well, don't you know I have some place downstairs for you all to sit and do what you want to do?"

"I know. But I didn't think you'd want me to take these books down there. They should stay in the library."

He looked around and finally said, "Just read then—just go ahead." He turned and walked out. I thought the matter was closed. I soon found out it was not.

His children and their spouses came for dinner that evening, which was not uncommon. Ed Smith, married to Maddox's daughter, Laura, was the chairman of the First National Bank, and Maddox's son, Baxter, was its executive vice president. Maddox was at his customary place at the head of the table. As I moved among them serving soup in my white jacket and bow tie with a napkin draped over my arm, Maddox said, "I have an announcement to make."

"Yes, Papa?" one of his children said.

Silence.

"Vernon can read."

More silence. Maddox went on.

"And he's going to school with white children."

No one made a sound. Finally, and with a great deal of emotion, Maddox said, "I knew all this was coming. But I'm glad I won't be here when it does."

The truth is that his guests were all quite embarrassed by this display because they knew I could read. They knew I was a college student. Maddox's children had hired me, through my mother. My ability to read was not a detail they had thought to mention to him. Why should they have?

For my part, the whole business seemed so absurd that there was nothing to say. I served dinner, poured the water and wine, and left them to themselves. This was not the last of it.

The next day I drove Maddox and two of his friends to lunch. One was his frequent companion, Jim Dickey, another widower who lived across the street from him. The other, ironically, was James Robinson, whose grandson (also named James) in the 1980s was the chairman of the American Express Company where I was, and remain, on the board of directors. The three of them sat in the back talking about various things. I was lost in my own thoughts until Maddox's voice cut through my reverie.

"Jim?" he said to both of them.

"Yeah, Bob?" they responded.

"Vernon can read."

What did Maddox mean to accomplish with this? I knew that some of the people who worked for him could read. Indeed, as I think back on it, I'm sure at some level he knew, too. But it was necessary for him to act as if he did not know it—at least not in any way that could change the way he viewed the brown faces who busied themselves in his service. The simple fact was that he never thought about those who worked for him in any way that did not directly affect their duties to him. We were merely entities who drove him around town, cooked his meals, brought him his food, and kept his house and yard in order. Why think about whether reading and mathematics meant anything to us? (Although I think he should have paid more attention to Lizzie's use of math.) In the end, that part of our lives just did not matter.

When I have told this story to younger people, they often ask why I was not more angry at Maddox. How could I have continued working for him under those circumstances? While I was certainly annoyed by what was going on, I did not think then—and I do not think now—that it would have done any good to lash out at this elderly man for his aggressive backwardness. Each of us has to decide for ourselves how much nonsense we can take in life, and from whom we are willing to take it. It all depends, of course, on the situation and people involved.

I knew Maddox, or more precisely, I knew his type. I was aware of and had borne the brunt of the forces that helped shape him. He had lived his life as though Booker T. Washington's program for black-white relations in the South had been enacted. To me, Robert

Maddox was not an evil man. He was just an anachronism. And with the brashness of youth I mentally noted (and counted on) the fact that his time was up. I do not mean just his physical time on earth—but I believed that the "time" that helped shape him was on its way out. His half-mocking, half-serious comments about my education were the death rattle of his culture. When he saw that I was in the process of crafting a life for myself that would make me a man in some of the same ways he thought of being a man, he was deeply unnerved. That I was doing it with money gained from working in his household was probably even more unnerving. These things, however, were his problem. As far as I was concerned, I was executing a plan for my life and had no time to pause and re-educate him.

I kept reading in Maddox's library, but he never again announced to anyone that I could read. This story does not have a happy ending, with the old man coming to see the error of his ways and taking on the role of mentor to the young man; I would find mentors in other places. The character of our relationship, however, did change slightly, but perceptibly, after he was forced to focus on who I really was. He became much more inclined to speak to me at times other than when he wanted me to do something for him. As we drove around, he sometimes tossed out a comment about a current issue with the expectation that I might know something about it. At the very least we could have a conversation. That held true over the course of the next few years when I worked for him during the summers and on vacations from school.

The story is told, and I am not sure it is true, that in 1961, when I escorted Charlayne Hunter through the mobs at the University of Georgia to desegregate that institution, Maddox was watching the well-publicized event on television. By that time he was no longer living in the house (in 1963 he would sell the property to the state of Georgia, where the governor's mansion now stands), and he was living in a smaller place in Atlanta attended by a nurse.

The nurse recognized me and said, "Mr. Maddox, do you know who that colored lawyer is?"

"I don't believe I do."

"It's your chauffeur, Vernon."

Maddox looked hard at the screen and said, "I always knew that nigger was up to no good."

I FIRST THOUGHT SERIOUSLY OF WRITING a memoir in the 1970s. Though still a young man, so much had happened to me—I had come so far in life, and black people had come so far during my lifetime—that the moment seemed right to tell the story of this process as I had lived it and seen it. An incident in the winter of 1970 prompted my thinking along these lines. My daughter, Vickee, who was eleven years old at the time, was talking to our house-keeper, Mrs. Gaines. We were all new residents of Westchester County, New York, having moved there from our home in Atlanta when I became executive director of the United Negro College Fund.

Mrs. Gaines, who had been with us back in Atlanta, came along, and her presence was greatly appreciated and much needed because my wife, Shirley, had multiple sclerosis and was at the beginning of what would be a long, difficult, and valiant struggle. We were all very far from home and depended very much upon one another. In the evenings, after Mrs. Gaines had prepared dinner, we would all sit down together, eat, and go over the day's events or whatever else came to mind.

One evening, Mrs. Gaines told a story about taking the bus from Cuthbert, Georgia, to Gainesville, Florida during the era of segrega-tion—a trip that had taken her further south and into even more harsh racial terrain.

She got on the bus and took a seat in the middle section, sliding over to be near the window. Only one other passenger was on the bus, a white man sitting up front. Not long into the trip, another white man boarded the bus, walked over to where Mrs. Gaines was sitting, and said, "Get up and move further back. I want to sit here."

Vickee had been listening with great attention. She asked, "Well, what did you do?"

"I moved," Mrs. Gaines replied, as if it were the simplest thing in the world—no emotion, just in a totally matter-of-fact manner.

Vickee was indignant and certain. "I wouldn't have moved," she declared.

Mrs. Gaines leaned over, touched Vickee on the shoulder, and said, "Yes, Vickee. You would have moved."

That colloquy between the generations opened my eyes. I had been in the thick of the civil rights movement almost from the time of my daughter's birth, as a lawyer, organizer, and, now, as the head of an institution that symbolized black aspirations. Yet it was clear that my child knew nothing of the world in which I, her mother, and Mrs. Gaines had lived. This was at the height of the "black power" movement. The music Vickee listened to, the images she saw on television, all suggested that empowerment and the choice of rebellion were open to all. She could not comprehend the oppression, the enforced servility, the downright meanness of life for blacks in the Deep South.

The three adults sitting at that table knew what could have happened to Mrs. Gaines had she refused to move. The white man, or the bus driver himself, could easily have beaten her up, left her beside the road, and called the sheriff, and she would have been arrested for vagrancy. All for refusing to do something that she should never have been asked to do in the first place. We knew how that story could easily have played out. Vickee did not. A whole universe of understanding was missing.

I decided at that moment that someday, I would try to do my part to bridge the gap—to tell the story of those times from my perspective; to explain how we had gone from the days Mrs. Gaines knew to a time in which a young black girl could be so confident in her humanity that she found it unfathomable that anyone could try to take it away from her. This is, I believe, the most important American story of the second half of the twentieth century, and there are many ways to tell it. In my case, a simple fatherly impulse to explain to his daughter "how he grew" has given rise to this very personal take on the black experience since the end of the Second World War.

Although it has taken me much longer than I thought it would to get to it, I am very glad I didn't follow my impulse to write the memoirs of those times while I was still living them. Distance and age

have brought me a sense of perspective that now allows me to attempt a more substantive and illuminating depiction of that era. My
thoughts are clear.

That is why this book effectively ends in the 1980s, when I began
a chapter of my life that is still being written. All that has happened
to me since then is too close to be considered true memories. Perhaps
sometime in the future, when I have had the chance to bring the
meaning of my life out of the public arena into greater focus in my
own mind, I will revisit this business of writing memoirs.

But in the meantime, I choose to stick with what I know and believe fervently about the progress of black life during the decades of
which I write. I hope what follows will be instructive to readers today, and for anyone in the future who wants to know something of
what these times were like, as well as the events that took us away
from them.

CHAPTER 1

MY MOTHER'S SON

WHEN I THINK ABOUT THE EARLY PART OF MY LIFE and how it helped make me the man I have become, it is so clear to me how lucky I was to have been born and raised in a world of structures. There was the structure of my family, the structure of the St. Paul African Methodist Episcopal (AME) Church, the Gate City Day Nursery, my schools, the Butler Street Colored YMCA. But above all else, I had my family.

I know for certain that the world my parents created for me, as I grew up in Atlanta, Georgia, has made all the difference in my life. And when I say "created for me" (and I should include my brothers Warren and Windsor in this), I mean that literally. It was as if the world had been built for the three of us, and it was just our job to make the best of it.

The principal architect, general contractor, and bricklayer for the whole enterprise was my mother, Mary Belle Jordan, with strong assistance from my father, Vernon E. Jordan, Sr. Although my father was a constant and steady presence, there was no question who was in charge of my brothers and me. It was my mother's plan that mattered. Her strategy for getting her black sons through childhood in the segregated South grew out of her approach to life in general: Make the most of what you have at the moment, do the best you can when it counts, and hope and expect good outcomes from your efforts.

This sounds simple enough on its face. But like so many of the rules and guidelines we all try to apply as we go through life, my mother's approach was easier said than done. Think of our situation. We were in Georgia—unreconstructed, unrepentant Georgia. At the time of my birth on August 15, 1935, the state was seventy years (one biblical lifetime) away from the end of legalized slavery. That was just a blink of an eye in history's terms, and the fallout from that history was everywhere to be seen.

Although slavery was officially over, there was no way for those old times to be forgotten because they really had not gone too far away. Thousands of blacks, my grandparents among them, had been trapped in a system of debt peonage that was slavery in all but name, eking out a "living" on "Mr. So-and-So's" property. All that was missing was the auction block. Sometime after my mother moved to Atlanta, members of our family had to go in the dead of night and literally steal her sister, my aunt Jimmie Lee, from the home of the white man for whom she worked as a maid and cook. It was like being on the Underground Railroad, only it was the twentieth century. Jim Crow was operating at full throttle. Lynching was a part of life in the South. Most blacks could not vote. This was a hard time to be a dreamer.

And yet here was my mother. A black woman—unlettered, unlearned, but with a Ph.D. in life—who had come out of the Georgia countryside into the big city to make a better place for herself. It was a breathtaking act of courage for her to dream and to expect that her sons would find their way in a world that had not, despite what she may have felt about it, really been built for them.

Although she sometimes called me "Junior" or "Vernon Junior," my mother's main nickname for me was "Man." She started calling me that when I was still a little boy. While away at camp or later in college and law school, she sent me letters with the salutation "Dear Man." This was her positive way to counteract what she knew would be the outside world's—the white world's—view of me even after I had officially passed into manhood.

So from the very beginning, I felt the tug of my mother's hope. It could not have been missed. I moved forward, propelled by her deep ambition and love for me—two things I never had a moment's doubt about and that moved me to accept her guidance and to want to vindicate her faith in me. It is an almost irresistible challenge when you have someone who thinks you are special and who works to see to it that you get the chance to shine. A bargain is struck, sometimes silent, sometimes spoken: their faith and commitment for your effort and success. If success is at all possible, you do not want to fail. You do everything you can to not fail. If there are times when things don't work out as you plan (and that often happens), a hard and honest effort fulfills the bargain. No matter what, you never break faith with those who support you.

This is not to say that I did not have a will of my own, or my own preferences. It just happened (nature or nurture?) that my mother and I were of the same mind on the main point: that I was to go as far as I could as quickly as I could. All children rebel at some points, but for the most part, I believed my mother was right. If she had a plan for my advancement, then I was all for it. I was so confident in my knowledge that she wanted what was best for me that I followed her instructions about the important things in life. Until she died, I never made a major decision without consulting her. Sometimes, I didn't even get the chance to consult.

"Vernon, Jr., now wherever you go to college, you're going to join the ROTC."

"I don't want to be in the ROTC."

"It doesn't matter. Wherever you go to college, you're going to join the ROTC."

"Mama, what do you know about the ROTC?"

"I don't know anything about the ROTC."

"Well then, why are you so insistent that I should join it?"

"All I can tell you is that all the white women I work for are sending their boys to the ROTC. There must be something to it."

There must be something to it. That was how my mother thought about things. She hadn't figured out exactly why the ROTC was so important to the white women. I don't believe she knew it was the upper class's method of keeping their young men out of harm's way as they performed their military service. But considering how things were between whites and blacks, the details didn't matter much. It was a simple, straightforward calculation. Whether you were talking about the ROTC, schools, medical care, political power—all the basics of life—white people were hoarding the best of the world and had frozen black people out. It just made good sense to pay attention to where whites were going and how they were using the enormous amount of resources and opportunities they had rounded up for themselves. Whatever was going on that could be good for us, Mama wanted us to be a part of it, and her contacts with the white world gave her an idea what to look for.

M Y MOTHER, BORN IN 1907, came to Atlanta in the 1920s from Talbot County to "live on the lot." When you lived on the lot, you worked as a servant for a family and lived above the garage, in the basement, or in some other house on their property. My mother had no extensive formal education. What she did have going for her was natural intelligence and an almost superhuman drive—and the fact that she was a very good cook. This combination would one day make her the owner of one of the best-known catering businesses in Atlanta. But in the beginning, she was just one of many black women and men who escaped the sharecropper's life to try to do better in the world. She used every scrap of what she had to try to do that.

The family she worked for had daughters who were about her age and just about her size. This turned out to be something of an advantage for Mama because they gave her clothes that didn't fit them any more or that they had grown tired of. So sometimes she was able to go to church in dresses she could never have afforded on her salary. She was one of the best-dressed ladies at St. Paul Church, wearing clothes that the white girls had tossed away. They called this "making do"—making the most of what you had. In my mother's case, making do in this way helped enhance her stature in the community. She was an usher at Sunday services, and the fact that she was always well turned out made a big difference.

This is an aspect of the black church that often gets overlooked. Although religious doctrine was important, the church played another critical role in the psychological lives of black people of my mother's time. It was the one sure place where they could go to achieve dignity and status. No matter what positions they held in the outside world, no matter that they were spurned and rejected by society at large, in the church blacks had the chance to be in charge, to manage affairs, to feel that they were a part of something. The yardman who lived with condescension and contempt six days a week could put on his Sunday clothes and be a deacon. The maid or cook, hostage most of the time to other people's whims or cruelty, could be an usher and tell people where to sit so that the program could proceed as planned.

I have a favorite photograph that tells the story. It shows several latecomers to church peering into the sanctuary through the small windowed portions of two swinging doors. The doors are shut tight because the service has started. The worshipers are anxious to get in. You can see it in their faces. You can also tell they are in their finest clothes, that they have put a lot into getting ready to go to church. They just didn't make it on time. At the immediate inside of the door stands an usher, this time a man. He knows how badly they want to get in. His face is impassive, yet his will is clear. They are going to have to wait. Church has started. There is serious business going on. Order must be upheld. On Sundays, America's second-class citizens had somewhere to go to get spiritual nourishment and to feel like whole human beings.

My father's story was much the same as my mother's. Born in 1908, he also come out of rural Georgia—Monticello, in Jasper County—one of seventeen children. I am convinced, although I have no proof, that our name, "Jordan," came from the white family who owned a large furniture store in the county. I presume that the Jordans owned one or more of my ancestors, since some slaves took the last names of their owners. But I have never had any real interest in all that.

What is more interesting to me is that my father, for whom I am named, was born Vernon Ulysses Jordan, but he grew to hate his middle name and changed it to Eulion. Where he got Eulion from I have no idea. With this small bit of self-refashioning, my father carved a unique space for himself. As far as I know, we may be the only Eulions in the entire world.

When my father met my mother, he was a chauffeur for a prominent white family. He went to church regularly. He even sang in the choir. That is where my parents met and got to know one another: in the church. My father had Thursdays off. He'd pick her up, and they would go out on the town. That's how it all got started between them. By this time, my mother had already gotten the idea that she wanted to become a caterer, and true to form, she decided to prepare herself by going to night school at Booker T. Washington High School, taking a class in home economics.

From the standpoint of that time, theirs was an interesting match—interesting in ways that would in the end prove to be too much for their marriage. Put simply, my mother was ahead of her time, and my father was a man of his time. By any measure, my mother would be recognized today as a feminist—though I am not so sure she would have been comfortable with all the associations that word currently calls to mind. If being a feminist means that you stand your own ground, work to achieve your goals, and do not see yourself as just an appendage to a man, my mother fit the bill ten times over.

Although she kept our house in order and cooked for us, it was clear that her life was outside the home. She was a businesswoman, not a housewife. That would be less of a problem today than it was during the time when my parents were married. Of course, black women have always worked outside the home. Enslaved women worked in the fields. After the end of slavery, black women worked out of economic necessity—and their husbands had to accept working wives. We generally have not had Ozzie and Harriet-type expectations of family life, since for most of us, that type of life was out of reach—even if we had wanted it.

Still, with all the adaptations that blacks had to make to our family situations, the expectation remained that the husband was the head of the household. It was "the man of the family" who was supposed to direct the course of family life. He was in charge.

That might work if the man was better suited to that role. It might have worked if the husband and wife were evenly matched in this regard, and the wife just decided to leave it to her husband so she could do other things. In our family's case, it would not have made any sense at all because my mother was more suited to being the prime mover. Her business skills shaped the way things operated. She was much better at planning than my father. She was better at handling money. She had the energy to pull it all together. And so my father, quite wisely I think, left it to her to do that.

He paid a price for this. His buddies taunted him. They would say, "Mrs. Jordan wears the pants in that family!" That kind of talk might seem harmless today, but in the 1940s and 1950s, this would hurt any man who had conventional ideas about the proper relationship between husband and wife. Whatever my father may have understood about the practicalities of the situation—my mother did have a flair for management—it could not have been easy for him. But what was he to do? Make her sit down?

I knew it bothered him. I knew because he would sometimes say so. The outside teasing just put the fine point on a conflict that was already deep inside him. He was happy about my mother's success. It benefited all of us. At the same time, there is no question that another part of him wanted a more traditional family, and a more "normal" wife. He saw things through until my younger brother Windsor and I were out of school, and then my parents divorced after twenty-eight years of marriage.

At the root of it all was the difference in my mother's and father's personalities. Where my mother was entrepreneurial and driven—always thinking about "how you get there" and always sure that there was in fact some place else to get to—my father was less of a risk taker and much more easily satisfied. My mother aspired to great things in life. I guess you could say my father just wanted the good things of life. He was a plain, honest, hardworking man who had his own code of discipline and order, and I loved and admired him very much. He taught me how to sign my name, and I've copied my signature after his. He kept the hedges trimmed, the car washed, his shoes shined. He could tell you at a moment's notice where everything he owned was, because for him, everything had a place. His steadiness was the perfect complement to my mother's charging determination.

When he went off to the navy in 1943, he made me and my brother real heroes in the neighborhood. Most of the other fathers were going into the army. My father was in the navy! He was a steward and, at times, an assistant to a gunner. When he came home on furlough, I was king of the mountain. I felt so proud and happy to walk down the street with him, to go to church with him, to be seen anywhere with him when he was wearing that uniform.

The truth is, any rituals that took us out of the house with my father meant the world to me. Every Sunday morning my mother would cook a big breakfast for the family. She would stay behind to clear away the dishes while my father walked me and Windsor to Sunday school. This happened no matter what: rain, sleet, shine. This is what the Jordans did.

My father belonged to the T. J. Chambliss Bible Study Group. While we went to our Sunday classes, he would be off in his group arguing about the correct interpretation of one or another passage in the Bible. They also spent a good deal of time arguing about politics and the situation blacks were in at the time, which my father was always more than ready to do. Our morning classes finished, Daddy would gather Windsor and me up and walk us to a nearby café to have a soda. By this time my mother would have gotten the house in order, and she would drive to the church to meet us for the eleven o'clock service.

After church, we usually brought someone home for dinner. Most often it was Sister Fannie Green, another refugee from rural Georgia who had come to the city to "live on the lot," in her case on Peachtree Street. After a big Sunday dinner, we sat around talking, and then my mother or father would drive Sister Green to her home on the other side of town. It is hard to imagine in this era of 200 television channels, computers, video games, and almost endless sporting events that driving Sister Fannie Green home could be a major form of recreation for two little boys, but it was. To top things off, Sister Green would give me and my brother fifty cents.

The routine of walking to Sunday school with my father, of sharing a soda with him and listening to him talk at the dinners with Sister Green or other members of our church, gave me a strong sense of security. I never had to wonder about what we were going to do, whether he would be there or not. With that issue settled, I could concentrate on being a kid, learning all the things I needed to learn in order to become an adult.

As for his hopes for me, my father would have been perfectly happy if I had just finished high school, gotten a job in the post office, bought myself a little white house with green shutters, gotten a car, married a nice girl, had two kids, kept my car washed, my grass trimmed, read the newspapers, voted in every election, attended Sunday school and church. He would have thought that was a very good life. And he was not wrong about that. That does describe a good life. But it was not good enough for my mother, and it was not good enough for me.

There was another aspect of my father's personality that influenced the way he went through the world and what he wanted for his sons. Although he was a smart man, he just did not have as much confidence in himself as my mother had in herself. As a matter of fact, he did not have as much confidence in himself as my mother had in him. I remember how she pushed and pushed to make him take the examination to become a postal worker at the army base at Fort MacPherson. "This is something you can do," she would say over and over. "You can do this." After a while he followed her advice and took the test, and everything worked out. He got the job carrying mail. This was a tremendous aid to our family. It insured that whatever ups and downs there might be in my mother's business (as there are in every enterprise), there would always be a steady, and good, paycheck.

In the end, it may be true that what you think you want in life is a function of what you think you deserve, or what you think you can achieve. Maybe it was not so much that my mother and father actually wanted different things. It was just that the difference in their levels of confidence helped set the expectations they had for themselves, and for me. My mother wanted to have and do great things because she thought it was in her power to have and do great things. And so, why not? She felt the same about her children. When we were little boys, my mother would talk about the Lab High School, an experimental school affiliated with Atlanta University. She had heard it was a good program and that was all she needed to know. "If it's still open when you're old enough, I want you to go to the Lab school," she would say, making it sound like the best thing in the world. Her ambition for us was just enormous, and she never missed the opportunity to let us know that.

My father seemed to tailor his desires to what he may have thought was a more realistic judgment of what could be achieved. Perhaps he saw himself as just facing the facts. Facing facts is a tricky business. What are the facts? Who makes them "the facts"? Why should anyone be bound by facts that someone else has drawn up? Who knows why my mother did not see how "unrealistic" it was to think that she could go from being a cook in someone's house to running Mary Jordan's Catering Service and being admired and respected by blacks and whites alike? Why did she, living in the heart of segregated Dixie, think her black sons could go as far as they wanted in life?

I GOT TO KNOW SOMETHING of the life my parents left behind when we went to the country to see relatives. For a city boy, these trips were like visits to a faraway exotic land, and they brought on the same intense feelings of excitement and anticipation mixed with a small sense of possible danger. We were going to see people we loved, in a place where we felt comfortable, but we had to pass through some very treacherous territory to get there. My mother packed lunches, because we would not be able to stop on the way; or if we did, we would have to go to the back of some restaurant not knowing whether the people would be hostile or just indifferent. Once we were in the car, pretty soon the aroma of my mother's fried chicken, and whatever else she'd prepared, filled the air. "Mama, we're hungry!" we'd say, almost before we'd gotten beyond the city limits.

Our trips were to visit three of my grandparents who were alive when I was a kid: Charlie and Annie Jordan, and Jim Griggs, my mother's father. My mother's mother, Julia, had died before I was born. Charlie Jordan was a carpenter who had retired by the time I was old enough to know him. He used to sit on his front porch drinking sweet water, which was literally that—water with a couple of teaspoons of sugar in it. What fascinated me about him was that he could tell time, with great precision, by where the sun was in the sky. We would ramble around his house and the surrounding land, have a big dinner that my grandmother had cooked, and then go to sleep at night on pallets on the floor, under quilts my grandmother had made.

We went more often to my mother's old home in Talbot County. This was, in part, because her father, "Pa" as we called him, would think he was dying about every three months. "Send for Belle," he'd say from his "deathbed." We would load up the car, going down there expecting the worst. We'd walk in and there he'd be, eyes low, lying under the cover. "Is that you, Belle?" he'd ask. After a few moments in her presence, which he missed so much, he'd say, "I feel better now," and he wouldn't die.

Pa was my favorite grandparent. He lived on the property of Mr. Robert Callier, for whom he had worked all his adult life. It was easy to talk to Pa about anything that came to mind. Once, while we were sitting on his front porch, I asked him, "Pa, sitting here today, if you could have anything in the world, what would it be?" He thought for a moment and said, "If I could have anything in the world, I'd want to be able to go to the bathroom indoors, in a warm place, one time before I die."

That stunned me. As a kid I'd been thinking about that question from my own perspective, and I had much bigger dreams than that.

Pa was so close to me that I expected his dreams would be pretty much like my own. He was not asking to have a million dollars, or a fancy car, or a big house. He did not say he wanted to learn arithmetic so that Mr. Callier could not cheat him every Monday as they settled accounts for the crops he was growing on Mr. Callier's land. Thinking back on the social situation at that time, it is telling that Pa did not say he wanted to be able to vote without intimidation or to have equal access to public accommodations.

My grandfather's ultimate aspiration was a basic creature comfort. His desire was elemental, growing out of the severe deprivation he'd suffered in his life as a sharecropper, and as a sharecropper's son. What I dreamed of, during a time of rising expectations, was beyond anything Pa could have contemplated. He certainly would never have dreamed that his twelve-year-old grandson would be able to go to college and law school and have the opportunities I have had in life. There was no way for Pa to really see the things that were in my brave new world. I understood that only vaguely then. It is much clearer to me now.

That summer brought another turning point in my education about life. Trips to the country put me in touch with my cousins and other children who lived in the area. As soon as we arrived, after changing out of our traveling clothes—we always put on our best clothes to take trips—we would find our cousin Bobby and go play with another boy named Bobby, a white boy my age. We did all the things one would expect—exploring, climbing trees, playing games, getting into fights. Although one Bobby was white and one was black, we were all just good and easy companions over the summers of my early childhood. That ended in the summer of 1947.

I came into my aunt Jimmie Lee's house as usual and, after greeting the adults, was getting ready to go outside immediately. My cousin was already there, and I said, "Let's go get Bobby," meaning the white boy. My aunt grabbed me by the arm, holding it very tightly, pulled me close, and said, "Listen. You must understand that he's no longer Bobby. He is twelve years old. He's 'Mr. Bobby' now."

Her words stung me, making me think about the ways of that

world in a way I never had before. "Mr. Bobby"? I was twelve years old, too. Why wasn't I "Mr. Vernon"?

I said to my cousin, "Forget about going to see Bobby. We won't do that any more." That was the death of our little interracial summer band.

M Y MOTHER HAD HAD A SON before she married my father. My older brother, Warren, was fourteen years older than me, and he was an important, though intermittent, part of my life as a young boy. By the time I was old enough to know him, he was really out in the world. As a matter of fact, he went away to the war during the same years as my father.

Even though Warren was, more often than not, out of my daily life, he was the big brother I looked up to, the one who went ahead and came back to tell me and show me all that was waiting out in the world. He was the first to get married (in a ceremony conducted by a very young preacher named Martin Luther King, Jr.) and the first to have children. Warren was our model.

In some ways Warren's absence during my childhood made him an even more romantic figure. When he was around, the time always seemed special. In would come this very handsome man, extremely popular with the ladies, who played softball very well—and he was my big brother! Warren introduced me to jazz music. It was from him that I learned to appreciate be-bop and first heard of and listened to Charlie Parker. One of the highlights of my life was in 1950, when Warren drove Windsor and me to Chicago, our first big-city experience.

Warren also figured into our excursions into the country. Atlanta was an urban area, but at that time, we did not have to go far out of the city to be in rural Georgia. Warren took us out hunting with Mr. Jenkins, a deacon at the Mount Zion Baptist Church. They hunted with dogs, and it was marvelous to see how Warren and Mr. Jenkins talked to those dogs and got them to do the most amazing things.

Most often, we went night hunting for possums and coons. We had no guns—we could not shoot in the dark. Instead, the dogs would tree the animals, and then we would come and shake the tree until they fell out or came down. The dogs surrounded them, and we maneuvered the frightened prey into a croaker sack. The possums we ate, the coons we let go. Then in the daytime, we hunted for rabbits. It was wonderful—dealing with nature, being outdoors in the woods with my brothers. I was very much a city boy, but because my family's roots were in the country, rural values and mores were never far away.

If Warren was the model of the absent big brother, Windsor was the little brother who was always there. We are a shade under two years apart, so I do not remember a time when Windsor was not in the picture. We went to camp and to all the various activities our parents planned for us together. In this relationship, I was the big brother—with all the benefits and burdens that come with the role. On the good side, at times I could exercise my big brotherly prerogative to persuade him to do things—chores, errands—that I didn't want to do. On the other hand, when we fought, Windsor always won because I was afraid to beat him up. I knew what my parents would say: "You're not supposed to beat up your baby brother."

My size played a role in this as well. Of the males in my nuclear family, I am the tallest at just a little under six feet five inches, having inherited my height from both my grandfathers. This was apparent very early on. It is not uncommon for kids who are big or tall for their age to have a sense of their potential physical power compared to other kids, and to voluntarily hold themselves back at times. I knew that if I wanted to, I could hurt Windsor and the other kids my age, and some even older, but I never was keen on doing that.

There is no question that between the two of us, Windsor was the more fun kid. I had my moments, but he was more exciting to be around and more devilish in many ways. During his senior prom, he and his date were driving along to get a late dinner when a great song came on the radio. Windsor pulled over to the side of the road, he and the girl got out, and they danced to the music right there. Even had I wanted to, I could never have done that.

O NE OF THE STRANGEST PARTS of being in the public eye is that people who don't know you believe they know you. Sometimes they believe it with their whole hearts. What they know is what they have read in the newspapers, seen on television, or heard second- or third-hand. This gives them just enough information to piece together what they think is a plausible version of your life and who you are.

This is understandable. We human beings always try to make sense of the world we live in—even when sometimes there is no sense to be made. We want it all to fit. "Ahh, that's how he's done that," or "She's got that because of this." Things have to be justified according to our own sense of the way the world works.

We are also curious about one another. When one of us gets a lot of attention—becomes famous—a story line grows up around that person. A powerful mixture of fact, fiction, extrapolation, and inference is taken and shaped into what can be called that person's "image." The image often has very little or nothing to do with who the person really is.

Over the years, I have been the subject of hundreds of profiles, probably in every form of media that exists. One recurring theme is that I have gone from "rags to riches" in my life. While I certainly did not grow up in the lap of luxury, the truth is that compared to most young black kids of my time and place, I had a pretty comfortable existence. I was never in rags.

The stories about how I "came out of the projects" have helped shape my image because "the projects" are symbolic to most Americans. It makes them think of extreme poverty, single mothers with lots of children, gangster youth, unemployed and uninterested fathers just out of prison. Often a moralistic tone creeps into descriptions of life there—a tone that demonizes people whose main problem is that they are poor in a society that doesn't have much use for poor people.

Of course, if you get out of the projects, a different spin is put on things. This is in the time-honored tradition of celebrating the man or woman who started with nothing and rose to prominence: "Up from slavery"; "He was born in a log cabin"; "He was raised in the projects." All these phrases play into America's love affair with progress; we are proud of the idea that people in this country can move from one status to another more easily than in other countries. If you follow the outline of the story as it is supposed to unfold, when you move up, you take the values of your beginnings with you. If you don't, you will be accused of having "forgotten where you came from."

While I have definitely moved from one status to another in my life, my starting point was not in the most impoverished and deprived segment of the black community, as all the talk about "the projects" would suggest. I am a product of the lower middle class. You could even say that as my mother's business prospered, we became, in economic terms, part of the black middle class.

We do not talk much about class in America. The focus is usually on race, for very obvious historical reasons. But we ignore class at our peril. It is easy to get a distorted picture of the black community and the individuals within it when class is taken out of the equation. We assume that every black person has the same values, experiences, and expectations. Therefore, their responses to issues and problems will flow along the same lines. They do not.

Class works in the black community in much the same way it does everywhere else. Lower-middle-class people the world over are strivers. They are not so beaten down that they cannot hope for a better life. Because they do have some place to get to, they are not as blasé about success as members of the upper classes. Stability and prosperity are within their grasp, and they reach for it. People in the lower middle class are not ashamed of this, nor do they feel guilty about it. They think it's what they are supposed to do.

I did spend the early part of my life in the projects. But they were not the projects as we think of them today. University Homes, where I lived until I was thirteen, was the first public project for black people built in the United States. It was not designed solely for poor people. During my time there, the residents came from a wide variety of economic and social levels. To the people who lived in truly deep poverty, sometimes in homes with no indoor plumbing, we were the rich kids.

The manager of University Homes, Alonso Moron (pronounced "muh-ROHN"), lived there. Moron was a Harvard-trained lawyer who would later become the president of Hampton University and would be a finalist to succeed Lester Granger as executive director of the National Urban League. (Whitney Young won out in the end.) Prosperous businessmen also lived at University Homes. Teachers lived there, too, along with the occasional street hustler. It was a mixed bag that turned out to have been a very good environment for black kids. We got to see black people get up and go to work every day in a wide range of occupations.

We had role models. The term has been used so much that some have become cynical about the concept. That's too bad, because role models are important. Children will have them no matter what. It is in the nature of young people to look to their elders for signals about what things are important and how to act—even if they aren't anxious to admit it. The only question is who they are going to be watching.

I had the example of my parents, along with many of the adults who lived in University Homes, to give me an idea about how I should go through the world. These were not some distant figures designated by the media as "role models." They were in my life on a day-to-day basis, flesh and blood. I could talk to them. Even if I didn't talk to them, I could observe them. Sometimes they did the right thing. Sometimes they made mistakes. The important point was that most of them were in there trying. This made a big, and very positive, impression on me.

There was something else going on in my environment that was of great benefit. University Homes got its name because it was right in the midst of Atlanta's complex of black colleges: Atlanta University, Clark, Morehouse, Morris Brown, and Spelman. These schools made Atlanta the Athens of black America. The building I grew up in was right across the street from Spelman, the noted black women's college. We were just down the way from Morehouse and all the others. It was very much like growing up in a college town, with all the advantages of that setup.

Famous people came to speak at those schools. Well-known professors taught there. It was the heyday of Dr. Benjamin Mays, the charismatic and brilliant president of Morehouse College who was such an inspiration to so many people in the civil rights movement. As a young boy, I used to follow Dr. Mays around campus, trying to imitate the regal way he carried himself. Black professors, college administrators, and support staff were in my view on a daily basis.

Then there were the students—some of the best in the country. They were there to become what W. E. B. Du Bois called the "talented tenth" and to take what they had learned back into their communities as teachers, doctors, ministers, social workers. These young people were all around me. Although I loved being close to Spelman so that I could watch the girls, it was also important for me to move among young people who were going somewhere. There was no way for me to think that blacks could not aspire to and achieve excellence. I could be one of them. Even if there were arbitrary rules designed to keep us from rising as far as we could, I never had cause to doubt that we had the ability to compete in the world if the rules could be made fair.

My parents insisted that I was going to be prepared to do my best in the competition. The family structure was in place. My mother and father also looked to other institutions for what they could contribute to my well-being. There was never any question in my mother's mind that I was going to go to college. It was just a given, and so she started from the beginning taking what she thought were the necessary steps to get me there.

Step one, of course, was to make sure I attended school regularly, which I did. There were other steps to be taken. My mother got involved in school herself. She was the president of the PTA at every school I attended: the Walker Street Elementary School, the E. A. Ware School, and David T. Howard High School. In fact, when she was head of the PTA at Howard High, she was also president of the PTA at C. W. Hill, where Windsor was in school. My high-school basketball coach, T. Herman Graves, served on the board of the PTA with my mother. He remembers her showing up at their September meetings with the agenda for the whole year planned out. The agenda was always followed. She did all of this while running her catering business and taking care of her other responsibilities.

Somehow my mother had the notion that if she got involved with the PTA, her children would have a better chance in school. If she really got involved—made herself the head of the whole organization—it would make our chances that much better. The teachers would respond to us differently because they knew we had a parent who was involved and interested and held a position of authority. She would have influence just by virtue of her position. If she worked hard at it, and became well known for that (which was what happened), things would be even better for us—a maximum effort for a maximum return.

The way my mother went about this also sent a message to me. School was a place where I went to learn, but it was also important as an institution. I came to see that it is a good idea to become involved with any institution or entity that is critical to your welfare. You have to be at the table to help set the agenda, or someone else will set it for you. There is no guarantee that those who are sitting there in your place will represent, or even be aware of, your interests. You can't take the chance.

Also, if you can be involved at the top level of an institution, by all means do so, even if it will mean (as it almost always does) giving up a good amount of your free time. It's worth the effort if important things are at stake. There couldn't have been many people with less free time than my mother. It took tremendous will to fit this into her life, but she did it because she believed the stakes (her sons' education) were high enough to warrant the effort.

Added to the work that we had to do as students, my mother wanted to make sure we took advantage of whatever opportunities school had to offer outside of the classroom. I saw Washington, D.C., for the first time in 1946, when I went to march in a parade down Pennsylvania Avenue as a member of the School Patrol. Both my brother and I were in the patrol. One day the teacher who was our leader said: "There's going to be a trip to Washington. You'll have to wear a blue shirt and white trousers. We're going to go on the train. The trip will cost $35." That was a lot of money in 1946— $70 between the two of us. I wanted to go so badly.

That night at dinner I said, in a matter-of-fact way: "There's a trip to Washington. The School Patrol is going. But it costs $35 a person." I didn't press it. I was hoping the message had gotten through. The next morning my mother said, "Vernon, Jr., here's your $35. Windsor, here's your $35."

My brother was surprised. "You really want us to go?"

She said, "Yes, travel is the best way to learn."

That was my first train ride. Schools all over the city were participating in the event, so there were black kids and white kids. All I remember about the train was that the white kids sat in the back and we black kids sat in front. This was the reverse of how it usually went on public transportation. Of course, the idea was to let the black kids sit right behind the engine and to keep the white kids safely and comfortably away from it.

When we got to Washington, the white kids stayed in a hotel. We were put up in an old art studio in an apartment building in what is now Logan Circle. We slept on cots. By this time I was familiar with slights of this kind. I knew it was wrong and that none of it made any sense. I just could not let this destroy the excitement of seeing Washington for the first time. I owed it to myself (and to my parents) not to.

Parading down Pennsylvania Avenue was exhilarating, but touring the city and the area around it made it all complete. I climbed the Washington Monument, toured various government buildings, and saw all the sites D.C. has to offer. The whole experience was fabulous, and as my mother predicted, it taught me a lot. I hated to leave, but I knew that some day I'd return. That day came sooner than I expected. The next year, the PTA decided to sponsor the trip. They had to pick two students to send. My mother was the president of the PTA. Somehow, I got voted to go.

ORGANIZATION AND STRUCTURE WERE THE KEYS to our existence. Windsor and I were always doing something: going to school, to church, to the YMCA, or to an after-school program at the Gate City Day Nursery, a Community Chest organization (now the United Way). Gate City was run and ruled by Miss Kelly, who was at once the softest and most stern social worker around. She had no qualms about using a switch on any of us when we got out of line.

We learned something new at each institution, and they all provided much-needed stability. Whatever the season, I knew that every Monday and Friday at five o'clock, we were going to go to choir rehearsal at St. Paul. My brother and I sang in the St. Cecelia Choir, which had been funded by R. A. Billings, the only doctor in our church. Dr. Billings paid the band director at Washington High to make sure that we were ready for the Vespers services that were held every fourth Sunday. Although sometimes it was a grind, being in the St. Cecelia Choir and attending the Vespers services gave me some of the happiest memories of my childhood. The music was wonderful—our theme song was the famous Brahms lullaby—and the program itself was very sophisticated and uplifting.

Dr. Billings was the team physician for Morris Brown College. If we had perfect attendance at choir rehearsal, he would take us to the Morris Brown football games and let us sit on the bench with the players. That was something else. We felt special and privileged. The generosity of people like Dr. Billings meant so much in a time when there were not many publicly funded programs for kids. He was another role model.

There was always a speaker at the Vespers service, and so we heard prominent men and women of the community talk about their lives and ideas. One Sunday it would be A. T. Walden, who was the most prominent black lawyer in the town, the man who prompted my earliest thoughts of being a lawyer. The next Sunday it might be Martin Luther King, Sr., the minister at the Ebenezer Baptist Church, or Warren Cochrane, executive secretary of the Butler Street

YMCA, but it was always a prominent member of the community or a religious leader. Whenever there was any reading or recitation to be done, I usually volunteered or was assigned to do it. I learned about music, and I got to see what it was like to perform before an audience.

About the only time I confounded my mother's organizational scheme was when I simply resigned from piano lessons. Like everyone else who gave up the piano as a child, I have lived to regret having been so hardheaded about this. I would love to be able to sit down and play "My Faith Looks Up to Thee" to my satisfaction. If I had just stuck with it, I could have the music I love so much literally at my fingertips. I just couldn't see this far into the future when I was a boy. All I knew then was that I just couldn't stand piano lessons.

I would be up a tree or playing ball, and then I would hear my mother calling (or blowing the car horn, which was usually how she signaled for us to come home). I had to stop what I was doing, go home, take a bath, put on dress clothes. Then came the hard part. I would have to walk past the guys who were still in the tree or still at whatever we had all been playing—on my way to piano lessons with my little brother.

At least I had it better than Jimmy Mayo. Jimmy played the violin. You could hear him practicing all the time, and he was very good at it. Still, violin playing was a bit rarefied for my gang, and the guys thought Jimmy was a little strange. On top of it this, his mother was trying to be an opera singer. It was just a bad deal all around for Jimmy. Later on, Jimmy would graduate from Morehouse College and would earn a Ph.D. in chemistry, so he must not have been too scarred by the experience.

My music teacher was Mrs. Rosalind Days. Her husband, Kenneth, also taught music. So on any given day there would be a few children sitting on their back porch waiting to take their lessons. I'd always find myself sitting there in front of, or just behind, some little girl done up in a pretty dress and patent leather shoes with ribbons in her hair. The girls, of course, had actually practiced their music. Few of us boys ever had. This was a serious problem for us because Mrs. Days was from the old school. She'd sit there with a ruler in her hand, and every time I hit the wrong note, she'd hit me. Here I would be, taking piano lessons, getting hit, and crying in front of the girls—just total humiliation. It got to be more than I could stand, and I just quit.

Given the force of my mother's personality, you'd think she might have made me tough it out. After all, this had been her idea. Looking back, I think she must have sensed the real depth of my misery over this and decided the game wasn't worth the candle. Her goal was not to break my spirit. It was the very opposite. She was trying to expose me to things she thought would enrich my spirit and make me a well-rounded person. She also may not have been too thrilled with Mrs. Days's choice of motivational technique.

While Mama acquiesced to my thumbs-down on the piano lessons, she continued to believe that learning an instrument should be on the agenda. After the piano debacle, she let me choose what I wanted to play. We went downtown, and she bought me a trumpet on credit. I was satisfied with my choice. Her mission to get me involved with music was on track. All was well.

With my mother at the helm, my direction in life was set early on. All I had to do was make sure I didn't do anything that would take me too far off course. Had I been a different type of person or had I not understood that her greatest desire in life was to help me rise in the world, I might have been inclined to "resign" from more things she had planned for me. The truth is, there was no objective evidence that my mother didn't know what she was talking about. Her plans for herself generally worked out. I was doing well. Under the circumstances, the best course of action seemed to be to accept her wisdom and forge ahead.

CHAPTER 2

AT HOME IN THE WORLD

THERE IS NO QUESTION that my mother's way of seeing the world and moving in the world is very close to my own way. Whether this is because I grew up watching her or whether her traits were simply passed on to me genetically can't really be known. But so much of her is in me. Just as work was at the core of my mother's life, it has been that way for me as well. My mother was willing to take risks as she built her career. I have been, too. She was restless. I am certainly that. As early as I can remember, I have been on the move. What can I do now? Where can I go? What else can I try?

What others may see as too chaotic or hectic a pace is just my speed. I actually get a great sense of comfort from always having lots of different things going at once. If one is prepared and organized enough to handle it, complexity can bring its own order to life. It certainly has in mine. I am never without something to do, and I have always liked it that way.

The differences between my mother and me are obvious. There is, of course, the matter of gender and generation. My mother was a black woman, born during a time when opportunities for blacks and women were severely limited. I sometimes wonder what would have happened had she been born in a place where people like her were valued as human beings and citizens. What if Georgia had thought it important to provide a good education and equal opportunity to all who lived there? What if the choices open to young black women today had been open to her?

Although I am very proud of what my mother made of her life, and her success was extraordinary, I believe that she would have made a great CEO of a company, president of a university, judge, general—anything that requires education, determination, perseverance, organizational skills, and savvy. I was lucky to come of age at a time when the doors were opening for black people. During the next generation the doors opened a little wider. With any luck, they will open even further for the generations to come. What my mother accomplished in her time, limited as her choices were, shows that black people have always had the ambition and talent to succeed. American society just was not ready to accept this in full flower. So my mother found something she could do, and she went to it. Over the years I have tried to follow her in that.

This started early on, with her encouragement. When I was about five years old, my mother ran the kitchen concession at Fort MacPherson. At that time, Fort MacPherson was just outside of Atlanta. Over the years, urban sprawl has brought it within the city limits. Because we were too small to be left alone and there was no one to look after us, Windsor and I often went to work with my mother. We were mostly underfoot, but we did have our own little business going on the side—my first taste of entrepreneurship. We would go off hunting for stray golf balls, take the best ones, clean them off, and sell them to the army officers. We did pretty well for ourselves. Even as a little kid, I enjoyed the sensation of having a task, carrying it out, and getting paid for my efforts.

I always wanted to make money, and I was never at a loss for ideas about how to do it. After selling golf balls, my next business venture was at home. Like almost every housing project, the buildings in University Homes had been built cookie-cutter style. The front of everyone's unit looked the same. We all had doorknobs, mail slots, and doorbells made of brass. When I was ten, I decided to go into the brass-polishing business. I got the materials needed and went door-to-door offering to polish the brass on each apartment. The residents were more than happy to say yes, so that was another profitable way to spend time.

Then I also used a fairly conventional way of getting spare change. Like many American kids, when I was a young boy I had a paper route. Again, my territory was University Homes. I was the junior partner of a slightly older boy, whose name I will not use because of one of the more creative parts of our association. We got up early in the morning to go get our papers for delivery. Before we went to work we had a little ritual. The two of us would go to a neighborhood store—we tried to pick a different one each day—and help ourselves to half a pint of milk and a cinnamon roll.

We were getting paid for delivering the papers. We could have bought our little breakfast. I could have eaten at home. It wasn't a question of need, at least not a physical one. I think it was just the thrill of getting away with it—of testing the limits as kids often do as they try to find out who they really are in the world, how far they feel comfortable going, and what they can and can't get away with. For the most part, I followed the instructions that were laid down by my parents, teachers, and other authority figures in the community. I was pegged as a "nice" boy. So these small acts of rebellion must have served some purpose at that stage of my life—the "good boy" trying to be "bad" for a while. I grew out of this pretty quickly.

My mother knew nothing about my "five-finger discount" breakfasts. Had she known, she would have hit the ceiling. What she saw was her resourceful son, rising at dawn to seek his fortune—or at least to get some more spending money. That was okay by her. That is what she wanted me to do. She didn't even mind it when I sold the fancy sandwiches she used to make for my lunch every day. I'd sell them to the teachers, who had more adult tastes. "That's good for the catering business," she would say. With the money I made from the teachers, I would go across the street from my school to buy wiener sandwiches for lunch.

The truth is that my mother used her business to make sure we had our own pocket change. Windsor and I worked for her when she catered parties. She paid us as though we were her employees.

There was no such thing as getting an allowance. What we got from her on a steady basis, we worked for. From the age of ten, I was a waiter passing hors d'oeuvres or doing whatever else was required. By the age of twelve, my father had taught me how to tend bar, and when my mother's regular bartender was not available, I substituted for him at some of the parties. As I got older, I tended bar as a matter of course. I was pretty good at it. I still am.

IT WAS THROUGH MY MOTHER'S BUSINESS that I had my first serious exposure to lawyers. From 1948 until about 1960, my mother catered the monthly dinners of the very exclusive Lawyers Club. The club's elite membership was drawn from the most accomplished (or at least the most socially connected) attorneys in Atlanta.

The atmosphere at the meetings was just about what one would expect: all white, all male, cigar smoke, plenty of good-natured banter, and whiskey, along with my mother's filet mignon wrapped in bacon. I moved among the guests as a servant, quiet and unobtrusive, for the most part ignored. This was not a two-way street. I was a teenager who happened to be intensely interested in the men of that club—how they made their living and how they dealt with one another outside of the public view. Of all the places we worked, weddings, bar mitzvahs, dinners, cocktail parties—you name it, we did it—I think I liked the Lawyers Club the most of all.

In the world as it existed at the time, the thought that I could one day be among those men was beyond far-fetched. And yet I was instantly drawn to the world in which they lived. These were the movers and shakers of their community, for the most part secure in their power and positions. This confidence allowed them to treat one another with an easy camaraderie that was admirable, and which was very instructive for what was to come later in my life. I wanted to be a part of something like that. Not necessarily with those individuals, but with a group of people who were doing similarly important things and who could meet to enjoy one another's company.

I was so interested in their operations that I sometimes neglected my duties. The club always had an after-dinner speaker. Instead of staying in the kitchen, helping to clean up, and getting packed to go home, I would go back near the dining area, stand at a discreet distance, and listen to the speeches. What they were saying did not always interest me, but I was interested in the way each speaker presented himself. It was during that time that I firmly decided that I was going to be a lawyer.

I felt it so deeply, even as I knew that the men whom I served could never in their wildest dreams imagine that I could share a profession with them. But being a waiter was simply a temporary phase for me. I knew what was to come, and what I would one day look like when the change came.

In the meantime, there was my mother's catering business to work in and other jobs that came my way. As a teenager, I was a camp counselor for part of the summer at the Butler Street YMCA. There is nothing like trying to handle twenty-five eight-year-old boys when it is too rainy to go outside and some way has to be found to harness what amounts to unbridled energy. My hat is off to all the elementary school teachers of the world. I sang so many camp songs, broke up so many fights, cleaned up after so many spills. Then again, I also heard many unintentionally funny comments, saw kids who didn't think they could do things (like learning to swim) become accomplished under the direction of the Y's staff.

For a time, I had a dishwashing job at Emory University, where I worked part-time during the school year and in the summers when I'd finished a session as counselor at the YMCA. I got the job when I was fifteen and kept it for most of my years in high school. This job gave me my first experience in managing people. I was the youngest person on the dishwashing crew, which consisted of older men. I think I may have been the only one there who could really read. In the land of the blind, the one-eyed man is king. So I was made the head of the dishwashing crew because I could read well, and my employer was impressed.

Naturally this caused some resentment. I was young, and they were older. One saving grace was my height. I had a tough time telling them what to do or, at least, having them actually do what I told them to do. The work would pile up, and they'd be downstairs playing cards. Our supervisor, a white woman named Mrs. Haney, was very, very mean. Everyone was afraid of her. When the crew disappeared on me, I'd have to go back and invoke the name of Mrs. Haney to get them back in line. "I don't care whether this gets done," I'd say, "I do know that Mrs. Haney sure does." As a management tool, this was a pretty blunt instrument. But it usually did the trick.

The jobs I held as a teenager reinforced my certainty that I was going to do something different in the world. My co-workers, in all likelihood, were doing some version of what would be their life's work. I was very much aware of the differences in our circumstances, of the fact that I was being prepared (and was preparing myself) to move to the next level. Most of the people who worked with me had little or no education and, therefore, almost no hope of moving anywhere beyond the next job that would be just like the one before.

Following my senior year in high school, I worked as a waiter at the Capital City Country Club in De Kalb County. The captain was a man who was always very busy—nice, but a no-nonsense type of fellow. After working there a while, I noticed the captain followed a curious ritual. As he performed some task, the cashier would read the day's menu to him three times before he began the day's service.

I never thought a thing about this until we went to the filling station one day and there was a contest going on. If you filled the car up, you'd get a prize. The captain had gotten a full tank of gas, so he was eligible to win. When the attendant handed him the form to fill out, he said, a bit too gruffly, "I don't have time for that—give it to my assistant," gesturing in my direction.

Then it hit me: He could not read. That was the point of having the cashier read the daily menu to him. He always claimed it was just a matter of efficiency, that he could keep doing little chores while others read to him. This was just a cover for what must have been a deep embarrassment.

I was embarrassed for him. And I was so sorry at the same time. What a strain it must have been, to go through life memorizing things so you could get through your job, having to hide the fact that you couldn't read to avoid ridicule. It was ingenious, but it was also sad. He was such a proud man. There was no way I could let on I'd learned his secret. So I took the form, filled it out, and we never said another word about it.

I enjoyed my time at the Capital City Country Club. Not only was the money good, but it provided another avenue for my budding entrepreneurship: selling liquor to my fellow waiters. Like a number of counties in the South at that time, De Kalb County was "dry." You couldn't buy liquor there. This was a real problem for the waiters at the club who enjoyed drinking. Most of them relied on public transportation, so it wasn't a simple matter of driving into Atlanta to get alcohol. That was where I came in. I had a car. I'd go to a liquor store on Peachtree Street in Atlanta, the last store before reaching De Kalb County, buy ten half-pints of Gilbey's Gin for $1.25, and sell it to the waiters for $2.00. Sometimes I'd make extra runs during the day.

Also, since they were without cars, I would give as many as I could a ride home—at fifty cents a head. Otherwise they would have had to take a cab from the club to the nearest bus stop and then get the bus home, which was much more expensive. The whole thing worked out to everyone's mutual satisfaction. They got their drinking in, and a cheap, hassle-free ride home. I made a profit.

My experiences with work during these years not only provided an outlet for my youthful energy—they gave me a sense of power and control over my life. By working and saving my money, I could have a few of the things I wanted. From my view, there was every reason to want to continue in this vein. My mother's sense of the importance of work, entrepreneurship, and frugality colored my whole way of thinking about this, both then and now. Her early experiences in life—the racism, the economic deprivation—evidently caused her to believe that it was important to have a plan in life or others would control your destiny. When we started working, she took Windsor and me to the bank to open our own savings accounts. We had our passbooks, and when we'd get our statements, Mama would note how the interest compounded on our principal. In her view, this was one of the most important lessons in life for us to learn.

I sometimes think it's hard for people who have grown up with the teachings of the church, as most blacks have, to feel entirely comfortable with what might be seen just as the pursuit of money. "It's easier for a camel to fit through the eye of a needle than it is for a rich man to get into the kingdom of heaven," we have been taught, along with "Money is the root of all evil." Even "Blessed are the poor" suggests that a person who wants to make money (beyond what it takes to buy food, clothes, and shelter) is somehow morally suspect.

Of course, there's another reason that some in the black community may feel ambivalent about pursuing money with a lot of energy. It was the naked pursuit of money that brought our ancestors to these shores, chained in the hulls of ships. People used money to buy us. They made money by selling us. Fortunes were built on this activity with no serious thought about the morality of it all. Even if the religious counsel against worshipping Mammon didn't cause a yellow light to flash among our people, history alone would provide a reason for caution.

Although this is understandable, it is ultimately shortsighted. No group in this country can hope to make strides for itself without economic advancement—on an individual level and on a group level. Ruby Hurley, who was my boss when I was Georgia field director for the National Association for the Advancement of Colored People (NAACP), said there were two things that white people understood: the dollar and the ballot. Those interested in maintaining white supremacy worked hard to keep blacks away from both. She was right. Both things have to be attended to if blacks are to make real progress in America and in the world. I have never had any doubt about this at all.

I DIDN'T SPEND ALL OF MY CHILDHOOD and youth working for pay. My primary occupation was student. I did well in my studies from the very beginning, and I got a reputation in school and in my neighborhood for being smart. This was both good and bad for me.

On the good side, I got to enjoy the positive reinforcement it brought from my teachers, my mother, and other adults. This kind of thing builds on itself. If people tell you that you are smart, you have the confidence and incentive to work to keep that image.

The downside was that there was something of a stigma attached to being too intelligent. Although the stigma affected both girls and boys, it was much worse for boys. I will never forget it. One day when I was in the eighth grade, a girl in our class was writing on the board. She had drawn two columns, with the headings "Girls in our class" and "Boys in our class." She listed everyone's name. At the end of the "Girls" column, she wrote "Vernon."

What was that about? Because I was the best student in the class—I answered the questions, did my homework, tried to please my teachers, spoke correctly—I was a "girl." That kind of thing was meant to hurt, and it did. Not that I thought there was anything wrong with girls. I liked girls very much. I just wasn't one of them. What had I done wrong besides trying to do well in school?

Even my father had a little bit of this in him. I do believe there were times that it bothered him that I was one of the smartest kids in my school. It wasn't that he didn't want to me to do well in my studies. He was just suspicious of the enthusiasm I had for it. In his mind, that meant that I was going to grow up to be what he would have called a "sissy."

At the base of all this was fear. If you think of where my father came from and the set of values he brought with him—a real man didn't sit around reading books—this was a foreign thing, having a son who seemed intent on outfitting himself for a world beyond what he knew. I remember once when I was in junior high school, our principal, Mr. Charles Gideons, came to our house for dinner. I heard my father muttering that he was worried about me. Mr. Gideons, who must have been a pretty good student himself to have grown up to be principal of a school, didn't seem concerned at all.

It took a while, but it dawned on my father that being smart and interested in school didn't mean that I was so greatly different from him, which may have been at the root of his reaction anyway. We had simply grown up in different times. Avenues were open to me that hadn't been open to him. I could prepare myself to be a man in a different way. In fact, it was absolutely essential that black boys prepare themselves for manhood by taking advantage of every opportunity to educate themselves so that they could compete with girls and boys of whatever race.

I am disheartened whenever I read that even today some black kids respond negatively to their peers who try to be good students. Those kids are accused of "acting white" if they throw themselves wholeheartedly into their books. If that is true, we really have something major to overcome. People fought and died, worked all their lives, so that black kids could get a decent education. There was a reason Southern slave masters tried to keep blacks from learning to read. An educated black person was out of his or her place—a threat by definition. How could any black person in his or her right mind give in to the idea that being smart is for white people and being dumb is for blacks?

We can't underestimate how much the signals that were being sent to black people during my youth influenced their thoughts about education. I was a good student during the 1940s and early 1950s in a school system that was separate and unequal. The state of Georgia spent less per capita on the schools I attended than it did on the white schools. We got the cast-off books the white kids didn't use anymore. In 1951, I was given textbooks that had been used by white students in 1935, the year I was born. I did the best I could, but I was operating at a distinct disadvantage.

The message sent to us from society at large was that black people didn't count. There was little purpose in striving to better ourselves. Under the circumstances, it is easy to see how some people living under that kind of oppression—and that is the word for it—would develop a distorted view of themselves. It's harder to imagine that there would be people who still had hope. As a testament to the human spirit, there were such people. Many people. They were the ones who helped make a difference in my life.

For every discouraging word I may have heard from some of my fellow students about my academic achievements, I had several more words of praise from my teachers. For every attempt by the outside community to make me believe that I was inferior, there were multiple efforts by my teachers to make me feel like a star. There is not enough good that can be said about black educators in the South who tried to instill a sense of pride and mission in their students. They meant so much to us. Working against huge odds, with few resources at their disposal, they taught us as best they could. They lifted our hopes. Anyone who showed the slightest amount of initiative was immediately taken up, backed up, and pushed forward by these really extraordinary people.

There was Mr. H. J. Furlow, my social studies teacher, a strict disciplinarian who taught us how to speak—how to "enunciate," as he would say. "Stand up straight," he instructed, "and look at people when you talk to them." He was a wonderful man. His wife played the piano at the Bethel AME Church, and each year Mr. Furlow played the Devil in Bethel's production of *Homeward Bound*. He was always a great favorite. People came from miles around to watch him,

In the early 1980s, I gave a speech at the Metropolitan AME Church in Washington, D.C., with Mr. Furlow in the audience. I noted his presence and told the parishioners that he used to grade our performances when I was back in school in Atlanta. When I was done, Mr. Furlow came up to the podium, interrupting the order of service, and said slowly in that deep tone of his, "Vernon gets an A." I loved it.

Ms. Amelia Thornton was an English teacher who took a great interest in me as well. Even to this day, I cannot write anything without feeling her presence over my shoulder, checking my grammar. Once, I did something I wasn't supposed to have done—I spoke to Ms. Thornton with too much of an edge in my voice. The next day she pulled me into an empty classroom and said, "You kept me up all night long last night. Don't you ever talk to me like that, boy." That was a tough moment, but it meant a lot to know that she was thinking about me, that she valued me enough to correct my behavior, and that she wasn't going to let go of me. That's the feeling they gave to us—"we will not let go of you"—even though the dominant community had said we weren't worth very much.

I remember one classmate, the beautiful Margaret Matthews, who was very athletic and participated in a variety of school activities. Ms. Marian Perkins, a teacher in our school, just took her on. She treated Margaret almost as a daughter, advising her about colleges and helping her grow into a graceful woman. Eventually Margaret became the head majorette, and in our senior year, homecoming queen. She went on to college, not far from where I was in school, which was quite convenient because I could call her up when I needed a date; there were no black girls at my college. Margaret eventually went on to become a teacher in Memphis.

Ms. Perkins's intervention in my friend's life made all the difference in the world. People like Mr. Furlow, Mr. Thornton, Ms. Perkins, and Mr. Graves, my basketball coach, are the true heroes of our community. Without their unheralded acts of kindness, bravery, and dedication, all the speeches by famous "leaders" would be worthless because there would be no one there to hear and no one capable of heeding their call.

With all of this said, it would be a mistake to be too sentimental about our situation. Yes, Ms. Thornton was wonderful. Yes, Mr. Furlow, Ms. Perkins, and Mr. Graves lifted us up. But no amount of odes to their greatness can hide the fact that we were being treated like noncitizens in a place we had helped to build. We worked. We paid taxes. We were human beings and Americans. Yet we were living behind an iron curtain.

Our school was neglected. I suffered personally from the effects of the dual educational system. Although I was at the top of my class, when the time came for me to go to the college of my choice, De-Pauw University, our pre-admission testing showed that I wasn't as prepared as my white classmates. Never once in my youth did I go to a school with enough resources to help its students compete on an equal basis with the average white student. During the months before I entered DePauw, I took reading classes at Atlanta University to help me get ready for college. My high school should have prepared me for college.

Inferior schools were only part of the picture. When we went to the Fox Theater or the Capitol Theater, we had to sit in the balcony.

When we rode on the bus, we had to sit at the back. If we went downtown to the courthouse, we had to drink from the "colored" water fountain. We couldn't go the University of Georgia or Georgia Tech. When we went to the ballpark, we had to sit in the bleachers.

What was happening to us was wrong. Even then I knew it was. That was the main reason I wanted to become a lawyer. When I was at the Lawyers Club thinking of those important men and wanting to be one someday, I believed that I could be important by helping to change the way black people were being treated. This was very much on my mind.

When the civil rights lawyer A. T. Walden used to speak at the St. Cecelia Choir's Vespers services, he'd talk about segregation and use a line from a popular song, "I'll be glad when you're dead, you rascal you." He was telling us very clearly that the end of segregation was as certain as death was to every living thing.

Mr. Walden was very active in the Butler Street YMCA, where I spent so much of my time. His office was right next door to the Y, and so I saw him often. If being at the Lawyers Club gave me some idea about the trappings of the legal profession, it was Mr. Walden, his activities, and his reputation that taught me about the substance of lawyering—that it could be used to bring about the social change we were all looking for. Mr. Walden, a graduate of the University of Michigan, was the man I wanted to walk, talk, and dress like.

Mr. Walden also stimulated my early interest in politics. He and John Wesley Dobbs were co-chairs of the Negro Voters League. Walden was a Democrat, and Dobbs was a Republican. At every election, the Voters League would issue its endorsement, choosing what usually amounted to the lesser of two evils. Atlanta newspapers waited anxiously to find out who the Voters League supported because it indicated which way the black vote in the city would break.

One year I was asked to spend two or three hours in Walden's office folding the letters of endorsement and stuffing them into envelopes for mailing. I saw this as a huge responsibility because it was a position of trust. The Voters League's endorsement was a closely guarded secret until the time came to announce it, and only I and members of the Voters League knew who that would be. This was my first turn as an insider. It made me feel a part of the political process. From then on, I was hooked on following politics at the local and national level.

I went to my first political meeting in 1948, when I was in the eighth grade. One Saturday morning, our adviser at the Butler Street Y, Ralph Long, took a group of us to a meeting of the Fifth Congressional District Republican Organization. Presiding over the meeting was Elbert P. Tuttle, a white lawyer who would later be appointed to the United States Court of Appeals for the Fifth Circuit by President Eisenhower, where he would issue some of the most important rulings on behalf of civil rights in the South. Tuttle's vice-chairman was a white man named Harry Sommers, who owned the Oldsmobile franchise in Atlanta, but what was most impressive to me was that the secretary was W. J. Shaw, a black optometrist whose shop was on Auburn Avenue, and that two other black men, John Wesley Dobbs and John H. Calhoun, were also members of the committee. The Republican Party in the South was open to all races—a legacy of the Civil War and Reconstruction, and a practice that had survived the movement of so many black voters to the Democratic Party of Franklin D. Roosevelt in 1932. Blacks played an active participatory role in the Republican Party in Georgia, and I have never forgotten that my first political meeting was an integrated occasion.

We were a political family. That is to say, my parents were always interested in the workings of society and the process by which things could change, and they encouraged us to be that way as well. We went to the NAACP mass meetings. My parents thought it was a part of our civic duty to be involved in that way. We got dressed up every New Year's Day and went to the Emancipation Proclamation Day ceremonies sponsored by the NAACP to hear speakers who were involved in the movement, people like Thurgood Marshall, Roy Wilkins, Mary MacLeod Bethune, Congressman William Dawson. The first time I ever heard anyone curse in the pulpit was during one of Bill Dawson's speeches. It was nothing very rough—a "damn" here, a "hell" there—but we were in a church. That was just deeply shocking.

Those events impressed me so much that they awakened in me a desire not to be simply a spectator. I wanted to be able to take control of the moment as much as I could. After one particularly inspiring presentation, I said to my father as we were leaving, "One day I'm going to make the Emancipation Day speech." He looked at me and said, "All right."

In HIGH SCHOOL, I belonged to an interracial council run by the Urban League. We met on Sweet Auburn Avenue with white teenagers and talked in very polite ways about the racial situation. We were pretty much dancing around the issues, but we all knew that we were on the verge of something. Our little group was an attempt to prepare ourselves for the new times to come.

In 1951, our bandmaster, Mr. Kenneth Days (the husband of the woman whose heavy hand with the ruler drove me away from piano lessons) told us that the superintendent of the schools wanted us to play for Senator Richard Russell as he went up Peachtree Street on his way (he hoped) to 1600 Pennsylvania Avenue. To black people, Senator Russell was evil incarnate. He was our senator, but he did not really represent the black people of Georgia. It would be more truthful to say that he was resolutely against us. The thought of playing for Russell was just too much for me and my band mate, Maynard Jackson, the grandson of John Wesley Dobbs of the Negro Voters League. Maynard and I said, "No, we're not."

There was a great stir when word of our stance got out. A meeting was called to discuss our position. After a serious debate, as much as it hurt, Maynard and I ended up caving in to pressure to play for Russell. This was one of those tough situations where any choice made would cause pain to someone. If we had we boycotted the parade, maybe taking some other students with us, Mr. Days might have lost his job. So we went and played with no enthusiasm. The storm passed, Senator Russell did not make it to the White House, and twenty-one years later, Maynard was sworn in as the first black mayor of Atlanta.

Although Maynard and I failed in our attempt to protest against segregation, I had another outlet for my beliefs. My interest in the civil rights movement fit neatly with another of my passions: making speeches. It was not for nothing that I had dreamed of delivering the Emancipation Day oration. From earliest childhood, when I delivered Easter speeches at church, I have been in love with making, writing, reading, and listening to speeches.

I started entering speech contests, through my school and various civic organizations. Most of my topics touched on issues I would later work on as an adult in the movement: voting rights, education, citizenship. I got my picture in the newspapers (both black and white papers) a few times for winning contests or participating in various conferences. When I was fifteen, I won an oratorical contest in Macon sponsored by the State Negro Voters League. My topic was "The Negro in America." "Preparation, perspiration, and perseverance," I said, were the three things needed "by the Negro youth of the day."

Looking back on my teenage self, I can see that I was beginning to come into some sense of who I was going to be. I'd always felt that I wanted to be a leader—my mother had encouraged this from the time I was a little boy. Now I was having experiences and successes that made it clear that I could, in fact, become a leader in some capacity. The more positive attention I received, the more convinced I became. The only question was: "Leader of what?"

At that time in the black community, if you were a good speaker and smart, the natural assumption was that you would become a preacher.

"Vernon, Jr., is going to be a preacher," Sister Fannie Green declared as we had dinner at our home one Sunday after church.

"No, he's not," my mother replied.

"Why not?" Sister Green asked.

"Because no son of mine is going to spend his life kissing the bishop's ass," my mother said.

I was completely shocked. That was the first time I had heard my mother curse. She usually managed to get her point across without resorting to that. The heat of her conviction also surprised me a little. In retrospect, I suppose it wasn't really too much out of character. My mother had little patience for foolishness, and she saw some of the political maneuvering within the AME church as being just that: foolishness. Compared to the freewheeling Baptists, Methodists operate under a fairly rigid hierarchy—with ministers, presiding elders, bishops, general conferences. She could see that it would take a lot of energy to negotiate that structure. To her it would be a waste of my career.

Despite my mother's opinion, I actually liked the idea of becoming a preacher. I have always admired the black church as an institution, the role it has played in the spiritual and political life of the black community—the songs, the preaching, the depth of feeling among the people. Whether it's the kind of church that shouts or one that does not—the denomination doesn't really matter—there is simply a feeling that is unique to the black church because we have had a unique history.

I saw this connection to the past through another of my mother's business ventures, "Lake Jordan." In the late 1940s, Mama bought property in Redan, Georgia, and had a lake dug on it. She put a trailer there and rented the lake out as a spot for black people who because of segregation did not have easy access to other lakes for picnics and recreation. She ran this for a little over a decade. Area churches soon heard about it and started renting Lake Jordan for their outdoor baptisms. I loved going out there to watch them in their long robes, the men and women dressed to the nines. They would sing the old spiritual from slavery time, "Wade in the water / Wade in the water, children," and then dunk people under to make them brand new. All this was very attractive to me.

While in college I was sent to Union Theological Seminary for a conference on the ministry, my first trip to New York. I spent four days listening to some of the great theologians of the era, Reinhold Niebuhr, Paul Tillich, James Robinson. The conference was designed for young men who were pursuing other disciplines but whom local pastors, advisers to the Methodist student movement, or professors thought should be exposed to concentrated discussions of theology. I believe their hope was that we might get a call from the Lord while we were there, and our paths would be set. It didn't happen. Or at least, I didn't hear from Him.

One of my great disappointments in life was that no preacher from the AME church ever took a real interest in me or in the other youngsters in the church. People would say within their earshot, "That boy's going to be called to preach." But as my mother observed, they were so busy running for bishop that there was no time for mentoring young people in their flock. No one came up to me and said, "This is what it's like to be a preacher." Had they done so, the law as a profession might have had some serious competition. Even though I have remained active in the AME church, my two models for ministers are two Baptist preachers, Gardner Taylor and Howard Thurman, both men who acted as mentors and friends to me.

Had I gone into the ministry, I know I would have had a church that combined a spiritual message with a lot of community outreach. I would have had a big gymnasium where kids could come and play games and where boys and girls would come to date and hold hands—a church as community center, seven days a week instead of just on Sunday. It was not to be. I had another calling that has allowed me to do some form of what ministers do. I have never had regrets about the path I chose.

IN BETWEEN SCHOOL AND WORK I managed to have a social life when the time came to do so. Most of my free time was spent in organized activities—day camp and sleep-away camp in the summers, the Butler Street YMCA during the school year. I did the normal things teenagers did at that time. Luckily I had a car, so I was mobile from the age of sixteen. Because I worked, I always had money to take my girlfriends to dances and to the movies. We ate at Joe's Coffee Bar, which had the best bologna sandwiches in the world. We

parked and necked in the backseat of my car, then got moved along
by the police when they caught us. Even though I was a city boy,
drugs were unheard of among my friends. We did do a fair amount
of drinking, with gin being the drink of choice. My buddies and I
would date girls from the East Side one weekend, and the next week
we'd date girls from the West Side of town.

Going to nightclubs was a favorite activity. Some of the dances we
went to started at ten in the evening and ended at two in the morning. There was a singer named Billy Wright who would start to sing
at ten minutes until two, "Let me go home, whiskey / Let me walk
out that door." Then you'd try to get that last slow dance with your
girl.

My date to the senior ball was a girl named Jeannie, who I'll always remember walked up to me one day in the cafeteria as I was sitting with yet a different girlfriend. She threw a bag of marbles down
on the table before me and said, "Since you want to play . . . "

All in all, it was a pretty good life for someone in my circumstances. I can say without fear of contradiction that I had a happy
childhood. I had everything I needed and a good deal of what I
wanted in the way of material goods. I had my family, with all the
good times and shared difficulties that brings. By the time I was in
my teens, my parents had realized their dream of owning their own
home. We moved out of University Homes to the East Side into a little house with green shutters, well-trimmed hedges, and a close-cut
lawn. We were living our own version of the American dream.

How did white people fit into this? The answer is, not much at all.
They were not a direct factor in my growing up. My thoughts about
white people in those days had mainly to do with the system they
were forcing us to live under. We didn't come into much contact
with whites on a social basis because we stayed within the context of
segregation. That we lived in the system did not mean that we accepted it. We knew the way we lived was wrong, that when we went
downtown there were certain rules to be followed because we were
black. We had to go to the bathroom before we left home and take a
drink of water so we could minimize direct contact with the dictates
of segregation.

I very much wanted us to be rid of all that, but that didn't mean I didn't live my life, that I didn't laugh, get angry, fall in love, have all the kinds of responses and emotions that human beings have. There was no "woe is me" aspect to my life. When I was in high school, my friends and I were not sitting around worried because we could not go the Varsity Club at Georgia Tech and get served. That was off-limits. We did not protest that. We were, in the main, just trying to get on with it.

Getting on with it involved developing a real sense that this part of my life was about the preparation to fight the battles we knew were coming. You could not fight without tools, and that was why education was so important. By the time I reached my teens, the attacks on the system of white supremacy in the South were coming fast and furious. My hero A. T. Walden had filed a suit seeking equalization of teachers' pay in the 1940s; the Supreme Court had outlawed white primaries that disenfranchised black voters and had held that the enforcement of racially restrictive covenants violated the Constitution of the United States. These suits and victories were in the news and heralded the beginning of a new world.

We paid a lot of attention to these developments, but we went on with our lives in the meantime. Ours was not a world of complaint. There was a concentration, on the part of my parents and other adults in the community, on going to work, providing for the family, and giving children the spiritual and organizational structure that would make us ready to usher in and participate in what we fully expected would be a brighter future. There was not much we could do about where we were. But we could do something about where we were going.

And so we had our church picnics. We knew when to go to parks in downtown Atlanta and where to set things up. Brother George Johnson made lemonade in big tin tubs with a fifty-pound block of ice in the middle. There were softball games and horseshoe tournaments. Our Sunday-school teachers, the pastor, and the young adults went about doing what they could to make sure everyone had a good time. We didn't let segregation, bad as it was, interfere with enjoying our lives.

There were oratorical contests, talent shows, Negro History Week celebrations. A great disappointment of my early life was that Frank Hill, a good friend, was chosen over me to play Joe Louis in one of our elementary school Negro History Week presentations. Each year our teachers chose students to portray the heroes of the black community. Every boy wanted to be Joe Louis. He embodied all our hopes for power, beauty, and grace. No one could touch him. When Joe Louis fought in the 1940s, you did not have to stay inside to listen to the fight. You could go out into the courtyard of University Homes and listen because every radio in the place was tuned to the broadcast. There were great cheers and much happiness when he won, and total despair when he lost.

The year Frank got to be the Brown Bomber, I was chosen to play William Grant Steele, the first black symphony-orchestra conductor. The "heroes" were announced one by one during a school assembly. When the name Joe Louis was called, the hall broke into thunderous applause, and Frank bounded out, shadow boxing, to receive it. And then later on in the program, when it was William Grant Steele's turn, there was tentative and polite applause—people weren't really sure who Steele was. I walked out in my makeshift tuxedo and tails with a baton in my hand and talked about conducting Tchaikovsky at Carnegie Hall, knowing full well that I was nowhere near as exciting to the audience as Joe Louis. Although I didn't see it at the time, my teachers were exactly right; I was better suited to being William Grant Steele, to being the one who brought something a little different to the proceedings.

Because so many areas of life were closed to black people, we found our heroes where we could. The "first Negro" to do this, the first to do that, confirmed that we as a people were on the move. There was no more potent a symbol of this than Jackie Robinson. With the popularity of basketball among black youth today, it may be hard for some to imagine how much a part of life baseball was to blacks, particularly in the South. When Jackie Robinson broke baseball's color bar, he was immediately elevated to the status of an icon within our community.

Robinson came to Atlanta with the Brooklyn Dodgers in 1949

when the team was on its way up from spring training. The Dodgers had arranged to play an exhibition game against the Atlanta Crackers, the local minor-league team. It is almost unfathomable that in my lifetime there could have been a team officially known as the Crackers. Even more surreal was that Atlanta's Negro League team was called the Atlanta Black Crackers. Robinson's arrival was a big moment, and there was no way my father, Windsor, or I would have missed it. We went to Ponce de Leon Park, thrilled at the prospect of getting a glimpse of Robinson. The seats in the park were divided to provide for maximum segregation. From first base to third, under covered stands, sat the white people. Out in left field and right field stood all the black people; there were very few seats for us and no cover. News of Robinson's presence brought out an overflow crowd, and rather than turn people away, the managers of the ballpark roped off part of center field to allow for more spectators. Any ball hit into the area beyond the rope was ruled an automatic double. Right behind that rope is where I stood with my father and Windsor.

When Jackie Robinson came to the plate, there were boos from first to third base. The people in left, right, and center field went crazy with applause. He did not get a hit the first time up. On his second at bat, Robinson singled to left field. A few cheers rose from first to third, but mainly boos. The fans in the outfield again cheered loudly. Then Robinson stole second base. From first to third, a few more cheers, and those in left, right, and center field went absolutely nuts.

The next batter hit a pop fly to right field, which was caught easily. Robinson tagged and went to third. George Diehl was pitching for the Crackers, and Country Brown was the catcher. Robinson took a lead off third base as Diehl got set to pitch. He threw the ball, Brown caught it and threw it back. Before they knew what had happened, Robinson had stolen home. The entire stadium erupted. Everyone cheered. The people seated from first to third momentarily forgot Robinson was black. In that split second, they saw only his tremendous skill. We blacks were cheering as if he had won something for us. And, of course, he had.

Witnessing Robinson's triumph would have been excitement

enough for the Jordans. Yet there was even more to come. Later on, the Dodgers' catcher, Bruce Edwards, came to the plate and hit a ground-rule double right over the rope into center field. We stood and watched the ball sail toward us. As it came near, the crowd spread out and I got separated from my father and Windsor. Looking around trying to find them, I saw a small mountain of what looked like a hundred men who had scrambled to get the ball. Very quickly, the pile grew smaller as each disappointed man got to his feet. From the bottom of the pile came this voice, "I got it! I got it!" I recognized it instantly. It was my father. That was a heroic moment for all of us. We took the ball home and wrote on it, "Ball hit by Bruce Edwards during the first game Jackie Robinson played as a Dodger in Atlanta." Windsor still has it.

When this happened, my father had been home from the war for four years, but his time in the service was not a regular topic of conversation at home. Men in his generation didn't talk very much about their feelings, but I think the war deeply affected my father emotionally. The first time I ever saw him cry was one evening when we were sitting, as we did every night after dinner, listening to the radio. In celebration of Veterans Day, the station replayed a very inspirational prayer that Franklin Roosevelt had given to be broadcast to all the troops overseas.

Windsor and I were sitting on the floor, and my parents were in chairs. At some point, I looked up to see tears streaming down my father's face, and he began to cry in earnest. Seeing a parent cry is one of the most unsettling things that can happen to a child. "What's the matter?" I asked.

He explained that when he had first heard the speech, he was on a ship in Okinawa. During that time he was wondering whether he would ever see his family again, and yet here we all were.

"I can't help myself," he said almost apologetically.

There was a real paradox to my father's situation and that of other black veterans. They had risked their lives fighting for their country and returned home to a place where they could not sit where they wanted on a public bus or go to state schools their tax dollars supported. Their children were shunted into inferior primary and secondary schools. It was just obscene. But my father never talked to us about it in those terms. The reality was what it was, and he came home and went back to work, although I believe he and the men in his Bible study class discussed his predicament when they veered away from religion to talk politics. If he had any bitterness about this, he kept it to himself.

THE PROBLEMS CAUSED by Atlanta's racial divisions helped define our lives in important ways. Race, however, wasn't the only issue. The class system within the black community entered into the equation as well. My family was comfortable financially, but we were never part of what could be called the elite of Atlanta's black society. We didn't concern ourselves with this except to the extent that it caused us any specific problems. There were times that it did.

Atlanta has long had a reputation as being a city where some members of the black community are extremely color conscious. There was certainly a lot of that when I was a kid. If someone called a person "black," that was considered cause to fight. This was all a holdover from slavery, when looking more like white masters meant, in some cases, better treatment for the light-skinned slave. Lightness was valued. Darkness was devalued. After slavery ended, this hardened into some version of a caste system within the black community. Color consciousness among blacks is just another component of white supremacy.

My early days in Atlanta were well before the "black is beautiful" movement of the 1960s offered a strong critique of that type of thinking. Color consciousness hasn't disappeared—there are still some people holding onto it. I would bet, however, that calling someone "black" today wouldn't mean the same thing it meant in the 1940s and 1950s. That's a great advance.

I have very dark skin. I have never seen blackness as being negative, in me or in anyone else. In school I dated whichever attractive girls would go out with me. As a precocious (and tall) eighth grader, I once made a pass at a girl in the eleventh grade. "I'd like to talk to you," I said. She replied, "You're too black to talk to me." So I didn't try to talk to her anymore. Interestingly enough, on my first day at Howard Law School I ran into this girl. She had taken some time off from school and had returned as an undergraduate. When I encountered her the second time and she knew I was a law student, she wasn't so stuck up.

In the end, you simply cannot let others define you in a negative way and make that a part of your view of yourself. The need to make another human being feel small, for whatever reason, is a sign of deep personal turmoil. You can't let someone else's problem keep you from doing what you set out to do in the world.

This business of color within the black community will, I believe, continue to diminish as a serious issue. It certainly won't determine people's careers or social standing to the extent it once did. It just can't anymore. With the doors to education open to more blacks than ever, there is simply no way to confine the opportunities for advancement to black people of any particular shade. When I go to college commencements now, I see handsome young black men and beautiful young black women of all hues who are going on to make something of themselves. For them, blackness is a state of mind—and a good and comfortable one, too. That is just the way it should be.

D URING THE FALL OF 1952 the National Honor Society at David T. Howard High School had a visitor. Paul Lawrence, a representative from the National Service and Scholarship Fund for Negro Students, came to my school to encourage its best students to think of applying to white colleges in the North. Traditionally black schools were great, he said, but it was important for us to know there were other choices we could make.

This effort was part of the spirit of the times—to get young black people to feel that the nation was ours, too, and that we weren't confined to any narrow set of opportunities or aspirations. Lawrence described how his organization had successfully placed students from Dunbar High, the renowned black high school in

Washington, D.C., into white colleges. "We could do the same thing at your school," he said.

Lawrence was a very tall, imposing man. I remember being quite impressed by him, and what he had to say. His message was something of an eye-opener for me. Although I'd wanted to go away to college, I hadn't really considered going to a white school. Lawrence's presentation broadened my perspective considerably. Suddenly I had something else to think about.

There was one thing I didn't have to mull over. I knew I didn't want to go to school in Atlanta. While I respected the traditions and the prestige of the black colleges there, they were simply too close to home for me. Familiarity with them didn't breed contempt, it just foretold a lack of adventure.

My best buddies of that time, Riley Ragsdale and Walter Lee, were also in the honor society, and they heard Lawrence's appeal along with me. The three of us had talked a great deal about what we'd do once we graduated from high school. As far as we were concerned, our college careers were all mapped out. First, we would go to Howard University in Washington, D.C.—a black school, far enough from home to be "away" but close enough for us to come home when we needed to. Then we'd get a house together, be sharp everyday, go to classes, drive our cars, date the girls. We were definitely set.

Lawrence's visit threw a monkey wrench into this. I was intrigued with the notion of doing something completely different, something out of the ordinary. The idea fit me perfectly. I am a loner by nature. The chance to go to a new place and make a start in unfamiliar surroundings complemented my basic impulse to be alone, even in a crowd. As much as I wanted to be with my friends, our plans could not compete with this very deep personal instinct.

At the same time, my interest in going to a white college was probably a natural outgrowth of my desire to change the way blacks lived in the United States. I had spoken about this myself in various places, and I had listened avidly when others spoke of it. Doing away with limitations and opening horizons was what it was all about. We had to take those chances, in order to go places we weren't "supposed to" or "expected to" go. I was confident I would succeed wherever I went, so why not do that in an unexpected venue?

I applied to Howard, but I also sent off applications to several predominately white colleges. Some of my teachers were less than enthusiastic about my plans. I had a bit of a problem with them when the time came to ask for letters of recommendation. They had gone to black colleges, most of them right there in Atlanta. Each tended to be very chauvinistic about his or her alma mater: "If Morehouse was good enough for me . . ."; "If Morris Brown was good enough for me . . . "

There was a tension within them. On the one hand, they were pleased that I was going to go to college and, presumably, to do well in the world. The vast majority of their students never made it to that point. At the same time, there was this notion that my decision to apply to a white school was a judgment of them, and of the schools they had attended. I was, in some fundamental way, rejecting them and rejecting something of which they were very proud.

For my part, it really was just about trying something different. Someone had made me aware of an alternative I hadn't known about. I saw it as a great challenge, to do something neither I nor anybody else expected me to do. This was in no way a statement of how I viewed my teachers. I admired them very much, but that didn't mean I had to follow the same path in life that they had followed. Moreover, it was largely their doing that I was the type of young man who wanted to go off and prove his mettle. Had it not been for the faith in me they'd shown over the years, I wouldn't have had the confidence to go off into the unknown. They had done their job. Some of them just didn't see it that way, but in the end, of course, they all went ahead and wrote very favorable recommendations.

My first contact with a white institution turned out badly. I was one of ten kids from Atlanta, and the only black one, who applied to Dartmouth College that year. I went downtown for my interview with an alumnus of the college, a local banker who was the head of the Dartmouth Alumni Association in Atlanta. Things went well at first. He noted my good grades and my extracurricular activities, and then he summed up by telling me that the reason I should go to

Dartmouth was that I could then come back to Atlanta and be a "Booker T. Washington for my people."

I didn't like that. I admire Booker T. Washington. He was a man of great accomplishment who built an institution, the Tuskegee Institute (now known as Tuskegee University), that survives today. What I didn't like was having this white man tell me what I should do with my life under those circumstances. Even if it was a noble idea (and he meant no harm; he thought he was saying something positive) his suggestion made it clear that he wasn't thinking of me as a person.

I was just a symbol to him, not a young man who needed to be given the chance to study his own mind and conscience to find out what was important to him in life—which is what a liberal arts education is supposed to allow students to do. When he should have been telling me how Dartmouth was going to help start me on that journey of self-discovery, he'd already made the discovery and passed it along to me. His presumptuousness put me right off Dartmouth College.

I'd also applied to DePauw University, a small school in Greencastle, Indiana. More than any other place with which I had dealings, DePauw made its case to me. Administrators wrote to me. Students wrote to me. The bank wrote to tell me how they would handle my money. Fraternities wrote warm letters of welcome. Members of the staff wrote to tell me how they would make sure I had everything I needed—all of them making it sound as if the school would disappear into a sinkhole if I didn't come to Greencastle. It was a magnificent recruitment effort. Of course, none of these people, save the administrators, knew that I was black. They'd just gotten the names and addresses of the accepted students and had gone into their recruitment mode.

As for Howard, I'd spent time there during the eleventh grade, having gone to Washington to be a part of conference on citizenship sponsored by the National Education Association and the U.S. Department of Justice. President Harry Truman was a speaker, along with Eleanor Roosevelt and others. I was a delegate sent by the Georgia Congress of Colored Parents and Teachers and the Atlanta District PTA, with the strong encouragement of my mother, who was still the president of the PTA at my high school and an officer in the Georgia Congress. I stayed at Carver Hall on the Howard campus. So I was familiar with the school, and I liked what I'd seen.

My parents, who supported my decision not to go to school in Atlanta, were very keen on Howard. At one point after I had been accepted at Howard and DePauw, I came home to find a letter on my bed. This was how my mother often communicated with me. She wrote, in part: "We want you to know we will support you in whatever decision you make about college. But we think if you go to Howard you might be more comfortable socially, academically, and financially."

I think this was something of a test. They wanted to see just how committed I was to going north for college and, at the same time, to give me a chance to know that I was making the decision for myself. Whether it was DePauw or Howard, my mother really just wanted to make sure that I went away to college for the same reason she had sent me and Windsor to Washington with the school patrol when we were in the fifth and sixth grades: The new surroundings would bring new experiences that would, in turn, create opportunities I might not have otherwise.

Both my mother and father were very excited about the prospect of getting me off to school. My mother took me downtown to Zachary's to upgrade my wardrobe. Not that there were any particular problems with the way I dressed. Slovenliness has never been an issue with me. Even as a teenager I was very meticulous about my appearance. The special trip downtown to buy clothes was a signal that the process of easing me out of high school and into the world of college had begun. My mother bought me a very well made and attractive blue serge suit and a dinner jacket and justified it by saying, "You'll need this when you're in college." I went home feeling on the edge of something.

MY BUDDIES WERE LESS SUPPORTIVE. Riley and Walter were none too happy about the possibility that I would go to a white college. What would happen to our plans for Howard? Hadn't we all agreed? It would not be the last time that decisions I made for myself put me at odds with friends.

Riley, Walter, and I had continued our practice of dating West Side girls and East Side girls. On a weekend that we were supposed to go out with the girls from the East Side, I had to work a party with my mother. The guys went out anyway, and my East Side girlfriend, Lessie, went with them. I was free the next night, so I made a date to see Lessie.

I picked her up, then we went out and wound up at our usual haunt, Joe's Coffee Bar, drinking gin. At one point Lessie looked at me and said, "I want to tell you something."

"What?" I asked.

She paused a moment and said, "Your friends are not your friends."

"What are you talking about?" I knew she meant Riley and Walter.

She explained. "Riley and Walter say you think you're better than they are because you aren't going to go to Howard with them."

I was dumbstruck. Could they really have believed I felt that way? My buddies weren't expressing disappointment that we wouldn't be together—that they'd miss me. I would have understood that. I felt the same way about them. Instead they were reading a bad motive into my decision-making process.

I, too, had enjoyed our dream about going to college together. But this was a very serious, very personal matter to me. I wanted to remain connected to them—we would all be coming home to the same place for school vacations—though not at the expense of following my own judgment about what was the right thing for me to do at that time.

Then Lessie, who was just a wonderful girl, said something that eased the deep hurt I was feeling at that moment. She said, "I want to tell you something else. Don't pay any attention to Riley and Walter You're smart. You go on up to your school." I've always been grateful to her for saying that.

GRADUATION DAY CAME. My whole family turned out for the ceremony in the City Auditorium. I was happy, but feeling a little bruised, still smarting from a failed run for student-body president earlier in the school year. Ever since I was in the eighth grade, I had wanted to be president of the student body, which could only be done as a senior.

I took my campaign very seriously. My running mate was Ethel Wardell, and we addressed the lofty issues of the day—citizenship, civil rights—the kind of things I talked about at speech tournaments. My opponent, Lonnie King, who would later be involved in the sit-in movement, took a different approach. He engaged in a little negative campaigning. He actually had a slogan that went up on posters: "Vernon wants the job too bad. Ethel makes everyone mad." Well, I did want the job very badly, and Ethel was a very smart girl and, as often happens, was resented for this.

We were allowed to make a campaign speech during the school assembly. I gave a speech quoting every philosopher I'd ever heard of—very serious, very earnest. My opponent got up and said: "Vernon's mother is the head of the PTA. My mother can't be the head of the PTA because she has to go to work every day." The crowd loved it. Then he went on to talk about the food in the cafeteria and that he was going to work to make it better. They loved that as well. As a finish to his presentation, he called some of his friends to the stage and they played a rousing rendition of "Begin the Beguine." The audience loved that most of all. That was enough. He won. I was devastated.

My mother was philosophical about the whole disaster. Even though she was always my greatest champion, she thought losing might have been good for me. It was one thing to be confident, she felt; it was quite another to be too cocky. Having tasted a good amount of success, she saw me drifting toward thinking I was entitled to everything I wanted. Naturally, I simply couldn't think of it that way. I wanted to win, and I was very hurt that I didn't. Although it may seem strange to say, after all these years, I still don't think I've gotten completely over it.

One thing that pacified me a bit on graduation night was that I had won the Atlanta Journal Cup. During those days, the paper that is now the *Atlanta Journal-Constitution* was two separate papers— the *Atlanta Journal* came out in the evening, the *Atlanta Constitution* in the morning. The Atlanta Journal Cup was given to the person voted the best all-around student in each high school in Atlanta. When I was chosen, I got my name and picture in the *Journal*, which by all measures qualified as a very big deal. My parents were quite excited about this, and I was happy because I knew that this was the fulfillment of their dreams for me. Considering it now, I can imagine even more clearly how they must have felt about this.

We marched into the auditorium in our caps and gowns. We got our diplomas; the valedictorian and salutatorian made speeches. I was presented with the Atlanta Journal Cup. When it was all over, I went off to a night of celebration with my friends. It was the end of something, and a beginning.

CHAPTER 3

DEPAUW

TWO DAYS AFTER MY GRADUATION from high school, I was on a train heading for Greencastle, Indiana. I had been invited to attend an Educational Guidance Clinic at DePauw University, which I had chosen to attend in the fall. The conference was a way of getting some of the things one would normally do during Freshman Orientation Week out of the way. It was optional, but there was no way I'd let that opportunity pass. I was going to go, and go alone. It was a heady feeling being a young man alone going out of state, out of one region into another. I'd been on trips before—to conferences, speech tournaments, family visits—but this one was different. This trip was about me and my future life in the most intensely personal way. I sat at the window for the whole trip, watching the landscape, the houses, the towns change as I made my way from the South to the North.

If I'd had any doubts at all about whether I wanted to go to school at DePauw, they were wiped away after this trip. There were about forty other incoming freshmen at the conference. We stayed in dormitories and ate at the campus dining hall. I was the only black participant and was not at all uncomfortable. This was the way it was going to be. I had chosen this path.

My uniqueness had a very positive side to it. Because I was the only "one," I became an instant object of curiosity and attention, almost like a star in some sense. I think it made a big difference that after a few years of participating in speech contests and presenting myself before an audience I was self-assured. Whatever came, I thought I could handle it.

It helped that I was able to do something during the week that made a favorable impression on my classmates. We were kept busy all day with various programs and tests. Greencastle wasn't exactly a hub of activity at night, so to fill some of the empty hours when we were back in the dorms, I drew upon my experience as a camp counselor. I knew lots of songs that my dorm mates hadn't heard. So I taught them, and in that more innocent time, singing them was a satisfying form of recreation.

The one jarring note came near the end of the week. John Wittich, the dean of admissions, gave me some tough news. He said that based on the results of tests taken during the orientation, I shouldn't want to come to DePauw; the academic work would be too hard for me. His advice was very specific: "Go to Ball State," he said, referring to a state school in Muncie, Indiana. He noted my ambition to become a lawyer, and all but said the idea was ridiculous. I should concentrate instead on becoming a high-school social science teacher, which would be more suitable given my test scores.

He further suggested that the social life for a black student at De-Pauw would not be promising. In other words, interracial dating was frowned upon. There were no black women enrolled at De-Pauw. He went on to say that even getting a haircut might not be possible. He seemed to be thinking of everything he could say that might discourage me.

I was not discouraged. I was not entirely surprised to find out that I was behind the other students, because I knew there were problems with the segregated schools I had attended in Atlanta. Fortunately, my image of myself was so set at this point that I assumed that whatever problem existed could be fixed. Certainly I should be given the chance to fix it, to take my best shot before I was sent off to Ball State. I was far more angry at Dean Wittich than I was dispirited. I said to myself, "I shall return." The week ended, I said good-bye to my newly made friends, and I went back to Georgia.

M Y PARENTS QUICKLY PUT TO REST my thoughts of going alone to begin my college days at DePauw. They were absolutely set on taking me to college themselves. And Windsor would come along as well. As much as I didn't want this, I knew it was useless to protest, particularly since my parents had made up their minds about it. So I went off to Indiana, family in tow.

Things worked out quite well. My parents were impressed with the school and the warm way they were received. What a moment for two people whose family had almost no history of attending college—my father's youngest brother, Uncle Lewis, was the first in his family to do so. On my mother's side, no one had gone to college. I was a typical eighteen-year-old, not overly concerned with my parents' inner lives. There was no real way for me to fully grasp what taking me to DePauw must have meant to them. *"We're taking our son to college!"*—of course they were supposed to come.

The school assigned a faculty member and an upperclassman to help first-year students and their parents with orientation. We each had a schedule of meetings with people in the community, to get us acquainted with the area. My family visited with the president of the local branch of the Central National Bank. There was talk and good food. To cap everything off, on Sunday morning, Dr. Howard Thurman preached.

Dr. Thurman was one of the greatest and most influential preachers the world has produced. He was a spiritual leader of the still-nascent American civil rights movement, and in later years he would give wise counsel to, among others, Martin Luther King, Jr., Whitney Young, James Farmer (who was his student), Jesse Jackson and, I'm very proud to say, me. It was Thurman who had led a group of black Americans to India in the 1930s, where he met Mahatma

Gandhi and was greatly influenced by Gandhi's theory of nonviolent revolution. His book *Jesus and the Disinherited* was a spiritual blueprint for the themes struck by leaders of the movement in the 1950s.

Of course I could not know as I sat with my family in church preparing to listen to Dr. Thurman that one day he would come to play a pivotal role in my life, as a mentor and friend, that his words would literally help keep me alive. On that Sunday morning in 1953, I was just a freshman and he had just begun his tenure as dean of Marsh Chapel at Boston University, the first black person to occupy such a position in a white institution. We were both far away from the times to come.

Dr. Thurman was awesome that day before a church filled with students and members of the town. Along with Dr. Thurman, we (the Jordan family) were the only blacks in the congregation. This was my family's first experience in an all-white church. We walked in, sat down, and noted with interest the two pulpits that are in every Methodist church sanctuary. Dr. Thurman stood in the higher one, in a purple robe. His sermon that day was, literally, the Lord's Prayer. He began, "Our Father," and for the next minute or so he didn't say anything. He went on, "Who art in Heaven," followed by another long pause, and then "Hallowed be thy name." He went on like that through the entire prayer, letting the meaning of each phrase sink in.

The Lord's Prayer, the most important one in the Christian faith, can be (and often is) said in a flash, without considering its meaning. In Dr. Thurman's skillful and divinely inspired hands, it was transformed. For one moment, on a Sunday morning, he led us through a deep consideration of what that prayer really says. Its simple power was restored.

You know you're in the presence of a good preacher when he or she finds a truth and reveals it to a congregation, and everything is laid bare. Howard Thurman held me spellbound. All I could think of after he finished was getting to him so I could shake his hand. I went over and told him how much I admired what he'd done. He didn't know me from anybody, but that would change.

WHEN THE TIME CAME for my parents to leave, we stood near our car, saying last-minute good-byes. Windsor was the first to peel off, anxious to leave because it meant he'd have a bedroom all to himself when he got back home. My departure was a net gain for him. He wasted no time getting in the car. My mother gave me $50 and wished me luck. This was what she had worked for, and now the day was here. There weren't any words to sum up the years and effort she had put into this.

Having now come to DePauw, and experienced the friendliness of the people, my father was totally sold on the school. He was generally much less communicative than my mother. Most of the time I had to sense what he was feeling because he wasn't in the habit of telling me or writing it down as my mother did. Now, he came over to me and said, "You can't come home."

I had no idea what he was talking about. "What do you mean, I can't come home?"

He said, "I mean you can't come home. You know those tests say that you don't read as fast as these boys and girls. When they've finished the book you may still be reading. But you just can't come home."

I had no idea he was concerned about that. I'd put that out of my mind because I was so determined everything would work out. But then, as I stood there in the face of my father's very realistic view of all that was at stake, I felt a little exposed.

"Well, what should I do, Daddy?" I asked.

"Read, boy," he said. "Read."

There wasn't much more to say. We shook hands, he got in the car, drove off, and left me to my task.

I had been in my room a week when my roommates arrived. Russ Foote and Roy Carlson were two Midwestern boys who were seniors and great friends. They had planned, in the same way I had planned with Riley and Walter, to spend their senior year in college together. Instead they arrived at school to find they'd been placed with me, a black freshman from Atlanta, Georgia. When they walked in and saw me sitting there, the look on their faces said it all. What have we gotten ourselves into? Though they were not hostile or impolite, I knew they wished things were different—that I wasn't there, that they could have their partnership as they had planned it.

For several weeks we co-existed. I went about my business. They went about theirs. One evening, I came back to our room from studying in the library. As I was putting away my books and papers, Russ said, "We've been talking about you."

That was interesting. "Really?" I said, with no clue as to where this was going.

"Yeah" he said. "We've decided something."

"What did you all decide?" I asked.

"Well, we've decided that you're no different than us."

This was even more interesting. "Oh," I said.

"Yeah. You snore. You sing in the shower. You do your work."

I didn't really know what to say to that. On one hand, that they had to think about it spoke volumes about their level of awareness. On the other hand, they were just two guys who had grown up without any relationship with a black person. It would be easy to recite the kind of negative things they'd probably read or had been told about blacks. The bottom line was that they were doing the best they could to make an overture to me. I accepted it. From that moment we began the process of becoming true roommates.

MY MOTHER HELD TO HER INSISTENCE that I join the ROTC, and as always, I followed her instructions. It was a disaster. The best way to put it is that I do not have what might be called "the military temperament." Of course I would fight to defend my country, but I had absolutely no interest in the ROTC program, what its officers and members were doing, how they were doing it, why they were doing it, and how I was supposed to fit into it all. But my mother had spoken.

Not long after signing up, I was instructed to report to our commanding officer. I walked into the reception area and greeted his secretary. She told me he was expecting me. I knocked. He told me to come in, and I did. No sooner had I gotten both feet inside the door and prepared to close it behind me than he bellowed, "Get the hell out of here, right now. And come back in here correctly."

I was perplexed. I backed out of the office, puzzled and alarmed at the same time.

"What was that for? What did I do?" I asked his secretary.

"You didn't go in the right way. You're supposed to go in, click your heels and salute and say, 'Cadet Jordan reporting, sir,'" she explained.

Although I thought this was nonsense, there was nothing to do but follow her instructions. He'd sent for me, so I had to go.

I went in, clicked my heels, saluted, uttered the correct words, feeling a little foolish. My performance satisfied the commandant, and he told me to have a seat. He explained that he had received my application to DePauw.

"I understand you play the E-flat tuba," he said.

"Yes, I do." During my senior year in high school, I had switched from playing the trumpet to the E-flat tuba.

"Well, we need a tuba player for the ROTC band."

"I don't want to play the tuba. I don't even want to be in a band anymore," I said, thinking this would end it.

It did not. "Doesn't matter. We need a tuba player. Consider it an order."

Not wanting to let the matter drop there, I went to the dean's office to try to get out of the ROTC. He wasn't sympathetic. "You're in the army now," he said. So, against my deepest wishes, I played the tuba in the ROTC band.

As IT DOES FOR EVERY NEW STUDENT IN COLLEGE, the first fall went by quickly. Before I knew it, I was back in Atlanta for Thanksgiving. My buddies from high school who had gone to college were all home. As it turned out, only Riley had gone to Howard. Walter had gone to Morehouse. Fate had wiped away every scrap of our little dream of a Howard trio.

I was anxious to get together with Riley and Walter to swap stories about our college adventures. The first night we got together, I made the mistake of wearing my ROTC uniform to our rendezvous at Joe's Coffee Bar. The fellows really went after me about it: "Hey, man, you're not sharp anymore. Got your little uniform on."

I was totally unprepared for this. That uniform was the one thing that made ROTC bearable. Even more important, I was proud to wear it home because I knew it would make my father, the old navy man, happy. As I had walked so proudly with him in his uniform during the war, he could now do the same with me. It never occurred to me that this could be a problem with my friends. Why should it have been? What did it have to do with Riley and Walter?

My friends, of course, couldn't know what this meant in my life and might not have cared even if they had known. They were holding on to their disappointment with my choice of school, and their faulty assessment of why I had made that choice. It's safe to say that if it hadn't been the uniform, it would have been something else. They were angry at me. For whatever reason, Walter had not joined Riley at Howard. Yet they didn't seem to be at war with each other about that.

There was no way to put matters back as they were. We were on our way to becoming different people, a process that had started back when I gave up on our plan for college. Maybe the differences were always there, masked by our high-school enthusiasm for one another.

I did try, over the course of the vacation, to make some headway with Riley and Walter. We might, I thought, build a friendship that took account of our differing circumstances. If real affection was there, that should have been possible. Nothing I tried seemed to work. Things were just the same when I came home for Christmas break: more overtures met by sarcasm and borderline rejection.

I went back to Greencastle thinking of how estranged I was from the people with whom I'd been close for so many years. With no hope of figuring this out on my own, I wrote to Ethel Wardell, who had been my running mate when I had run for president of the student body at Howard High. She had gone to Spelman College. Ethel was my friend, and I knew she was in love with Riley. In fact, Riley would later leave Howard and marry her. If anyone had a clue about what was going on, she would.

"What's the matter with Riley and Walter? What have I done wrong?" I asked.

Ethel wrote me back and said at one point—very seriously, taking a cue from Rudyard Kipling—"Vernon, you're walking with kings and you've lost the common touch."

As soon as read this I sat down and wrote her a one-sentence reply, "Dear Ethel, Kiss my ass."

There would be no more efforts to patch things up. We'd all have to do the best we could in the world.

As all of this was happening, I noticed there was a hint of surprise among some of my teachers and others back home in Atlanta that I could afford to go away to school, especially a white school. That sort of thing was rare, and strictly for upper-class blacks. In their eyes my family didn't belong in that category. I was the son of a cook and a postal worker. We lived on the East Side, instead of the more socially correct West Side.

It apparently hadn't dawned on some people that a family like mine could manage their lives in a way that allowed them to send a child off to college. They just didn't know my parents. Though my mother and father disagreed about some things, they agreed on their goals for the family, and they lived in pursuit of achieving them. This meant that they worked hard, and especially in my mother's case, were fanatical about saving money. There were few extravagances in our lives. I remember a time when my father wanted to play poker for money, and my mother was dead set against it. Resources were to be husbanded for the good of the household.

When I think of what made the difference in my life and the lives of my friends who were, for the most part, similarly situated, I would have to point to my parents' willingness to make short-term sacrifices for long-term gains. Some of my friends' parents were unwilling to do this. It was not always the case that they had less money than we had. In some cases, they may have had more. But they also had different values. If people had known the sacrifices my parents made, there wouldn't have been any sense of shock about how they were able to pay for my schooling.

Evidence of this slightly bemused attitude, which first showed itself during my college application process, continued well into my time at DePauw. I came home on vacation once and was invited to speak and review the Sunday school lesson at the Friendship Baptist Church, which served a largely middle-class congregation. The superintendent of the Sunday school, a very prominent businessman who had invited me, introduced me by saying: "Vernon Jordan goes to DePauw University, a fine school in the Midwest. He's there because he received a scholarship."

When I rose to speak, I said: "It's really wonderful to be here and I thank you for your kind introduction. But I'd like to make one factual correction and that is that I am not at DePauw University on a scholarship. I'm at DePauw because my mother cooks really good food for white people and my father carries the mail at Fort MacPherson."

My host may have been embarrassed, but sympathy for him was the last thing on my mind. It was important for me to set the record straight. To my way of thinking, he had insulted my parents by diminishing what I knew from my day-to-day life with them was their measured, diligent, and really heroic effort to put my brothers and me on the right track. They worked hard, my mother was creative, and they saved their money. As a result of their sacrifices, my parents had accumulated enough money to allow me to get an education at the college of my choice.

My host wasn't malicious. He was acting according to his understanding of the rules of life that had been pounded into him. He could sense the question hanging in the minds of the congregation as they sat looking at me. What's he doing in a place like that? I lived on the wrong side of town. My achievement instantly made all their cherished beliefs ripe for rethinking. He felt it was his duty to explain this strange turn of events in a way that might soothe any anxieties that might have been out there in the congregation.

THINGS FELL PRETTY MUCH INTO PLACE once I settled into the routine of school. If the work was much harder for me than it was for most of my classmates, it wasn't apparent. We all complained about the work we had to do, and we all fretted over tests. I certainly was never at the top of my class, but I held my own.

I worked during school to cover day-to-day expenses. I was a babysitter for faculty members. And my experience with my mother's business came in handy for my main job, which was head waiter at the Longden Hall dining room. That's how I first met Richard Nixon. He was then the vice-president, and he came to DePauw during my senior year to dedicate the Roy O. West Library. There was a luncheon for him afterward in the Bowman Gymnasium, and I, along with another classmate, was chosen to be a waiter at the head table where Nixon sat. We were introduced to him, and it was a great thing to be able to write home and tell my parents that I'd met the vice-president. I have a wonderful (almost surreal) photograph of me at age twenty holding a coffeepot, standing at Nixon's table in 1956.

Home never seemed too far away. My mother's letters arrived with precise regularity. She wrote to me every day—sometimes letters, sometimes just short notes of instruction or items of interest from the newspaper. She'd done the same thing for my father when he was away during the war. If she had nothing in particular to say to him, she would stick our homework into an envelope and send it along. Keeping in touch was extremely important to her. At the end of her missives to me, she would always write, "If you make a dime, save ten cents," and "If you trust Him, He will take care of you."

One of my deepest regrets is that I didn't think to keep track of all of my mother's letters. As so often happens, we take for granted the things that are around us all the time. Because she had been in the habit of leaving me notes and writing to me even when I was at home, I tended to take the messages in the letters without focusing on the physical pieces of paper. I simply didn't see them as the heirlooms they should have become.

A good part of my energy was taken up with a number of school-related organizations and activities. There was no way I could ever give up public speaking. I very quickly looked around for a way to indulge myself. Not long after I got to DePauw, I read about the Margaret Noble Lee Extemporaneous Speaking Contest, to determine the school's best orator.

I mentioned to William Allison, one of the four black students at DePauw, that I was thinking of entering the contest. Allison was an upperclassman, also from Atlanta. I hadn't known him before I got to DePauw. We came from very different backgrounds; his whole family were college graduates. When we discovered that we were from the same hometown, his first question to me was, "Who are your parents?"—trying to figure out my place in the social order. I replied, "You won't know my parents."

Allison came to my room one night and was horrified when I opened the door wearing a stocking cap to make my hair lie flat. "Man, you can't do that here!" he said. He had one of those "What will the white people think?" responses that sometimes arise in black people who feel intimidated in a predominately white setting—like refusing to eat watermelon in public. Because I was living in a room with two white people, his reasoning went, I had to change the way I treated my hair. I didn't care what Allison or anyone else thought; I was not giving up my stocking cap.

When I told Allison that I was thinking about entering the Margaret Noble Lee speech contest, he was adamantly opposed. "No, no, you shouldn't do that," he told me. "That would be a big mistake. The Lee contest is very serious. You could end up being really embarrassed." He was talking to me as an upperclassman to a freshman, thinking I would be in way over my head. "That's much too sophisticated for you," he said. "I wouldn't waste my time with that."

For a brief while I took Allison's words to heart. Then I talked to my speech teacher, Dr. Forrest Seal, about it, and he was very enthusiastic. "By all means do it," he said.

I entered the contest, and to my amazement, when I had made it to the third round, there was William Allison as one of my opponents. He had never told me he was going to enter the contest. I've never understood why. To his surprise (probably great surprise), I won the round. There was one more after that, and then I made it to the finals, along with three other speakers.

One of the good things about going to a school in a small town is that everything that happens there commands great attention. There's no competing entertainment. When the four of us gathered to give our speeches in East College, we were before a capacity crowd. My topic was "The Negro in America," a subject I'd been talking about since I was fifteen years old. I felt comfortable with that. I did my best, and I won.

This set the course for the rest of my time at DePauw. Winning the contest in so public a forum shaped the way people viewed me. From then on, everyone knew there was something that I could do, and that something was positive.

For the next four years I gave speeches on campus and off. Kids at school would mention me to their folks, or to others in their hometowns, and I'd get invitations to speak at their churches. I traveled along the back roads of Indiana to speak before small country Methodist congregations, always the only black person in the room. On more than one occasion, children of the congregation would rub my hand as if they thought the black was going to come off.

Although Indiana is above the Mason-Dixon line, it has a tough history regarding race. For a time it had the largest and most active chapters of the Ku Klux Klan in the country. It was a mess in the 1920s and 1930s. When I was there in the 1950s, it wasn't exactly a racial utopia. My hosts, by virtue of having invited me to speak there on what was called "Race Relations Sunday," tended to be among the more enlightened (or were striving to be enlightened) members of the community. They were, for the most part, prepared to hear my message.

This was both fun and excellent training. I was talking to people whose instincts were basically sound, who were inclined to do the right thing, but who just didn't know how to translate their feelings into practice. They were searching. That's a universal phenomenon. Whether it's race relations, how to deliver services, how to put together a deal—whatever—the question is very much the same: What notes do you strike to inspire people or help them get to the place they want to be? I had to think about that a lot during those times.

I entered other oratorical contests as well. One of the more important ones was the Indiana Interstate Oratorical Association Contest at Franklin College, which I won during my sophomore year. In the finals, I was up against another young black man from Indiana State University. His speech made me very angry; he was essentially apologizing to white people for *Brown v. Board of Education,* which had been decided the previous spring. I think his coach had told him this might be a way to win. The novelty of having a young black person suggest that the Court had gone too far in calling for the end of segregated education in the South would win him points. He could appear even-handed and statesmanlike. It was a bad gambit. He looked foolish.

His talk hit me personally because when I arrived at Franklin College for the contest, the sponsors were surprised to learn that I was black. The all-white fraternity house where I was to stay did not welcome black guests, not to mention black members. A mad scramble ensued to try to find some place for me to stay. The last thing I wanted to hear was anyone, particularly a black person, say that segregation should not be destroyed with all deliberate speed. Between my housing fiasco and the speech apologizing to white people for *Brown,* I had more than enough incentive to win.

In the finals that night, I didn't talk to the audience; I talked to my opponent. He was sitting in the front row, and he was my target. I felt it was important for me to tell this young man that he had it all wrong—we can't deal with white people like that. And when I beat him, it was the first time a DePauw student had won the contest since Andrew J. Beveridge, a future United States senator from Indiana, did so in 1896.

DePauw sent word of my success to the Georgia press, black and white. There were some curious responses. My parents received a letter from a Georgian who had spent time near Greencastle. She expressed her surprise and pleasure that another Georgian had gone to DePauw. Then she offered that as soon as she'd seen the news item, she'd wanted to come by and say hello to my parents, but she and her husband had to stay home and supervise their "nigger hands." My picture had not run with the article that appeared in the white papers.

Then there were other reactions. Some of the very people who had discouraged me from attending DePauw immediately changed their tune. Suddenly it became very important that I was at that particular type of school (a white school) doing well. "That's my boy!" they'd say, starting a pattern that has continued throughout my life. I've so often found myself facing the skepticism of others whenever I've taken a unexpected turn in life and then accepting their congratulations when things turned out well later on.

I WAS ALSO PAYING ATTENTION to events beyond the campus, as the efforts to end segregation were taking dramatic steps forward. There was, of course, the U.S. Supreme Court's 1954 ruling in *Brown v. Board of Education*, and a year later, in December of my junior year, word came from Montgomery, Alabama, of the boycott of city buses in response to Rosa Parks's refusal to move to the back of the bus. Leading the boycott was the Reverend Martin Luther King, Jr., the young preacher from Atlanta. King's reputation had grown considerably since the day he had officiated at my brother Warren's wedding. With Montgomery, he became a figure of worldwide renown.

When I was home for Christmas that year, it was a great thrill for me to hear King give the NAACP's Emancipation Day speech on New Year's Day at Bethel AME Church. I went with my father that day and heard, for the first time, King give his "I Have a Dream" speech, which the rest of the country would hear him deliver at the March on Washington seven years later. King's words were so powerful, his delivery so inspired, that I knew right then and there that I was going to actively participate in the civil rights movement. There was just no doubt in my mind about that.

I knew early on my love of public speaking could help set the terms of my involvement in that arena, and I used every chance to practice. During my junior and senior years, I continued to give speeches on and off campus. This helped when I got involved in student politics at DePauw and became the treasurer of the student body. I also got involved, *one time only*, in local politics. In 1956, I signed up to work for a candidate for Congress running in the Democratic primary My chief job was to encourage the black voters in Greencastle (all 176 of them) to come out to vote. I handed out pamphlets, gave talks, and canvassed the black community. The night of the victory celebration, word came that it would be better if I didn't show up. Clearly the black vote was wanted and needed for the primary but was undesirable as the candidate prepared for the general election. That was the end of my campaign work in Indiana.

Then there was my involvement in the Methodist Student movement, which took me off campus into the "real world." We'd go to Chicago and Indianapolis to visit settlement houses and soup kitchens, where I was exposed to some aspects of life that I'd never thought much about. Our adviser was Reverend Elmer Harvey. He wanted very much to turn me into a preacher. It was his idea to send me to the conference at Union Theological Seminary, hoping in vain that I'd get "the call" from the Lord. He would be one of many people who would take an interest in my future, giving me advice that I didn't always follow, but appreciated nevertheless, because it showed that people cared.

If I'd listened to William Allison I wouldn't have entered the Margaret Noble Lee speech contest, and who knows how different my time at DePauw would have been had I given in to doubts about my ability (and my right) to participate on an equal basis in the life of the school. Maybe things would have worked out anyway—just at a later time. There is no question that this was a pivotal moment that helped set the contours of my career at the school and that my career at the school has been essential to all that has come since. To his great credit, Allison came up to me after I had won and admitted that he had been wrong to try to dissuade me from participating. "I didn't know," he said. "I just didn't know."

D URING OUR TIME TOGETHER, my first roommates and I came to enjoy one another's company very much. When Russ and Roy were to graduate, at the end of my first year, I decided to give them a graduation present. I invited them to Atlanta to stay at my home. They had never been to the South. So they accepted eagerly, thinking it would be something of an adventure. I was certain that it would be.

We traveled by bus, stopping in too many little towns along the way. When we arrived in Louisville, Kentucky, we got off to stretch our legs and to go to the bathroom, which turned out to be a real learning experience for Russ and Roy. They had never experienced legalized segregation, and when they saw the signs saying "White" and "Colored," they were momentarily confused.

"What do we do?" Roy asked.

"Well," I said, "you go this way," and pointed in the direction of the arrow showing the "white" rest room. "And I'll go that way," indicating where I was to go. "We'll meet right back here."

They were struck by how casual I seemed about this. I explained that this was just the way things were. It certainly wasn't something I liked. Nor did I for an instant accept this as the way things should be. Changes were definitely coming, but as things stood, we had to go our separate ways. Russ and Roy lost a little bit of their innocence that day.

We made it to Atlanta, and my parents welcomed my roommates graciously, with my mother cooking her best Southern dishes. This wasn't the first time I'd brought friends from college home with me. Earlier in the year, I'd brought down Robert Smith, another Southern boy who had grown up in South Carolina. When Robert came, our neighbors wondered at this curious sight: a white college boy staying in the home of his black classmate, right in the middle of a segregated neighborhood. Surely nothing like that had ever happened in our little corner of the world. As it turned out, it wasn't only the neighbors who marveled at the sight.

Robert slept in my bedroom. My mother later told me that at some point during the first night we were there, Daddy came into the room to just look at us as we slept. It was simply hard for him to believe what he was seeing. A young white man was sleeping under his roof—under his rules and protection—in the same way that Riley and Walter, or any of my other friends, would have. My father was not so much impressed with Robert, who was just a typical fellow, but the symbolism of the bedroom scene moved him to the core. It was all just light years away from the backwoods of Georgia that had helped shape his expectations. That a son of his would come home from college with a white classmate and interact with him as an equal was beyond anything he could ever have contemplated. He had to come and take a look.

By the time Russ and Roy visited my home, the sense of strangeness had worn off, but the message of their being there was still the same. Who could have known that day when Russ and Roy walked into our dorm room and had their hopes dashed that a mere eight months later they would be eager and very welcome guests in my own house? The three of us went a long way, in a relatively short amount of time, that year. I am so glad I saw their honest (if a little naive) "discovery" that I was "just like them" as a genuine effort to make human contact, which can never be wrong. It made my first months at DePauw easier, and it has left me with many fond memories. You can never have too many of those.

D ESPITE THE COMFORTABLE ROUTINE I established in college— schoolwork balanced with interesting extracurricular activities— there were some issues about being a young black man in an overwhelmingly white school during the 1950s that couldn't be settled so easily. As Dean Wittich had suggested, my social life was somewhat problematic. There were fairly small issues—"Where do I get a haircut?"—and bigger ones: "What do I do about girls?"

What to do about hair is something that bedevils many black students who go to college in places that don't have enough blacks to support a barber shop or hair salon. So black kids road trip for dates and road trip to get their hair cut or styled.

Although the number of blacks in Greencastle and its environs was small, the town did, in fact, have a black barber. His name was Bernie. In perhaps the most perverse twist of fate I've ever encountered, Bernie the black barber wouldn't cut black people's hair.

One of the few times in my life when I've been really angry was during my freshman year when I walked into Bernie's shop with a black schoolmate named Lenny Yorke, and asked, "How many have you got?"

Bernie was standing there cutting a white student's hair.

He said, "It doesn't matter."

"What do you mean it doesn't matter?"

"Like I said. It doesn't matter. I'm not—"

Before he could finish, I had the front of his collar clenched in my fist.

Lenny grabbed me and said, "Leave him alone. Let's just leave."

We left. I talked to the other black men on campus and we decided to go to Bernie to talk things over.

I said, "Bernie, how about cutting our hair?"

"No. No. I'm not going to do that." He was obviously concerned about his white clients. So I said, "We'll come to your house. It doesn't have to be here."

One of my friends spoke up. "You used to do it. You used to do it and sell whiskey before you found the Lord. Cut hair, sell whiskey on Friday and Saturday, and then go to church on Sunday."

"No. I don't do that anymore."

He just refused.

Some time later, I was supposed to go out with some friends and their parents. We were going to the Old Trail Inn—a fancy place for

Greencastle. I wanted to look right, so I made a decision. I called Bernie that Sunday and said: "Bernie, my daddy is a lawyer in Atlanta. He called me last night to say he's coming up here to take me to dinner for Dad's Day. I've told him about what happened, and he said to tell you that he'll be here by eleven, and if you haven't cut my hair by the time he gets to this campus, he'll have your ass in jail by sundown."

Bernie thought a second. As far as he knew, my father could well have been some rich black lawyer who'd sent his son up North to college. Then Bernie made a decision: "I'll meet you at the shop in twenty minutes." When I got there, he was waiting. He let me in and as I sat down, he said, "I really don't know how to cut this type of hair," touching the hair on my head as if it were some sort of alien substance.

I said, "Bernie, you're lying. Just cut my hair, please."

After that, I had my father send me a set of hair clippers. I cut hair for some of the black kids in the community, and when I needed a haircut, I'd hitchhike into Indianapolis. Eventually the university got a barber, a white man, who took all DePauw students. He was a nice man, and he did the best he could, but I would be exhausted by the time he finished. He was just sweating through the whole process, out of sheer nervousness. Getting a haircut from him was an ordeal. It was far easier hitchhiking to Indianapolis.

Figuring out the haircut situation was one thing. What to do about girls was something else again. Put plainly, my social life was warped compared to that of my classmates. The white guys on campus were free to fall in love with and to date the girls who were all around them. They didn't have to travel anywhere for companionship. Everyday interactions—sitting in class, eating at the dining hall, attending sporting events—could lead to romances that would be supported by the surrounding community. It was a natural, entirely expected, thing.

That wasn't true in my case. Blacks and whites could not date one another on campus. The rule wasn't written down anywhere, but we all knew the law existed—enforced by habit, custom, and the threat of social sanction. This gave rise to the predictable result: There were white girls at my school who were interested in me, and I was interested in them, but we were not free to act upon our mutual interests in the same way that white couples on campus could.

I don't want to exaggerate the difficulty of this. After all, I had grown up in the segregated South. I dated within my community. The problem at DePauw was that my community was now a white one. The better way to characterize my predicament is to say that it was inconvenient. Since there were no black females for most of my time at DePauw (two came when I was a senior, and I dated one, once), I followed the convention of young men in all-male colleges throughout the country—I took road trips.

One of my frequent dates was Myrna Smith, a co-ed from nearby Earlham College, a Quaker school. I'd bring Myrna to mixers at DePauw and socialize with her at Earlham. As a general rule, I avoided parties unless I had a date. The thought of standing around as the "extra man," while everyone else was paired off, was just too depressing. Adding to the discomfort was that it was purely external forces (not my own deficiencies as a potential companion) that accounted for my being alone more often than I wanted to be.

Aside from the surrounding colleges, there was Indianapolis and even Chicago, which I visited from time to time, where I could meet black girls. I fell in with various discussion groups—not unlike today's book club gatherings—that were set up to talk about issues of the day. Discussing issues was all fine and good, but the real point for me was meeting the girls who came to those groups. It was a wonderful way to meet young women who were both smart and pretty.

Indianapolis was nearer than Chicago, and it was there that I established my closest contacts within the black community. In my sophomore year, I went to a party one evening and met a girl named Harriet Wilson. She invited me to dinner at her home to meet her family. Her father, Clifford, was an executive at Eli Lilly and her mother, Mary, was a music teacher. Besides Harriet, there were four other children: Rose Marie, Sharon, Clifford, and Fred. They very quickly became my surrogate family.

I would come into Indianapolis, and whichever sister was home would be the one I'd take out. If none of them were at home, I'd hang around talking to Mr. and Mrs. Wilson. They treated me like a member of their extended family. I spent some weekends there and a few vacations. We went to church, to picnics, to parties. What a gift for a young man who was so far away from home with no family in the area. The Wilsons came to my graduation, acting every inch the proud family members watching their "son" end his college career.

Constructing a social life was just tougher for me. It took extra time. This turned out not to have been such a bad thing. I met some lovely people in the process, and I also learned a lot about human nature and the strange interaction between white and black Americans.

Peg Taylor was in her junior year when she asked me to take her to a dance given by her sorority, Tri-Delta, at the sorority's house. I was a sophomore. I'd seen her around campus, and we talked just as students do. Peg was extremely smart. When she graduated, she won the Walker Cup, the award for the best all-around student in the class. She said to me one day, "Vernon, I'd like for you to take me to a dance at Tri-Delt."

"Are you sure about that?"

"Yes, I'm sure. I want you to take me to the dance."

I knew we were treading in dangerous waters, but I liked her. So I agreed.

Peg went back to her sorority house and mentioned to a friend that she was going to go to the party with me. The girl went and told the "house mother," who in turn got on the telephone immediately to Peg's parents about the looming problem. In the meantime the leaders of her sorority house called a meeting.

A friend of mine, Bud Gilbert, heard about this and came over. "You've split Tri-Delta right down the middle," he said "They're fighting over whether Peg should take you as her date to the party." I had known there might be a problem. That it happened so quickly was a bit of a surprise.

Peg talked to her parents for a long time that night. Her father was beside himself. He made her promise that under no circumstances would she go to the dance with me.

At about 1:00 A.M. the next morning, Peg called me, crying.

"I'm sorry, Vernon. I don't think we should go through with this. I promised my father I wouldn't go with you."

I told her it wasn't a problem for me. She was still my friend, and I understood perfectly the position she was in. Peg was not at fault. She was just a free spirit who had wanted to make a statement. I was someone she liked, and there was no good reason we couldn't go to a dance together. I was well known on campus and, seemingly, well liked, probably by many of her own friends. Dating was a different matter. Peg was stunned by the reaction of her sorority, so much so that she resigned her membership.

Peg and I remained good friends throughout the rest of her time at DePauw. She had a car that she would loan to me whenever I needed to pick up Myrna or go visit the Wilson sisters. So, ironically, it was the girl I couldn't date who helped me date other girls.

IN MY SOPHOMORE YEAR, at the encouragement of my friends at DePauw, I tried out for "Duzer Du," the school's drama society. For my audition, I read from Tennessee Williams's *The Glass Menagerie*. My reading went well, and I was accepted into the group. And then two buddies of mine, Frank Staroba and Art Beer, decided that they wanted to write a play and asked me and my roommate, Bill Welty, to collaborate with them on the story.

We called it "Backwater," and it was based very closely on my experiences as a black student at DePauw. We wrote it and performed it—with me in the lead role—at a little theater on campus for three nights in the spring of 1955. It was a play of protest, and it got a lot of people's attention.

I played a character named Jefferson Gray, a senior at DePauw from Birmingham, Alabama. The play opens with my roommate inviting me to speak at his church for "Race Relations Sunday"— just as I was doing in real life, giving speeches at nearby churches on "The Negro in America." In the play, I deliver my speech, and afterward there is a reception. The white parishioners are so nice to me that I tell my roommate that I have decided to settle in the town.

Some people at the reception hear what I've said and become really alarmed; it was one thing to have me visit and give a nice uplifting speech, but having me as a neighbor was quite another.

So the next day, I go downtown to the offices of the president of the local bank and the president of the chamber of commerce, looking for work. And there's no work for me. They refuse to hire me. Then I go to the barbershop, and the barber won't cut my hair—just as had happened in Greencastle. Then I end up in a classroom with one of my roommate's former teachers, a lady who is the embodiment of everything good and wonderful in the world. I talk to her about whether I should stay after all, given the problems I would face. At some point my roommate joins us. He has gotten really nervous and upset because he is under pressure from his parents and from the community about having brought me there. And the teacher tries to work it out between us.

But before long, he and I exchange angry words. When he says something that really offends me, I move to hit him, forgetting the letter opener that I have been fiddling with throughout the scene. When I look up and see my hand gripping the letter opener, poised to strike, I see a switchblade instead. That really stirs me up because of all the stereotypes about blacks and knives. And then I let the weapon drop from my hand, hang my head, hunch my shoulders, and begin to weep.

The play's climax comes right after that. The president of the bank and the president of the chamber of commerce go to the minister (at whose church I had spoken) and tell him, "You have to preach on this subject because we can't have this guy come live in our town." The preacher doesn't want to do it. He's basically a good man, but he yields to the pressure of the establishment.

In the middle of the sermon, he begins to hallucinate, to go crazy actually. And then, all of a sudden, very dramatically, the stage lights go out and then return with just a spotlight on me, and there I am—on the cross. You could literally hear gasps from the audience, for there was the image of the black man as Jesus crucified by white townspeople.

This was way too much for many people in that small, conservative Midwestern town. Although the play ends with a hopeful effort at reconciliation, all anyone remembered was the sermon scene. House mothers across the campus said it was blasphemy to have me on the cross. That was not the only problem. I suspect they hated the mixing of racial symbolism, which equated persecuted blacks with Jesus and prejudiced whites with those who executed Him. It may have hit just a little too close to home.

Later that spring we took the play on the road and performed it at Dennison College, Ohio State, and other schools in the area. At each stop, the students got the message, even if some of the older audience members did not. I got a message myself, from my political science professor, Harry Voltmer, who returned a paper I had written for his class. On it was a bad grade and the following comment: "Too much acting, Vernon."

As I APPROACHED THE END of my career at DePauw, I could look back on my four years and feel satisfied about how things had worked out. I'd participated at a very high level in the life of the school. I had made good friends, some of whom I'm still in touch with to this day. My best friends were David Mornitz and my roommate, Bill Welty. Bill came from Hoopston, Illinois. When he'd go home, his friends who knew about me would chant: "Bill lives with a nigger. Bill lives with a nigger."

David and I were especially close. This was not without some risk for him socially. To have a black person as your "best friend" went beyond the more casual friendliness that I experienced with most of my classmates. We had an allegiance to one another. We became so close that David asked me to be the best man at his wedding, which was to take place soon after our graduation in June 1957. Like Peg Taylor and the Tri-Delta dance, this effort foundered on the rocks of parental disapproval. Neither his parents nor his fiancée's parents wanted me in town, much less in the wedding party.

Under heavy pressure, David rescinded both his request that I be his best man and my invitation to the wedding. It hurt a lot to have this kind of ugliness interfere with our friendship, and it struck a truly sour note during a time when we were all happy about graduating. But I didn't hold it against David or Joan, his fiancée. They felt they had to do what their parents wanted them to do. I was inclined that way myself. It happened that what their parents wanted them to do wasn't honorable. David and Joan's parents lived totally in one world, but their children had one foot in that old world and the other in the world that was coming.

I had no hard feelings. In fact, David and Joan came to visit me not long after graduation. I later visited them in their home, and I have kept up with them over the years. Decades after this bad episode, Joan apologized to me for her parents' actions. She went on to apologize for herself, saying that she wished she'd had the courage to put her foot down and refuse to give in to their prejudice. I accepted her apology, but I'd known long before that what she and David were up against.

I N THE SPRING OF MY SENIOR YEAR, a chapel service was held to recognize the members of Phi Beta Kappa. The names of all members of the society were read aloud in celebration of their achievement. After the ceremony, Professor Jomé, an economics professor, came up to me quite agitated.

"Vernon, I am so worried," he said.

"Why?" I asked.

"I didn't hear them call your name in the chapel today."

I said, "Professor Jomé, there are people who graduate Phi Beta Kappa, summa and magna cum laude. And then there are people who just graduate, and I'm one of those."

Professor Jomé was taken completely aback. "All the colored students graduate Phi Beta Kappa," he said. He was so upset that there were actually tears in his eyes. He'd been one of the professors who had treated my parents so kindly when they first brought me to school. He'd kept an eye on me during the next four years, and he just assumed that I would have my key. I did not, and that didn't bother me at all; I was so happy to be graduating. Not only did it represent a triumph over doubts about whether I would make it through, it also meant that I could begin to work toward my goal of becoming a lawyer. This time there was no question that I wanted to go to Howard Law School. That was where the most prominent civil rights lawyers came from, and that's where some of them taught. I knew that I wanted to be involved in that field, so my choice of a law school was easy.

Four years after they had left me standing near my dormitory, my entire family convened again in Greencastle to watch the end of my college career with great hopes about the beginning of the next phase of my education. This was a big moment in the Jordan and Griggs family. I had done something that only one other person in that combined clan had ever done: I'd graduated from college. It was a special time for another reason. My brother Windsor, who had gone to baking school in Chicago at the American Institute of Baking, was going to graduate just a few days after me. So my family had double cause to celebrate. Uncle Prince and Aunt Lennie, from my mother's side, came along to attend both ceremonies.

Like all college graduations, there was the usual mix of the bitter with the sweet, a hint of sorrow at the thought of friendships that would never be the same (no matter how much we promised otherwise) and joy at the prospect of beginning life with all the things learned during the four years gone by.

The best moment of all came for me when my father shook my hand after I'd received my diploma and said with great warmth and deep emotion, "You can come home now."

CHAPTER 4

CHICAGO INTERLUDE

I DROVE A BUS for the Chicago Transit Authority during the summer of 1957. It wasn't what I'd planned to do in that time between college and law school. I'd left DePauw certain there was at least some type of office job out there for a newly minted college graduate and soon-to-be law student. That wasn't the case, which became clear in pretty short order.

I was in Chicago because of my childhood friend Frank Hill, who had done me out of playing Joe Louis in elementary school. Frank had come up to Purdue University at the same time I was at DePauw and later transferred to Illinois Tech, in Chicago. I'd visit him there from time to time, sometimes driving a car borrowed from one of my school friends. We drove around a lot, and when I'd get tired, Frank would drive. The only problem was that he didn't know how to drive a stick shift. I'd put the car in first gear and go to sleep. Whenever we'd come to a stop sign, he'd have to wake me up to use the clutch so the car would not stall.

Near the end of my senior year, I mentioned that I was looking for work, and Frank said, "Why don't you come on up here and stay with me for the summer? There's bound to be something for you to do."

Frank's suggestion was more than welcome. I love Chicago, and have from my very first visit there. Frank lived in a rooming house run by a woman who was a retired schoolteacher. He spoke with her, and she agreed to take me on as a tenant. Although it meant I wouldn't be coming home before I went off to law school, my parents, who were also confident that I'd get a job, were happy that I'd be living with someone they'd known from the time he was a boy.

After Windsor's graduation ceremony, right there in Chicago, my family dropped me off with Frank. My mother especially wanted to see and inspect my home away from home. She knew this was yet another experience that could be valuable to me, and that I had really left the nest, but she was still a mother and wanted to make sure everything passed minimum standards. With that mission accomplished, my family went on to Detroit to visit relatives before returning to Atlanta. I was left with my childhood friend to begin one of the best (and most educational) adventures of my life.

Almost as soon as I'd settled in, I put on my suit and began to go around looking for work, bright and eager. I said all the things I thought would open the door: "I just graduated from college"; "I'm about to attend Howard Law School." Nothing went as I had expected. Rejection followed rejection. No one would hire me.

One day, on the train home after another fruitless interview, I noticed a group of men sitting across the way from me—laughing, talking, just kidding around. It was obvious that they were co-workers because they all wore the same blue uniform. On closer inspection I could see that they were bus drivers. Then it hit me. Maybe it was time to redefine my goals since nothing was turning up in the way of an office job. If I didn't do something quickly, my plans for a Chicago summer would come to a rapid end. I went over to them.

"How did you all get a job driving a bus?" I asked,

"You have to go over to the Merchandise Mart," they said, and told me where that was.

Instead of going home, I went straight over to the Merchandise Mart and told them I wanted a job. As luck would have it, they were happy to see me because the city was in great need of drivers. They said the first step was to take a written exam, and if I did well enough on that, I would then have to take a driving class. If I passed, I could be a driver. I took the test that afternoon, and the next day I was back there in class to learn how to drive a bus. By that time I'd been driving for many years and was quite comfortable behind the wheel. The class went well, and in no time at all, I was a bus driver.

As a temporary worker I was given the least desirable time slot, which meant I worked the night shift from 12:45 A.M. to 9:30 A.M.—six days a week, for $2.10 an hour. Filled with all the strength, energy, and bravado of youth, I'd sometimes volunteer to work an extra shift. I thought nothing of bringing in one bus in the morning, then taking another right out for another run.

But it was the world of the night, with its special tone and atmosphere, that really opened my eyes. I'd been out late in Chicago before, but it was not the same as carrying out a job after midnight. Without the congestion and the traffic of the day, I could see and think about the city from a different perspective. I came to feel as if I had a more in-depth knowledge of the place and of the people who lived there.

My route took me through working-class and, largely, black neighborhoods. In the main, my typical passenger was just like me: a low person on the totem pole, who didn't have the power to just say no to working the most difficult hours. Then there was Chicago's rich multi-ethnic mixture, so different from Atlanta's more predictable Anglo-Saxon and black combination—blacks, Poles, Italians, the Lithuanian and Estonian women who cleaned the office buildings long after all the professionals had gone home and were safe in their beds. I wasn't their regular bus driver, but we soon struck up a form of camaraderie. Their husbands would be waiting to pick them up, often at some place other than the normal bus stop. I'd generally agree to let them off where they wanted, if it didn't interfere with my schedule too much. No one ever complained. It was like a mini-version of a United Nations without the conflicts.

There was always an unexpected adventure. My first day on the job was the first day that the bus fare went from twenty to twenty-five cents. At one stop a frail, elderly woman got on the bus, wild-eyed, almost falling-down drunk. She stuck out a palm with two dimes in it and said, "I ain't got but twenty cents. This is all I have. But I'm going to ride this bus today." I said, "Yes, ma'am, you are," and put the extra five cents in myself.

I'd pick up a busload of happy people fresh from a carnival on Western Avenue, along with the thieves who were there to pick their pockets. Once, while making a turn on State Street, I noticed a man had fallen asleep at the back of the bus with his wallet exposed. At the next stop a man got on, eating a slice of watermelon in the middle of the night. He saw the sleeping passenger, too, and sat next to him. As I glanced into my rearview mirror I noticed the man with the watermelon easing a hand toward the wallet.

I shouted, "Don't touch that wallet!"

The sleeping passenger woke up, and the man with the watermelon dashed to the door. Even though it wasn't a bus stop, I had to make a split-second decision: Did I want them fighting on my bus? I decided I didn't, so I stopped, let him out, and started to drive off. The man with the wallet evidently didn't want to let this go. He went to the door himself, and I let him off, too, figuring they could handle their problem on their own. The last thing I saw was the would-be victim chasing the would-be thief down the street off into the night.

As a bus driver I became a member of a type of community with its own rules and expectations. I saw the same people, largely at the same time, every day. I got to know some of their names. Even when I didn't, I learned things about those who rode the bus on a regular basis just from steady observation and because they'd tell me things.

There was something about the night that freed people (or compelled them) to reveal parts of themselves. It reminded me of the times I used to take the train from Indiana to Atlanta. Almost inevitably, I'd find myself in a long conversation with some salesman who just wanted to make contact with another human being who wasn't a customer. I've found that frequent travelers are often very lonely people.

It was the same with some of my bus passengers. Out of loneliness or exasperation, they'd talk to me about issues in their lives at work or in their families, in much the same way people talk to bartenders or hairdressers. Women would tell me about how their husbands had mistreated them, beaten them. Men would talk about what a rough day they'd had on the job and how no one appreciated their struggles. The ladies of the evening would use me as a sounding board to marvel at the weirdness of a particular client. I had no stake in these people and they had no stake in me. Without the vulnerability of a shared attachment, they opened up.

There were some connections made. I had one rider, a man in a wheelchair, who was lifted onto the bus by a younger man, a family member, I supposed. One morning I saw him wheeling himself near the stop. I pulled over, opened the door, and asked if he wanted to ride. He said yes. Since no one was with him, I jumped out and helped him onto the bus. Once we started to roll again, he told me no bus driver had ever done that before. "Why don't you come by my place," he said, meaning the delicatessen where he worked. I went by there a couple of times and had huge, delicious, corned beef sandwiches and soda—all on the house. I can still see him, out of that wheelchair, balancing himself along the counters as he talked to me and served other customers.

One of the most interesting things I learned during this time was that there are some women who just love men in uniforms—it doesn't really matter what kind. I saw this more when I would work the day shift. Women were just more likely to flirt with me, or to accept my flirtations, when I was in uniform. Girls would get on, we'd exchange glances and pleasantries, and then they'd give me their telephone numbers when they were getting off at their stop.

Given my route, this made sense. A bus driver has a steady income, the job requires dependability—the driver must be the kind of person who will show up, keep to the schedule, follow the route. A man like that could make a very stable life for a woman. I must have been considered quite a catch. This was a surprising, and fun, part of the job. There were some parts that were less amusing.

Not long after I started I got a visit from the union representative. "Brother Jordan, how are you? Glad to have you with us," he began. Then he started talking to me about how he wanted me to pay union dues. I was making $2.10 an hour, and I wanted to take home every penny of it. So I responded like the perfect pre-law student, saying something to the effect that because I was a temporary employee, I didn't think I should have to pay any union dues. "Fine," he said. I got no argument from him, and I thought it was all over.

At the end of my shift one morning, I was in the locker room tying my shoe. I happened to look to my left, and I saw two feet. Almost at the same time I noticed two feet on the other side of me. Others quickly appeared. I jumped up to face four strapping men who just stood staring at me. One look at them and you'd know exactly why Chicago is called the "City of the Big Shoulders." My back was against the lockers. I knew what this was about. One of them began, "Brother Jordan . . . "

"Where do I sign?" I asked before he could even finish—or start.

It really made no sense for me to have balked at paying the dues. The union was good for me. It helped raise my salary that summer. When I came back to Chicago the following summer, things were even better. It just took a little time—and encouragement—to help me see this.

All in all, working this job was unlike anything else I'd ever experienced. The driving was the least of it. I was in a position of real responsibility, not unlike the captain of a ship. If there was a problem—a troublesome passenger, lost items, difficulties with the bus—people looked to me to solve it.

One of the worst things that could happen on a bus route was to get off schedule, because it could then throw everyone else off. When this happened to me once, the driver behind me asked if he could pass and get back on track. The buses ran on a trolley system, with electric cables connecting the bus to a power source. Passing me would require detaching my cable, something I hadn't done at that point. I said sure, but I told him that I'd never detached and reattached a cable before.

"Oh, it's no problem, I'll help you put it back," he said. "Just let me get by, and I'll stop back."

I got out, pulled the cable down, and stood there holding it with the sparks flying in the pitch-black night. He got back onto his bus and drove away, leaving me there in the dark to figure out how to fix the cable. I was furious and scared. After all, I was dealing with live electricity, and no one could ever accuse me of being mechanically inclined. It could have been a disaster. But I did have to learn how to do it myself, and I soon found out that the cables came off pretty frequently. I learned the hard way that night.

I T WASN'T JUST THE JOB that helped pull me toward adulthood. Living in the big city, out from under the influence of parents or school administrators, was liberating. I was a free man for the first time in my life. Law school was still to come, but I was a twenty-two-year-old emancipated male. The person who had boarded the train for Greencastle four years earlier was gone for good. I could go when, where, and with whom I pleased. It was up to me to set the agenda. And I did that with great enthusiasm.

Frank knew Chicago inside out, and he had good ideas about all the right places to go for fun. Despite our conflicting schedules—when I was coming home from work, Frank was leaving for work—we easily established ourselves as an effective social team. I'd spend the day sleeping as best I could, and then I'd wait to go out with Frank when he came home.

Chicago was a great town for music—especially during that time. I went dancing, to the good nightclubs. All of the big names came through there, and Frank and I went to see them: Sarah Vaughan, Dinah Washington, Erroll Garner, Ramsey Lewis, Ahmad Jamal. They were in their prime, and I was just at the right stage in life to appreciate them.

It wasn't all about entertainment. Benjamin Mays, whom I'd followed around Morehouse's campus as a child, happy just to get a glimpse of him, came to town. I rushed down to listen. His text was the parable of the rich man, who'd had a good harvest and was asked what he would do with the proceeds. When he said that he would build a bigger house and bigger barns, God spoke to him and told him that something else was required. Mays was speaking directly to Morehouse men and other blacks who had prospered, ex-

horting them to use their money to support the schools that had educated them and the churches that had nourished their faith and to
give aid to members of the community who had been left behind. I
wasn't a Morehouse man, and I hadn't yet prospered materially in
the way Mays meant. Still, I felt he was talking to me as the man I
fully expected to become one day. It was as if he had given me a personal order that I was duty bound to obey. Mays was such a tower-
ing figure, I wouldn't have dreamed of disappointing him.

Chicago was also a center for black enterprise. Many of the oldest
black businesses in the country were formed there, and I was very
much aware of that—and in awe of it. I actually made a pilgrimage
to Johnson Publications, which published *Jet* and *Ebony*, two magazines that were in the homes of almost every aspiring black family
during that era. I didn't know anyone there, didn't have an appointment; I just wanted to see the place where it all happened and drink
in the atmosphere of success.

All of this—taking in the music, Reverend Mays's call for the uplift of the black race, the success of a black company, my own im-
pending enrollment in law school—created a feeling of endless
possibilities. Every aspect of the black experience—cultural, intellectual, spiritual, economic, and political—seemed to work in concert
toward a future that appeared determinedly bright and wide open. It
was a great time to be young.

But there was another part of being young: persistent hunger. As I
recall, Frank and I always seemed to be hungry. Perhaps it was just
our age or the fact that we were running around so much, but I remember thinking about food quite a bit. Both of us were forever on
the lookout for ways to get a good meal, and sometimes we weren't
too scrupulous about how we got it.

At some point during that summer, we discovered an easy way to
get a good home-cooked meal: We'd go to wakes—not the wakes of
anyone we knew, but any wake that we could find. We fell into this
by accident. There was a custom among some in our neighborhood
to put a wreath out on the door to indicate that a wake was in
progress. Walking together one evening, Frank and I saw a wreath
and just got it in our heads to go inside to see what was going on. To

our surprise, and great happiness, someone offered us food just because we were standing there.

From that time on we would repeat this routine—not habitually,
just on occasion. The easiness of the operation made it difficult to resist trying it again. Once we'd found out who had died, male or female, young or old, it was a fairly simply matter to know how to
proceed. No one was in the mood to question people who, by all appearances, had come to pay their respects to the dearly departed. We
were just a part of a roomful of "mourners." As long as we presented the right demeanor (and we always did)—hands clasped before us, furrowed brow, with the appropriate look of concern or,
depending upon the age of the deceased, an expression of mild
shock, there was never a time when anyone doubted our bona fides.
And almost invariably after we viewed the body, somebody would
say to one of us, "Young man, are you hungry?" or "Young man,
would you like some dinner?" And we would invariably say, "Don't
mind if I do."

ONE ISSUE REMAINED UNRESOLVED for most of that summer:
Even though I knew I was destined for law school, my interest in the
ministry had not been laid totally to rest. It was always there in the
background, never able to drown out thoughts of law school but
present enough to make me want to keep that option open. During
my senior year in college I had applied to several seminaries, Garrett
at Northwestern and Drew University in New Jersey, bouncing the
choices of the law and the ministry around in my head.

This was very much on my mind that summer in Chicago because
I had to tell the administrators at the seminaries what I was going to
do. My conscious mind was dead set on law school; still, for some
reason, I found it hard to cut loose from the thought that I should
become a preacher.

My romantic life entered into the equation in an interesting way. I
was going out with a young woman named Peggy, whom I'd met at
one of those "talk about the issues, meet pretty girls" discussion

groups. Peggy, who was about five years older than I was, worked as a dietitian in Chicago. Although she and I got along very well, we did have some problems because she had converted to Catholicism and had all of the superconviction of the recent convert. Peggy was a very serious person, and she insisted that we go to counseling to try to make sure we could continue life in the right spiritual frame of mind. These meetings were almost always a wreck because I'd sit there arguing with our counselor about various points of religion.

Peggy really was dead set against my going into the seminary. If I went in, I would come out an AME minister. Then she couldn't marry me because I wouldn't be a Catholic. She told me flat out that if it was a choice between me and Jesus, she would choose Jesus. We went back and forth about this for a good part of the summer. I liked Peggy a lot, but I knew that the choice between law school and the seminary was really a decision that I had to make for myself, not to please her.

Ultimately, it was becoming clear that law school was the better place for me to be. I had envisioned myself in the profession for too long to let go of the dream, and it was an idea that my mother had nurtured in me as well. It was what I felt most comfortable with— what I had the truest calling to do. The adult response was to accept that fact and get out of the holding pattern of keeping my options open.

Speaking, having a public role, being involved in the issues of the day—these were all things that attracted me to the ministry. Preachers have been leaders within the black community since slavery, so it was natural for me to pause over that possibility as I thought of useful roles to play in life. Lawyers can do the same things, and I was part of a new generation that had other choices about ways to make a difference in the lives of black people. I could be involved in the civil rights movement as a lawyer just as easily as I could as a minister.

Then there were other concerns that I referred to when I wrote to the people at Garrett, telling them that I had decided not to enroll in the seminary. I explained, only half kidding, that I had "discovered sin" and that "I liked it." I felt uncomfortable about some aspects of the life of a preacher—mainly, the complete obliteration of the public-private distinction in one's life.

Ministers are on emotional, social, and intellectual call twenty-four hours a day. It's a profession that is lived from the inside out. One doesn't work as a preacher, one is a preacher. A whole set of expectations come with that title, some of them realistic, some wholly irrational, but they are there, nevertheless. The demands are enormous, not only for the preacher but for the preacher's family as well. This is not the life for a loner, for one who enjoys communicating with people but who must have a well-defined and inviolate zone of privacy. Given my personality, it made much more sense for me to become a lawyer.

THAT CHICAGO SUMMER was not without controversy. My landlady, with whom I had generally gotten along, evicted me near the end of my time there. She was a very attractive woman who could carry on intelligent conversation. She also had a slightly bawdy side that moved her to tell funny stories and make risqué comments. She was living a very full life. In the beginning, we seemed to get along very well. But as time passed, she became a little too aggressive and personal in her attentions.

Frank had his own bedroom, and our other roommate, Howard Anthony, had his, and I slept in a little room near the day room. One morning while I was getting ready for work, she walked into my room, combing her hair, with nothing on but her panties. She was a beautiful woman, but I had absolutely no interest in her and really resented her presumptuousness.

"How are you this morning?" she asked, as if nothing were out of the ordinary.

"I'm just fine," I replied evenly. Whatever she thought, this was certainly out of the ordinary for me.

From then on we were friendly, but there was always an undercurrent of tension. When my girlfriend from Atlanta came to visit a couple of times, my landlady was unfriendly to us both. It was a bad situation. Adding to it was the fact that her mother didn't like me either, and it was her thumbs-down that eventually did me in. Mother and daughter had a very complicated relationship. The mother lived in Milwaukee and was passing for white. My landlady, who by appearance was obviously black, wasn't allowed to visit her there lest she give away the secret. The mother always came to Chicago. Whatever my landlady's shortcomings, I've always felt sorry for her because of this particular reality of her life—not to be able to visit your own mother so that she could pretend that she had no connection to the black world. It was tragic and, given my closeness to my own mother, unfathomable to me.

To prepare for her mother's visits, she would clean the house—washing and scrubbing as if we were about to receive a foreign dignitary. During one of these visits, I made the mistake of bringing home two of my classmates, David and Joan, whose parents had asked me out of their wedding earlier that year. We went out to dinner, and I invited them back to the house for drinks.

We sat talking for awhile, not loudly at all, and her mother suddenly emerged from her room. "What are you doing here at this time of night?" she demanded. "We're just having a drink," I said calmly. Her hostility was so totally irrational that she could only have been reacting to the sight of two white people who would now view her as a black person. Her cover had been blown in a small way, even though it was highly unlikely that she would ever cross paths with David or Joan or that they would ever have an acquaintance in common besides me.

After that, my landlady decided that I had to go. When Frank heard about it, he was as angry as I was. It was just crazy. I was being put out of a place to stay for no good reason at all. In solidarity with me, Frank decided to leave as well. The quick and easy solution for us was to move into the YMCA, which is where I spent the last days of the summer.

In the crisis of the moment, I didn't tell my mother, who had continued her practice of writing to me and expecting letters back. She was frantic when she didn't hear from me and didn't know where I was. In those days, we didn't call on the telephone unless someone had died or was on the verge of death. I fully intended to contact her once I'd gotten settled.

When she found me, she asked, "Why did you move?"

I told her that I'd had problems with the landlady, although I wasn't specific about the nature of the problems.

My mother said, "I knew there was something wrong with her the first time I saw her. I was always uncomfortable about that woman." She'd never hinted that to me before, but she was always very good at reading people; I have no doubt that she really did sense that I might have problems with my living arrangement.

Although this was a fairly sour way to end what had been a great adventure, I didn't dwell on it. Nothing lasts forever, and I went into this period knowing full well that it was a phase destined to be short-lived. My thoughts turned quickly to my immediate future, where my real life would begin.

CHAPTER 5

HOWARD LAW SCHOOL

IT WOULDN'T BE A STRETCH to say that Howard University saved my soul. As much as I have always appreciated my years at De-Pauw—if I had to do it over, I'd go there again—Howard will always be special to me for the place it was and for what I found there: a wife, a career, and a reaffirmation of my faith in the mission of black people.

Looking back, I can see that my experiences at a white college and at a black law school served as perfect bookends for my formal education. It was good that DePauw came before Howard. Four years in a white environment, during the time that I passed from boyhood to manhood, taught me how to handle myself in territory that was not hostile, but which was, in a true sense, foreign. My time in Greencastle and the surrounding area was a psychological "Grand Tour," showing me what was in the world where I would later compete, preparing me to return to a safe place at "home" (Howard) to begin work on that project.

In going to Howard in 1957, I'd come full circle. After a childhood spent in University Homes watching the black students and professors in Atlanta's University Center—certain that one day I would be among them—here I was in the exact setting I had dreamed of: Howard University, the capstone of black higher education. It had taken me a bit longer to get there than I'd expected, but I had made it.

That's certainly how I felt even before I got to campus that September. With all thoughts of going to seminary dispatched for good, getting to law school, making it through, and becoming a civil rights lawyer emerged as the uncontested goal of my life. My path was clear.

Though I'd managed to save some money during the summer, as always I had to be extremely vigilant about finances and creative in my efforts to have some of the things I wanted, even as I lived within my means. While wrapping up matters in Chicago, I defrayed the cost of getting to Washington by signing on with a company that transported cars for clients who were going to a particular city or town but did not want to drive their cars a long distance. It was my job to deliver a car from Kansas City to Philadelphia. From there it was a simple, inexpensive train trip to D.C.

The car was great—a '56 Chevrolet four-door, which I took on a tour before heading east. First Chicago, then Greencastle, then on to Indianapolis to visit the Wilsons. After that, I made a stop in Columbus, Ohio, to see some of my elderly relatives, who fed me very well and sent me on my way with even more food. Of course, Atlanta would have been too much of a detour, and I knew I wouldn't see my family again until after I had become a law student. Except for that sad thought, I couldn't have been in better spirits. I was a young man, out on the open road with a wonderful car (all to myself), headed exactly where I wanted to go.

As things turned out, when I got to where I wanted to go, the place was closed. The school term was to begin on a Monday, and I came into Washington the Saturday before, only to find everything at Howard closed except the administrative offices. There was no way to get into my dorm to drop off my belongings before delivering the car to Philadelphia. The last thing in the world I wanted to do was to cart all of that back on the train with me.

My only hope was to go to the administration building and find someone who could help. To my good fortune, and surprise, the dean of the law school, George Johnson, was in his office. After I introduced myself and explained my predicament, he said, without missing a beat, "Well, leave everything here until you get back"—which is exactly what I did.

DESPITE MY LOFTY THOUGHTS about going to school at what was considered the pinnacle of black educational institutions, I was somewhat underwhelmed by what I saw of Howard during my first weeks there. At the time, it seemed to be the only federally supported winter resort in the country. I ran into a number of students who just didn't seem too serious about our enterprise—who appeared more interested in partying than anything else. Not that I had anything against partying, I was just momentarily taken aback by what seemed to be the too-easy manner of the place. It struck me as much less academic than what I remembered of DePauw, or what I envisioned of law school.

My first impression was wrong. I had really drawn an unfair comparison. DePauw was a small school in a small town. Student life made up the bulk of what Greencastle was all about. We were a group of kids in an environment that had little to compete with the academic and social offerings of our college, its small graduate programs, and the fraternities and sororities.

Howard was a large school in a city with an identity all its own. There was a medical school, a law school, a dentistry school, and other graduate programs, along with an undergraduate student body. The students in each of these programs had their own agendas and their own way of expressing their commitment to their education. Howard was simply too big and diverse to have one particular academic "style" that everyone could be expected to follow.

In truth, my law-school classmates took school very seriously. We had to. Our professors wouldn't let us do otherwise, given the school's reputation and the mission with which it was so closely associated: producing lawyers for the burgeoning civil rights movement. Everyone at the school had a real sense that the future of black America was very much tied up in what we were doing at Howard Law School.

We had good reason to think this way. Enrolling at Howard connected me to an institution with a long-established role in the life of black America. I had wanted to be a part of this for a very long time. My doctor, my dentist, some of my teachers, and a good many of the leaders of the community in Atlanta had gone to Howard. Mr. L. D. Milton, the president of the only black bank in Atlanta, was the chairman of the board of trustees at Howard. Mordecai Johnson, Alain Locke, E. Franklin Frazier—all these men were associated with Howard, and I knew about them and admired what I'd heard. Howard was our Harvard.

In addition, Howard was, as Thurgood Marshall told us in a law school assembly, "Charlie Houston's law school." Marshall was referring to his idol and mentor, Charles Hamilton Houston, whose name is not nearly as well known as it should be. He was the dean of the law school in the 1930s, overseeing its rise from an obscure night school to a top-flight, fully accredited day school.

After leaving Howard, he went on to head up the NAACP's legal efforts to end racial discrimination. It was Houston, along with his former student Thurgood Marshall and William Hastie, who perfected the strategy of using the Fourteenth Amendment to bring about the piece-by-piece demolition of the South's system of de jure segregation. He died seven years before I got to Howard, but his influence was everywhere.

Howard professors did research and helped prepare briefs for many of the important cases of the early part of the civil rights era. The NAACP Legal Defense and Educational Fund, under the direction of Marshall, did dry runs of their Supreme Court arguments at Howard. I went to every one that I could, sitting in rapt attention with my classmates as the lawyers prepared to argue cases that would determine the course of our lives, and the lives of our children, for years to come. All the great civil rights lawyers were right before us: Robert Carter, Thurgood Marshall, Robert Ming, William T. Coleman, Jr., Frank Reeves, Louis Redmond, Constance Baker Motley, Jack Greenberg. They'd go out into the hallways to take a break, and we'd stand around, keeping a discreet distance, just thrilled to be in their presence and to overhear their conversations. At some point we'd sidle up to them, introduce ourselves, shake their hands, and stand in awe.

Howard was the only law school in the country that offered a course in civil rights law, which I took enthusiastically. The man who taught the course, James Nabrit, also taught me constitutional law, and he was one of the best teachers I've ever had. Nabrit was a Morehouse man and a graduate of Northwestern Law School. A superb teacher and a superb lawyer, he had argued *Bolling v. Sharpe,* one of the four cases that became known under the heading *Brown v. Board of Education.* He would later become the president of the university. When he died in 1997, it was my honor to give the eulogy at his funeral.

Even when we weren't dealing with civil rights, my other professors were very conscious of the fact that we were being trained to make a difference in American life. Not that everyone was going to go off to become a civil rights attorney—most of us would not, of course. Just the fact that we were becoming professionals was a strike against the prevailing rules about blacks' limited place in American society. The movement was never an abstraction at Howard. It was a living, breathing part of our existence.

All of this was reinforced for me every Sunday in Rankin Chapel, right there on campus. No matter how late I'd stayed out on Saturday night, no matter how much drinking I'd done, I went to chapel on Sundays. The habit of a lifetime, my interest in preaching, and the need for spiritual renewal and reflection drove me there. The chapel was the center of the campus. The best preachers and the most noted intellectuals in the black community came to speak at Rankin, offering the message of the Gospel along with a message of social justice: Daniel Hill, Howard Thurman, Gardner Taylor, William Holmes Borders, Kelly Miller Smith, Martin Luther King, Jr., Ralph David Abernathy, Samuel D. Proctor, Vernon Johns—great men all. When *Brown v. Board of Education* was decided and the ruling was announced on the radio, Vernon Johns (who had preceded Martin Luther King, Jr., as pastor of the Dexter Avenue Baptist Church) and a fellow preacher were in a car driving along a highway. Upon hearing the news, they pulled over to the shoulder of the road, got out of the car, went around to the front, and knelt in prayer. The bumper was their altar.

Mordecai Johnson, the president of the university, talked to us about Lincoln, Jesus, and Gandhi. Johnson was much taken with Gandhi and offered the Mahatma's life as an example to us. It was important to remember, Johnson said to us one day in chapel, that Gandhi started his career as lawyer, and when he died, all his possessions could fit on top of his briefcase. While we appreciated Johnson's basic point, we really weren't thinking of following that prescription to the letter. Still, having those aspirations voiced and reiterated on a weekly basis was, for me, an integral part of the educational experience at Howard.

One sermon in particular stood out. Dr. Evans Crawford came to Rankin in 1958, when I was twenty-three years old, and spoke of how every individual should create his or her own tensions in life. In other words, we should not let others create tensions for us. Giving over that power allows others to set the agenda for what is, after all, your own life. You will always be dancing to another person's tune, called for reasons that often have very little or nothing to do with you and your needs, and everything to do with problems, issues, and concerns they may have in their own lives.

Dr. Crawford's words brought to mind the difficulties I'd had with my high-school buddies, who wanted to make me feel bad about where I'd chosen to go to college, who refused to accept my earnest efforts to keep our friendship alive. Almost five years had passed, but what had happened still rankled. If I'd let them, they would have run my life under the guise of being my friends. Over the years I've had to repeat to myself, almost on a daily basis, Dr. Crawford's admonition. It is at the core of my personal philosophy. I live by it.

E ARLY ON, I could see that my social life at Howard was going to be very different from what I'd known at DePauw. Evidence of that was in plain view from day one. Girls—the most absolutely gorgeous black girls—were just everywhere. And they were available for dating. I'd entered a heaven on earth. It would be hard to exaggerate what a difference this made in my life. After all the awkwardness, the forced unreality of my situation at DePauw, I was now in a place where I could act as a normal young man; no traveling long distances to make dates, no suppressing crushes (mine on other people, and others' on me) to keep social peace. I was free to seek a companion, and—just as important—to be sought after. It was all very natural, very human. Life was much easier and happier.

Everyone at Howard either lived in the dorms or lived in apartments out in the city. And we all ate in the same cafeteria—undergraduates and graduate students alike. You could pick out the graduate students by their white medical jackets or white dental jackets or, in the case of the law students, our shirts and ties. I guess that also made it easier for the female undergraduates to pick us out from the rest of the crowd, but I wasn't complaining. I had four years of lost time to make up, and it was terrific.

It was also liberating to be out of the small-town world of Greencastle and in the big-city life of Washington, D.C. On Georgia Avenue was the Howard Theatre, where I could go hear Erroll Garner or Art Blakey, Dizzy Gillespie or Billy Eckstine. And on U Street were all the bars and nightclubs where I could stop and take in the music and the lively atmosphere. The city was still mostly segregated in those years, so a lot of the well-known black leaders would go to Georgia Avenue to eat and drink and have a good time. The big restaurant was Billy Simpson's, where at the corner table one might find Adam Clayton Powell or Charlie Diggs, who were black members of Congress. Sometimes, on a special date, I would go to a restaurant downtown that served black customers, but by and large my social life revolved around Georgia Avenue and U Street.

As for male companionship, I had my dorm mates in Carver Hall. Carver was all male, of course—there were no co-ed dorms at Howard then—full of high spirits, interspersed with hard work. We discussed everything: our dreams about our careers, where we wanted to live, what we wanted for our families, the girls we wanted to date—everything. It meant a lot to have a society of young black men to talk to and compare notes with. I hadn't had that before, at least not so many in one place.

I spent a lot of time at Carver Hall, and not just because I lived there. I also had a job answering the telephone at the front desk. Though I had a lot of course work, I found it inconceivable not to take advantage of an opportunity to make a little pocket change, especially since my classes ran from 8:00 A.M. to noon, which gave me the afternoons free. We were supposed to study during those hours, but I liked working, and I also took a second job at the registrar's office for a couple of afternoons a week.

Working at the front desk at Carver Hall, I got to know a lot of my fellow students—and a lot about them from the telephone messages I took. What really struck me was how smart they all were, especially the guys from Virginia Union University, a black private college in Richmond that seemed to produce one great student after another. One of them, Doug Wilder, was a year ahead of me at the law school. I could see even then that he was destined for great things. He got along well with people, and he was a great raconteur. And so it was not surprising to me, thirty years later, that he became the first black governor of the state of Virginia.

My best friend that first year at Howard was my roommate, Joseph E. Lockeridge, a minister's son from Fort Worth, Texas. Joe was the leavening in my bread at Howard. If we were walking down U Street and I said, "Joe, let's stop here and have a beer," he would reply, "Brother Jordan, we've got to go study." So I would go study. He also suggested to me that I study at the Library of Congress as opposed to the library at the law school, because I always got distracted there by the co-eds who were doing their homework among the law students. And so Joe and I would take the streetcar down New Jersey Avenue to the Library of Congress, a fairly long trip, and study there.

Joe was a calming influence on me. We liked each other a lot, and I guess the best way to put it is that we liked each other's differences. Joe was a sturdy, sensible guy. He was, as they say, like the tree planted by the river. Slightly older—he'd actually been in the army—he knew enough of the world to have a good sense of perspective about things. Visually we were quite a pair: I was tall and string-bean thin, and he, much shorter with a slight build. We looked like Mutt and Jeff.

Joe used to wake me up on Sundays: "Brother Jordan, Brother Jordan. Wake up. We've got to go to church." So I have Joe to thank for making sure I heard all those great preachers who came each week to Rankin Chapel.

After law school, Joe went into politics and became a member of the Texas legislature in 1967, along with Barbara Jordan and Curtiss Graves. Those three were the first blacks since Reconstruction to be elected to that body. Joe's life was tragically cut short when he died in a plane crash in 1968.

I MOVED INTO MY OWN APARTMENT off campus my second year in law school, and it quickly became a meeting place for some of the guys. They would come over almost every day, just around dinner-time. I was from the South, so when it was time to eat, naturally, I'd feed them. I'd fry a chicken, make meat loaf, or beef stew, pulling together whatever little I had to share. That was part of my heritage. This went on for some time, and finally I realized they were beginning to rely too much on my open-handed Southern hospitality. My bank account couldn't take it. So one day the fellows came over.

"Hey, what have you got?" they said.

"Just one pork chop," I replied.

They got the message.

Before leaving DePauw I had pledged a graduate chapter of Omega Psi Phi, a black fraternity. The Q's, as we are called (the Greek letter omega resembles the letter Q) are famous for being extremely devoted to the fraternity. So much so that many undergraduate brothers actually get branded with the Omega sign. Loyal as I am, I'm not one for brands—or any other kind of markings on my skin. Pledging a graduate chapter allowed me to avoid that, and all the other extreme initiation rituals that one can find among college fraternities.

I joined the Omegas because Clifford Wilson, the patriarch of my surrogate family in Indianapolis, was an Omega man. Mr. Wilson was my sponsor, and he, along with some of his fraternity brothers, shepherded me through the initiation. They were all middle-aged, middle-class black men, and the way they chose to introduce me to the fraternity fit their profile. It was all pretty mild-mannered and tame—the very opposite of intense. I'd come into Indianapolis to meet with them, and when we'd finished, they'd pick up some beer (this was in the days before our heightened awareness about mixing alcohol and cars), drive me the forty miles back to Greencastle, turn around and come back home. They were big brothers to me in the truest sense.

After those beginnings, the fraternity system at Howard was something of a revelation. Unlike DePauw, there were no fraternity houses on Howard's campus. I do remember visiting an Omega graduate chapter that had a house not far from school, just to see how they differed from DePauw's fraternities. There were pledges there who were "crossing the burning sands," which means they were undergoing the final round of initiation into membership. One of the pledges was bent over and a brother, completely drunk and out of control, was paddling him. It was just too much. I stepped forward and said, "Look, you can't hit him anymore."

The brother, and those who were standing around him, looked over at me as if I were crazy. "Who the hell are you?" one of them asked.

"I'm just a brother."

"So what? Who says I can't hit him anymore?"

I said, "You're too drunk to do this. You stop hitting him, or you hit me."

That brought on a few more choice words from them, but no one made a move toward me. The paddling stopped.

I went on. "Listen, if you're going to paddle a pledge, paddle him. But not this way. This guy is full of whiskey. You can't let him paddle this kid. If he makes a mistake and hits him and hurts his spine, there won't be any excuse that he was drunk and didn't know what he was doing. You're all standing around helping. You're all in it."

Whether the thought of possible group responsibility for potential injury gave them pause or whether the moment simply had been spoiled, they decided to let the pledge go that time. I had no use for that type of thing. There was just nothing in it for me, so I avoided that part of fraternity life as much as I could.

This is not to say it was all bad. What Howard fraternities and sororities lacked because they didn't have the kind of permanent housing that promotes Greek life on other campuses, they more than made up for with their spirit and style. They managed to make themselves an extremely strong part of the social life of the school.

On certain days, the fraternities and sororities would meet on the commons in the middle of the campus to sing their various hymns and songs. This group-inspired spectacle was always impressive and very moving, even to a confirmed loner. When one of the brothers used to ring the Q bell and sing, "Ring those bells, let them peal loud and strong," I felt a surge of pride and comfort, giving over to the pleasures of belonging to a group, even as I knew that I could never surrender totally to the group dynamic.

One day, as I stood in the commons in the center of Howard's campus watching the women of Delta Sigma Theta sing their "Sweetheart Song," my attention was drawn to one of the sisters as she sang a solo. I knew who she was, and I had always thought she was just beautiful. But there was something about that moment that reinforced the feeling. All I could think was, "There must be some way to get a date with this girl."

Her name was Shirley Yarbrough, and she was, like me, a native of Atlanta. As a matter of fact, she and my brother Windsor were about the same age, and they had been good friends in high school. I knew Shirley's mother, Rosalee, and I had been aware of Shirley back in Atlanta, but only vaguely. We did not go to the same high school, and she was a year behind me. There was no real occasion for our paths to have crossed much in those days. Things were different now, and I was determined that we would get to know one another better.

Whenever I'd see Shirley around campus (she was a senior), I'd be as friendly as possible—"Hello, home girl!"—hoping to establish and strengthen the ties between us. Shirley responded in kind, and I was encouraged. There was one problem: I had a rival, a young man named Chester. Shirley had been "pinned" by Chester, a sign in those days that they were "going steady." I had a sense that she liked me well enough, so I was fairly certain I had a chance to move her boyfriend out of the way. What I had to do was make sure that I kept contact with Shirley. I asked her if she could help me get a date with a girl who was a friend of hers. Of course that wasn't really what I wanted. I wanted as many excuses to talk to Shirley as I could find. Once, when she went home on a trip, I volunteered to safeguard an enormous teddy bear she kept in her room. That earned some points for me.

In addition to great beauty and intelligence, Shirley had a composed and cool air about her that served as a perfect complement to her quick wit. She loved clothes and was always well dressed. What intrigued me most (and made me fall so hard for her) was that she never made a fuss about me. Law students were among the most popular men on campus, running second only to medical students. Undergraduate women in particular were very keen on us, and they always made us the center of fawning attention. To be honest, those attentions were not totally unwelcome. It was just that they were, at a very basic level, transparently mercenary.

Things were not like that with Shirley, who was very different from the other women I encountered. She was always courteous and nice to me—playful, very open, but nonchalant. She responded to me as a good friend and serious person. That's how we started.

Shirley and I saw each other a lot in the dining hall. I saw her at chapel—sometimes we went together, sometimes we'd just run into one another there. As the weeks went by and we became closer friends, she started studying with me in the library on campus. Sometimes we would go to the Library of Congress to work. Joe Lockeridge had known what he was talking about, because I loved being in the grand old building. It was just the right touch for inspiring me to get through the sometimes dry reading all law students have to do. And studying together led to something of a turning point in my relationship with Shirley.

One night, as I walked Shirley home to her dormitory after the campus library had closed, we ran into Chester. He was not too happy about the time Shirley and I were spending together, and when he saw us that night, he was adamant about asserting his position. He said to her in his best lord-and-master tone, "You've got five minutes to get home."

I thought it was funny. But I kept a straight face and said, "Well, Shirley, I guess I'd better rush you home, right?"

Shirley wasn't too thrilled about what had happened. Later on when she called to talk to me, she mentioned (casually) that she had returned Chester's pin. That was her signal. I had been waiting for it. We kept our practice of studying and eating together, but we also started to go out on real dates.

Even though Shirley had given him back his pin, Chester wasn't totally out of the picture—at least not as far out as I thought he should have been. I was becoming very serious about Shirley and was anxious to have her make a total commitment to me. From my end, there was still Peggy from Chicago, the woman who had wanted me to become a Catholic so we could get married. She was, in effect, my version of Chester.

Each year, Howard was the site of an event called the Barristers' Ball. I decided to go to work on Shirley's complacency just a little bit. I invited Peggy to come out from Chicago to go to the ball with me. Shirley heard all about it, as I knew she would. Not long after that, I invited her to come and watch my first-year moot-court argument. When I'd finished, we sat around talking. She mentioned the ball and noted that she'd heard I'd gone with Peggy. She was not as cool as usual. It was plain that she had the same feelings about Peggy that I had about Chester. We'd both come to the same understanding.

NINETEEN FIFTY-EIGHT, my second year in law school, was a time of endings and beginnings. One afternoon I came back to my apartment to find an envelope with two letters in it, one from my mother and one from my father. They'd written to tell me, each in their own way, that after twenty-eight years of marriage, they were going to get a divorce. My father had already moved out of the house some time before, and they had kept this from me as long as they could, to spare my feelings. I sat down and cried.

My parents had not been getting along for some time. I knew that much. The tensions that had always existed between them because of their different personalities and aspirations simply strained them to the breaking point. With no young children to shepherd into adulthood—by now my brother Windsor was on his own, too—there was nothing more to hold them together. The break was almost inevitable.

I knew this, but I still cried. Then I asked myself, "What are you crying about? These two people have been married for twenty-eight years, and they've both decided there's no point in going any further." The tears were for myself, not my parents. When I thought more about their situation, I actually had a sense of relief that they would no longer have to live life just going through the motions. It made sense for a son to mourn the loss of his parents' marriage. The family that had nurtured me, that I'd looked forward to my own children being a part of, wouldn't exist anymore. Even though I hated it, just hated it, I simply had to accept the adult reality that men and women often grow apart.

My father moved in with his mother and sister for a time, and they took care of him. Eventually, he remarried. Mama's circumstances were very different. She didn't get married again, nor did she show any outward interest in starting a new household. From age fifty-one, she carried on alone. After the divorce, my mother had no substantial life outside of her work, which was the thing that sustained her. This is not to suggest that the change was easy. Once, when I gave a speech at a church, my mother arrived to find that my father and his new wife had also come to hear me. As I watched from the podium, waiting to speak, my mother got up and walked out. Later she apologized to me, although it wasn't necessary. "I'm sorry. I promise, I'll never do anything like that again," she said. "I just couldn't take it."

One might think that marriage would be the last thing on my mind as I recovered from the searing experience of my parents' divorce. But by then I knew with absolute certainty that Shirley was the woman I wanted to marry and that I could not let her get away. At the end of my first year in law school, she had graduated and moved back to Atlanta to take a job as a caseworker for the Fulton County Welfare Department. She was very excited about that.

There were no summer clerkships for first-year black law students in those days, so at the end of the term, I went back for a second summer as a bus driver for the Chicago Transit Authority. Letters were not enough for us, and Shirley and I kept in touch by telephone as the summer went by and I returned to school in the fall.

I had raised the subject of marriage with Shirley before she had graduated. I told her, as we stood behind the Founders Library one afternoon, that if she would marry me, I would be somebody one day. Now, with her in Atlanta and me in Washington, I asked her again and she accepted my proposal. There's no doubt that the unraveling of my parents' marriage made me anxious to establish my own family. Our parents accepted our decision, even though it posed a logistical problem. We would be separated until I graduated. Shirley was as serious about her job as I was about law school. There was little point in her quitting and then trying to start things over with the county. Besides, we knew we'd be together permanently as soon as I graduated.

Shirley and I were married in a very simple ceremony in Washington. Just a few of our friends attended, and Joe Lockeridge was my best man. We had no money, and no time, for a real honeymoon. So we had a short one instead. We spent the weekend together in Washington and went to the Howard Theatre to see Erroll Garner and Nina Simone. On Monday morning, Shirley was on the train back to Atlanta so that she could return to work. I went back to my classes, a married man.

WITH A WIFE TO SUPPORT and one final year of law school to get through, I went back to work for Robert Maddox in the summer before my third year at law school. We were both older, of course, and he had become much more mellow than I remembered from my first turn working for him. He didn't get around as much, so there wasn't as much for me to do.

Although Mr. Maddox had gotten used to the fact that I could not only read but was in law school, he could still be surprised by little things that indicated that blacks and whites were not two separate species. One evening he announced that he wanted me to take him to the Chastain Theatre, which was running a Shakespeare Festival.

"I'm sorry, Mr. Maddox," I told him. "I can't take you. I've got a date with my wife. We have tickets to the Chastain Theatre tonight, too. I'll find somebody else to take you."

While Mr. Maddox was certainly annoyed that I'd refused to take him to the theater, he seemed even more amazed that his young black (he'd say "Negro" at best, "nigger" at worst) chauffeur had a wife whom he was taking to see one of Shakespeare's plays. This was not as big a surprise to him as finding out that I could read, but he did find it intriguing.

"No, no, I'll find somebody," he said. I let him do that.

ALMOST ANY LAWYER will tell you that the third and final year of law school is of questionable value. By that time, most people have gotten the message that law-school classes are supposed to impart. The most significant thing that happened to me during my third year—an event that pretty much overshadowed all things academic— was that I became a father. Shirley gave birth to our daughter, Vickee.

That whole process, pregnancy to birth, held me in complete thrall. There are few sights more beautiful than a pregnant woman— especially if the pregnant woman is your own wife. I remember seeing Shirley once at the top of the stairs at the Terminal railroad station when she was very far along in her pregnancy. She had on white pants and a yellow blouse, looking cute and radiant at the same time. I thought, "My God. She's carrying my child." In that moment the magnitude of my responsibility hit me with gale force. It just took my breath away.

When Vickee was born I was almost afraid to hold her, fearing that I might be too clumsy, make a mistake, and drop her. She was so small. I had no experience with the day-to-day care of babies. Frankly, I didn't get the chance to gain much with Vickee. I could not stay around too long after her birth because I had to return to Washington to finish law school. Shirley, with a new baby, remained in Atlanta to be near her family, as well as mine. Her mother helped with Vickee, and Shirley was able to go back to her job with the county. The separation was difficult, but there was little point in having her move up to Washington with an infant for my last months at Howard, since it was clear in our minds that we were going to settle in Atlanta.

GRADUATION FROM LAW SCHOOL was very different from my college graduation. The proceedings were much more low-key and lacked the drama of a college commencement. Most of the school-related energy of the year had been dissipated in the effort to nail down post-graduation jobs. There was very little left for displays of sentimentality.

Many of my fellow law students were like me, in that they had come to Howard with a plan to go back to their communities to practice. Doug Wilder had gone back to Virginia, Joe Lockeridge was going back to Texas, and I was going back to Atlanta. The thought of working at a big law firm or a corporation never seriously entered my mind, and I am sure it never entered the minds of my classmates. We knew those jobs were off-limits to us. This was true not only in the South but all over the country. The profession was very closed to racial minorities (and to women as well, I might add).

We knew that wherever we were going, we would have a general practice—wills, criminal defense work, real estate—serving black clients and black businesses. But we also knew that if we kept our eyes and ears open, we could also identify some civil rights cases and that we could then play a role in the movement.

At the same time, there was another group among my classmates who could not resist the temptation of government jobs in Washington. Just as so many black people without college degrees found security and a good-paying job working for the post office, a substantial number of black lawyers in the late 1950s and early 1960s went to work at jobs in the Justice Department, the Commerce Department, and other federal agencies. The good salaries were not the only attraction. Some of my classmates choosing not to return to their small hometowns in the South, preferring the more cosmopolitan life in Washington. Many of these lawyers made good careers for themselves, and several rose to judgeships or heads of administrative departments in the decades to come. But that was never part of my plan. I wanted to go back home to Atlanta and get started practicing law.

My family came up for the commencement exercises, and they were all very happy and proud of me. By then, however, we had gotten somewhat used to the idea that I had all the tools I needed to make it in the world. What mattered now was execution: I just had to carry on with the plan.

The other thing that distinguished my Howard graduation from my graduation from DePauw was that my parents were no longer together. The nuclear family that had celebrated with me in Greencastle had fractured. Instead of a happy band driving north together, my parents came to Washington by different routes—my mother by car, my father on the train. Daddy stayed in a hotel. Mama stayed with me in my apartment. There were no outward displays of hostility between them. They were cordial to one another, and we managed to get through it all with good humor and only a little strain. Still, it was all a little strange to be sharing that particular moment together when all our positions had changed so much. We had moved into completely unfamiliar terrain that would have to be negotiated over the course of the rest of our lives. If there were ever any lingering doubts in my mind that adulthood was full square upon me, they were obliterated during those summer days. I left Washington as the head of my own family, with a brand new career to build—wiser about life—but still hopeful.

MR. HOLLOWELL

WHEN I ARRIVED HOME in Atlanta as a newly minted lawyer in June 1960, there was no "Welcome Home" sign from the Georgia bar. But at least I had the job I wanted. I was working for Donald Hollowell. Mr. Hollowell was one of a group of black attorneys in cities and towns across the South who acted as "co-operating attorneys" with the NAACP, serving as local counsel when the Legal Defense Fund pursued a case in their area. At Howard, all of us who were interested in practicing civil rights law knew the names of these attorneys, especially those from our hometowns. And so we set our sights on finding work with them.

For a young man who wanted to become a civil rights lawyer, or any type of lawyer for that matter, there was no better teacher and mentor than Don Hollowell. He was, quite simply, one of the most gifted trial lawyers in all of Georgia. With his keen intellect and quiet determination, Mr. Hollowell was perfectly suited to the difficult task of practicing law—specifically law in the service of social justice—in Georgia during the 1950s and 1960s.

Mr. Hollowell's job was not easy, and I appreciate the scope of his achievement even more deeply now. What courage it took to do what he did in my home state! For all the problems many black lawyers face today (more restricted job prospects, glass ceilings once jobs are gotten), Mr. Hollowell's position during his early years at the bar, and even when I went to work for him, would be unfathomable to the young black lawyers of this current generation.

Imagine being a black lawyer in Georgia in 1952, when Mr. Hollowell opened his practice in Atlanta. There are fewer than fifteen practicing black lawyers in the whole state. You spend your time working on behalf of clients—unpopular because of their involvement in legal cases, unpopular because of their very existence. You crisscross the state, going to backwoods towns and villages untouched by time and progress, where a black man in a suit is a provocation, where judges refuse to honor you with the title of "Mister." This was the way Mr. Hollowell lived his life in the law, at considerable risk to himself, for the eight years before I began to work for him. By the time I arrived, he was forty-three years old, well seasoned, and in the prime of his life as an attorney. As has so often been the case with me, I was blessed that the timing was just right.

Because Shirley and I had always planned to settle in Atlanta and because I knew of Mr. Hollowell's reputation, it was natural to try to sign on with him. I got my chance through a mutual connection. Kenneth Days, my old bandmaster from David T. Howard High School, and Mr. Hollowell were fraternity brothers—they were Kappas. Mr. Days kept up with me through my mother, and he knew I was graduating and looking for work. He talked to Mr. Hollowell about me during the beginning of my third year in law school. This led to an informal meeting between us when I came home for Christmas break.

We had a good conversation. I saw firsthand how committed Mr. Hollowell was to his practice, to his community, and to the cause of civil rights. He had grown up in Kansas, gone into the army and then to Lane College in Jackson, Tennessee, and Loyola University Law School in Chicago, and he was very active in his church. I could see that he was climbing the mountain I wanted to climb. And it was clear that he needed help in his practice; he couldn't do all the work on all the cases by himself. The only question was whether he could afford to hire another lawyer.

I went back to Atlanta for more formal talks with Mr. Hollowell the following spring. On this visit, he invited Shirley and me over to dinner at his home. The evening had been going smoothly; we were enjoying the wonderful food and talking pleasantly. At one point, while Shirley was serving herself some of the delicious sweet potato soufflé, a dollop of the dish got away from the spoon and landed right in her cleavage. It was one of those absurd moments that seem so important to young people when they're trying to be on their best behavior but which are totally meaningless if the person they are trying to impress is really serious about them. We found it hard to see it that way at the time, certain that our every little move counted. I thought to myself, "Oh, no. So much for my job." Shirley was mortified. There was absolutely nothing for us to have worried about. I imagine Mr. Hollowell probably found the whole episode more amusing than anything else.

There were no guarantees in my job search. So in addition to Mr. Hollowell, I talked with other lawyers in town. I even went to see A. T. Walden, my childhood hero, at his office next door to the Butler Street YMCA. He was still the most prominent black lawyer in Atlanta, but he did not have a law firm. What he had was more of an association, with several lawyers sharing the same offices but each conducting his own business. Mr. Walden was very warm to me when I came to meet with him, but he made it clear that he did not have a job to offer. "You come in here and you go to work, but you don't get any pay" was how he described it to me. "You will have the association with me, but you have to develop your own practice." While I liked being independent, at that period I did not need independence as much as I needed a paying job. I could not, with a family, have the responsibility of building a practice straight out of law school. As much as I admired Mr. Walden, I kept looking.

There was one lawyer in particular whom I thought might be a possible second choice to Mr. Hollowell, even though his practice was primarily real estate. But this man proved to be unsuitable almost upon sight. We agreed on a morning interview, and I walked into his office to find a half-empty bottle of whiskey sitting on his desk for all the world to see. I knew before we got started that working for him just wouldn't do.

There were sisters in white at the St. Paul AME Church who had been waiting for me to graduate from law school so that I could draw up their wills. If they were to walk into the office and see that whiskey bottle, they would think I had thrown my life away. There would be no end of talk about it. He and I went through the motions, but there was no way I'd have taken a job with him under those conditions.

In the end, I went to work for Mr. Hollowell for a salary of $35 a week. As happy as I was to have a job—particularly that one—it wasn't enough to make ends meet, even with Shirley continuing to work at the Fulton County Welfare Department (and drawing a bigger salary than I did). I had to supplement our family's income. So I went back to working parties with my mother; a lawyer by day, a waiter and bartender by night. My mother's clientele remained the elite white people of the city. As a result, there were times when I would wind up serving hors d'oeuvres or drinks to a lawyer with whom I had been searching titles in the courthouse earlier that day.

The other black lawyers in town thought this was just awful. It was a very small world of college-educated blacks. The world of black lawyers was even smaller. To them, it was a matter of racial pride. By going to college and getting a law degree I was advancing in the world. My progress was the progress of the race. By taking a job as a servant, I was pulling the train backward, and dragging the black race along for the ride. "Man! What are you doing?" they would say to me.

Mr. Hollowell, who was always very gracious, never said a word to me about my moonlighting. I did good work for him, and that was enough. He knew the strong ties I had to my mother. He also knew that I was a man and that I had to do what I felt was right for my family.

And it was the right thing for me to have done at that time. I wasn't ready to play the role of the financially independent lawyer, because it would have been just that: a role, a fantasy. I understood why some were dismayed by my choice. I just couldn't let that bother me. Shirley and I had our own dreams—a house, security for our family—of our future. Like selling golf balls, polishing mailboxes, washing dishes, driving a bus—working for my mother was a means to an end. And I had no qualms about it, for this was a business of which I was very proud. This was a business that had paid my tuition. I saw nothing wrong with the job, because life is about doing what you have to do in order to get where you want to be.

MR. HOLLOWELL threw me right into the thick of things. I graduated from law school on a Friday, and the following Monday I was out serving papers, beyond excited about having entered the world of the law at last. This was something of an experiment for Mr. Hollowell, who had never had a law clerk before. He was by himself in practice, and he desperately needed the help. I became his factotum, doing all the legwork that's involved in law practice: looking up cases, gathering documents from the courthouse, talking to parties involved in cases, driving him to various appointments. If we had to take a trip out of town, to visit a client in the state prison, for example, and he told me to pick him up at 5 A.M., I'd be there at 5 A.M. Whatever he required, I did. I was very much taken with him—was in awe of him, in fact—and it was extremely important to have a man like him think well of me.

From the very beginning of my time with Mr. Hollowell, I worked on cases that raised some of the most troubling moral and social issues of our time, often in the most excruciating way. One in particular left the deepest mark on me. In the earliest moments of my career, I witnessed one of the most raw examples of injustice imaginable. The state of Georgia killed a man for what amounted to an argument with his girlfriend.

The month after I began work, Mr. Hollowell got a call from the president of the Atlanta NAACP, Mr. C. S. Hamilton. There was a young man named Nathaniel Johnson, he said, who was in the Tattnall County State Prison awaiting execution after he was found guilty of raping a white woman. The case had been handled by a white attorney who had convinced Johnson to plead guilty on the theory that he wouldn't be given the death penalty under those circumstances. The ploy backfired. Johnson was sentenced to die in the electric chair. The lawyer, belatedly, decided to fight for his client and challenged the sentence, taking it up to the Georgia Supreme Court, losing every step of the way. He did manage to prepare a writ of habeas corpus, which would have allowed a federal review of any constitutional issues involved in the case. The lawyer argued that the state had violated Johnson's rights under the Fifth Amendment to the Constitution and various provisions of Georgia's state constitution. That petition failed, in part because the relevant right was guaranteed by the Fourteenth Amendment, not the Fifth.

Mr. Hollowell agreed to take matters from there, and he was prepared to argue on the basis of violations of Johnson's rights under the Fourteenth Amendment. I drove Mr. Hollowell to the state prison to meet the client. We walked into the visitors' area to find Johnson, an extremely handsome man, sitting in a prison uniform, shackled to a ball and chain, smoking a cigarette. After our introductions, he told us his version of the story. He and the woman who had charged him with rape had been lovers, introduced by a mutual friend who had told Johnson that the woman, who was married, could not have children. Over a period of time, the pair had had sex without protection, evidently because Johnson didn't think it was needed. One day the woman announced that she was pregnant and demanded money from Johnson for an abortion. When he refused, she became angry and told her husband that she had been raped. Johnson was arrested in the middle of the night, with no warrant, and as things turned out, no real chance of getting a fair trial.

A hearing was set for the day before the execution, so Mr. Hollowell and I were in the U.S. courthouse, before Judge Frank Scarlet, trying to get a stay of execution pending the hearing on our habeas corpus petition.

"When is this supposed to take place?" he asked, meaning the execution.

"Tomorrow," we said almost in unison.

Scarlet was unmoved. He quoted Oliver Wendell Holmes, "Justice delayed is justice denied." As far as he was concerned, delaying Johnson's execution another moment would be an unjust result. He also viewed this as a state matter in which the federal court had no useful role to play.

We left Judge Scarlet's courtroom and went immediately to see Johnson in his cell. He was vibrating with fear. We told him that the judge had denied his request for a stay, that there were still avenues to pursue, and that we were going to pursue them.

That same evening we went to Reidsville to see Judge Carr, a state court judge who also had the power to issue a stay. He was adamant. "I'm not going to issue a stay in this case," he said. "This was a heinous crime."

Judge Carr was the key to it all. He had to act. So we rushed back to Atlanta to prepare a writ of mandamus, which is the means of making a recalcitrant public official do what he or she is supposed to do under law.

The next morning we were in the chambers of W. H. Duckworth, the chief justice of the Georgia Supreme Court, to make our case. In the middle of this literally deadly serious matter, Duckworth asked me, "Son, where do you play basketball?"

I shook my head and said, "I don't play basketball anywhere."

We left the chambers empty-handed.

Governor Ernest Vandiver was our last chance. His counsel was Henry Neal. If we could get to Neal, we might be able to get to the governor. Neal's office was our immediate next stop. While we stood in the waiting area, we heard his secretary announce, "Mr. Neal, there are two boys here to see you." Neal then told us in no uncertain terms that Governor Vandiver was not going to stop the execution of Nathaniel Johnson.

Mr. Hollowell was still not done. We left Neal's office and went upstairs to the Board of Pardons and Parole, knowing that this was our last chance to do something, anything, to save Johnson's life and allow his federal claims to be heard, as they should have been. While we were there, the head of the Board of Pardons and Parole, who had heard about our efforts, walked in and said, "Hollowell, you're too late. The process has begun."

Johnson had been executed, probably while we were running frantically from office to office trying to save his life.

That was a moment of complete despair—deadening, almost paralyzing in its intensity. We had tried so hard, thinking of everything we could, chasing down every legal avenue that was open to us, believing there was some way within the system to give this man a chance, and it was all to no avail. This was not like losing a case where your client has to pay money or has to go to jail—even for a long time. Nathaniel Johnson was dead. He was gone. There was no way to bring him back.

With nothing really left to say, Mr. Hollowell and I left the state capitol building. The combination of fatigue and utter demoralization had wiped out any chance that I could be productive at work, so I asked for the day off. I decided to walk home. Although it was before noon, the temperature was already scorching. This was a brutally hot Georgia summer. I walked along replaying the previous forty-eight hours in my head over and over, thinking of how our client had been killed by a poisonous combination of incompetence, hatred, and indifference—and then the tears began to flow. The more I cried, the weaker I got, and before I knew it I looked down and realized that I had totally lost control. I had urinated on myself as I was walking along, and my beige summer suit was wet. There was nothing to do but keep walking. The sun was beating down so intensely that by the time I got home, my suit was completely dry.

I GOT UP THE NEXT DAY and went back to work. We had to carry on. There was another capital case in the office, one that involved a charge of murder against a fifteen-year-old boy named Preston Cobb. Cobb had been sentenced to death, and his case had drawn national and international attention because one so young was going to be put to death by the state. It seemed uncivilized to many observers, and the whole affair became a cause célèbre, with well-known people like Eleanor Roosevelt weighing in on the subject.

I'd heard about the case from one of my cousins and wanted to know more. So I drove out to Monticello, Georgia, where Cobb's family lived and which was also my father's hometown. There was a very prominent black doctor who lived there, Frederick Douglass Funderburg, who had an interest in the case as well. I went to his home, and he put me in touch with a young man who had been dating Cobb's sister. That young man, in turn, brought Cobb's mother to Dr. Funderburg's house to meet with me. This was a very volatile situation. Cobb was accused of murdering a well-known white landowner in town. Everyone was on tenterhooks about it, so we acted with great caution. We wanted to make sure that no one knew what was going on. So we turned out all the lights and waited for Mrs. Cobb's arrival.

She came, and I explained to her who I was and that I thought Mr. Hollowell could help her son. In those days, the rules were very clear: lawyers were not permitted to solicit clients directly. The rules against champerty and barratry were meant to keep lawyers from drumming up business by encouraging people to fight, sowing discord within the community. People like Preston Cobb and his family, who were living under state-sanctioned oppression, were disadvantaged by this because they were often in serious need of help and didn't know where to turn.

We could help, I explained to Mrs. Cobb, but she had to come to Atlanta to request our services. This was a big step for a woman who was essentially living on a plantation, just like my aunt, whom we had spirited away from a sharecropper's life in the dead of night. But Mrs. Cobb agreed, saying she would take the train. "I'll be wearing a red dress," she said,

Mrs. Cobb came to Atlanta and engaged Mr. Hollowell as her son's attorney. Preston Cobb's case, unlike that of Nathaniel Johnson, was being followed by the world. We got some especially good coverage from Tom Johnson, who was then a reporter for the *Macon Telegraph*, and would later become the head of CNN, which shows the effect the media can have on the course of legal cases. Public scrutiny made all the difference in the world. Eventually, Preston Cobb got a new trial in Jasper County, and Mr. Hollowell and Horace Ward argued his case. This man's life was saved.

In another case, we represented James Fair, an eighteen-year-old black man accused of murder in Early County, who had been sentenced to death in a manner that defied any notion of measured justice. The proceedings against Fair had moved with lightning speed. He had been arrested, tried, convicted, and sentenced within forty-eight hours. We went to Reidsville to argue the motion for a new trial. Mr. Hollowell and I were joined by C. B. King, an NAACP lawyer from Atlanta.

Every day at the lunch break, the white court officials and lawyers went across the courthouse square for lunch at the whites-only café, while the three black lawyers went to the local grocery for sliced bologna, a loaf of bread, a jar of mustard, and some Coca-Cola, which we ate in Mr. Hollowell's automobile.

On the third day of the trial, a black woman seated in the balcony dropped a book, which got my attention. When I looked up, I saw her beckoning me to meet her at the courthouse entrance. "We've been watching you lawyers eat bologna sandwiches for two days now," she whispered to me when I got there. "Don't eat today. After court today, come to my home for lunch." She gave me directions.

And when we got there, we saw a beautiful sight—a table set for royalty. Her best silver, china, and crystal, a lace tablecloth, beautifully folded white cloth napkins, and the most exquisite Southern cuisine I've ever eaten. Some ten black women and their husbands joined hands with us for grace. Our hostess's husband said the blessing.

I shall never forget one sentence in that prayer: "Lord, we can't join the NAACP down here, but thanks to your bountiful blessings, we can feed the NAACP lawyers."

THE INTERSECTION OF RACE AND SEX in Georgia was always treacherous territory. Nathaniel Johnson had died because of this. His was an extreme example. Sometimes, other interracial situations brought about less dramatically tragic consequences. We had another client, a young boy from Meriwether County who had dialed the wrong number attempting to reach his girlfriend. He wound up on the phone with a white girl, who struck up a conversation with him. She asked him about his girlfriend and why he wanted to talk to her. The conversation turned personal, and the boy made some comments about the size of his penis. The girl said she didn't believe him and wanted to see for herself. Neither of them knew that the girl's father was listening in on another extension. The boy was arrested and charged with making lewd statements. A matter that should have been handled by a strong parental reprimand was treated as a serious legal case. This young boy could have gone to jail for a very long time.

His mother hired Mr. Hollowell and we went to Meriwether County. The first day, we walked into the courthouse and went up to the counsel's table. The bailiff said, "You boys can't sit here. Colored people sit upstairs."

Because I was young and not in the mood for this sort of thing, I asked, "Have you ever seen anyone try a case from upstairs?"

This was not the way to go, and Mr. Hollowell quickly spoke up to make sure that the verbal sparring didn't go much further. He calmly asked to speak with Judge Knight, who was still in chambers. After their talk, Judge Knight ended up ordering the bailiff to allow us to sit at the counsel's table.

Mr. Hollowell's rapport with the judge continued. He worked things out so that our client would not have to serve any time. There was, however, one condition: The boy had to leave town. His mother agreed to this resolution, and the matter was closed.

Word had gotten out that two black lawyers were in the courthouse working on a case. When we walked out of the judge's chambers, we noticed a number of black spectators sitting, as they were required to, in the balcony. As we started toward the door, they rose, almost as one, to come downstairs to follow us out. Once outside, we found that another small band of blacks had gathered on the courthouse steps. No one said anything to us. They were just silent, watching. The chances are overwhelming that they'd never seen a black lawyer appear in that courthouse. The whole scene was exhilarating (I had the sense they admired us), but it was also a little sad to know that we were so rare a sight.

At the car, we stood for a moment with our client, his mother, and the local undertaker, who had suggested to the mother that she engage Mr. Hollowell to represent her son. The woman expressed her gratitude, pulled out a wad of cash, and paid Mr. Hollowell right on the spot. Our client, too immature to fully understand what he and his family had been spared, was about to turn away in silence when Mr. Hollowell said sternly, "Boy, you say thank you to your mother."

As THINGS TURNED OUT, Mr. Hollowell and I soon had help in the office. Not long after I came on board, he hired Horace T. Ward, a young man from rural Georgia who had gone to Morehouse and then on to Northwestern for law school, finishing a year before me in 1959. Horace and Mr. Hollowell had known each other for ten years. Horace was the first black to apply to the University of Georgia's law school. Mr. Hollowell, along with Constance Baker Motley of the NAACP Legal Defense and Educational Fund, represented him. When the judge in the case decided that Horace had to exhaust his administrative remedies, that is to say, he had to appeal to the very state entities that were responsible for maintaining segregated educational facilities in Georgia, he decided to go elsewhere rather than pursue what looked to be a futile and time-consuming process.

In another example of how small our world was, Horace had met my brother Windsor before he'd met me. Northwestern was almost adjacent to the American Institute of Baking, where Windsor had gone to school. The two of them got to know each other there.

Horace also knew my mother. She was active in the NAACP, and when she became aware of his efforts to get into the University of Georgia, she encouraged him very strongly to go the distance. At the time Horace came to work with us, the battle had been joined again in the form of *Holmes v. Danner*, a case that had come into the office the year before. Now Horace was a lawyer working to make sure that other black students had the opportunity to do what he could not do: attend the University of Georgia. This has been so much the story of black advancement: one person making a first move, being rebuffed, and then supporting those who rise up to make other attempts when the right moment appears.

Hamilton Holmes and Charlayne Hunter were the two in Georgia who came forward to carry on Horace's original effort. Both had been star pupils at Turner High School in Atlanta. Like Horace

Ward before them, they had applied to the University of Georgia and had been turned down. Hamilton was attending Morehouse and Charlayne was at Wayne State when they decided to challenge the university's rejection of their applications.

The *Holmes* case was considered extremely important by members of the civil rights community. Thurgood Marshall had sent Constance Baker Motley down to work directly with Mr. Hollowell on the case, reuniting the older lawyers Hollowell and Motley with their former client, Ward, in the service of desegregating Georgia's universities.

I spent a good amount of my time during my first months with Mr. Hollowell doing the discovery and the legwork in preparation for the trial of the case that was to take place that coming December. Horace and I were sent down to Athens, Georgia, to go through the university's admissions records. At some point the university balked at this process, and Mr. Hollowell had to go to court to get the untrammeled right to discovery. This allowed us total access to the university's records. We needed to establish the criteria by which other students were being admitted to the university. If we could find people who were being let in with profiles similar to those of Hamilton's and Charlayne's, we could then make our case about the unfairness of the process.

Discovery can be a daunting task, not unlike looking for a needle in a haystack. Ms. Motley, Horace, and I went back down to Athens to start the search. There were thousands and thousands of student applications to go through, and we spent about three weeks in the registrar's office sifting through file after file. We brought along two students from Atlanta University to help out. We explained to them what we were trying to do and the kinds of things we were looking for, and they plunged in, too. The registrar from Atlanta University agreed to become an expert witness to help us analyze the admissions records.

That period was one of the richest times of my life. It was at once serious, fun, educational (watching Constance Motley, whom I'd first seen at Howard, was a lesson in lawyering all by itself), socially relevant, and uplifting. We were, with no doubt in my mind (then or now), the "good guys" in the drama. Lawyers can't always count on feeling that way about their cases. I've never felt it so sharply since then.

We were heavily into this process when I had an experience every lawyer dreams of: I found the "needle." There was a letter from a member of the board of regents to a university official on behalf of a young woman who had applied to the university. The letter extolled the virtues of this applicant and stated what a credit she would be to the school. As it turned out, this young woman had a profile almost identical to Charlayne's. She was admitted, whereas Charlayne had been told that her credentials were not good enough to qualify her for admission. This was exactly what our legal team was looking for. We had our smoking gun.

I knew how important this document was to our case—and how important it was to me personally to have found it. When I showed it to Ms. Motley and the others, they were ecstatic—the celebration was open and vocal: "This is it!" Mr. Hollowell and Ms. Motley thought the letter would go a long way toward helping us win the case, when combined with all the other information we'd gathered from the files. To have this type of validation, especially after the Nathaniel Johnson tragedy, was intoxicating. So much so that I thought nothing of the potential dangers of my next task, which was to go from door to door (day and night) serving subpoenas on the regents and the young white woman who had been admitted, as well as the chancellor and other university officials who had been involved in this episode. Having gotten what we came for, we closed up shop and went back to Atlanta to prepare.

T HE TRIAL BEGAN IN DECEMBER. Our days were spent commuting from Atlanta to Athens, a 150-mile round-trip. We had no real choice, for there were no hotels for us to stay in. Every morning we'd pile into two cars. Hamilton, Charlayne, and their parents would ride in one car; I would drive the other, carrying Mr. Hollowell, Ms. Motley, and Horace. My eye was always on the road, but this was a time for me to listen and learn as we went over what we wanted to accomplish for the day and, on the return trips, what we thought of how the day had gone. When we'd get back into Atlanta, sometimes we'd continue the discussion of the day's events over a bottle of whiskey or gin. What I had then was a very concentrated and high-level introduction to all aspects of the culture of the legal profession.

The intensity of Ms. Motley's focus was just immense. Thinking of every possible twist and turn of the case, how to respond to each one—her brilliance as a strategist was something to behold. She and Mr. Hollowell functioned as a tag team arguing the case in court, and as soon as she saw an opening, she would pounce. During the trial, I got the feeling watching her that she was sitting there like a barber sharpening his razor on a strop. No one was better prepared for courtroom battle than she was. She planned every detail of her direct examination, anticipated every possible issue that could be raised on cross-examination, and prepared a response to the hypotheticals.

My enduring memory of Constance Baker Motley is of her kicking off her shoes when we brought her back to the home of Edwin and Mamie Thomas, where she was staying in Atlanta, there being no hotel that would take her there, either. She had worked from sunup to sundown, and it was only when she got to the Thomases' house that she could truly relax.

Although we were going into hostile territory each day, I don't recall anyone expressing fear of physical danger. Perhaps we were so obsessed with the details of the case that we pushed any concerns of that sort into the background. Make no mistake. We were in Klan country, and in the country of those who adhered to the Klan philosophy but just didn't want to put on a sheet. Not long after our case was over, two black military men were driving in the area near Athens. They weren't wearing their uniforms, which might or might not have protected them, but they were in a nice car. They got stopped by some Klan members and were killed right there on the road. Perhaps our lack of fear can be traced to Mr. Hollowell. Traveling the dangerous roads of Georgia practicing law was old hat to him. A calm leader makes for calm troops. His demeanor set the tone for the rest of us.

Then there were the people of Georgia, at least those who were our supporters, who came to court every day to watch the proceedings. This was never just Hamilton's and Charlayne's case. Of course, if we won, they would benefit personally. At the same time, everyone knew that if we won, all other black children in Georgia—in the country for that matter—would have a significant victory. So black people came to court, a little confused at first. Accustomed to Georgia's segregated state courts, they hung back, not sure where they were supposed to sit. We were, of course, in a U.S. federal court, which was not segregated. It took a short while before they figured this out, and then they sat where they wanted.

W E WON THE CASE. The court ordered the University of Georgia to admit our clients. Our victory was front-page news in Georgia and throughout the country. For the university, the loss was more than just a defeat on campus social mores, it was potentially an economic disaster. When the rumblings about school desegregation started, to make sure institutions of higher learning held the line, Georgia passed a law stating that any college or university that admitted black students would lose its funding from the state. So even though we'd won the day, we knew the matter wasn't really finished. Even if it had wanted to, the university could not have capitulated, given the existence of that state funding law.

Instead of finishing out their terms in their respective schools, Hamilton and Charlayne decided they wanted to transfer immediately, so we went full-steam ahead. Mr. Hollowell and Ms. Motley had been called to Macon, Georgia, to deal with other motions that had been filed in the case, so Horace and I were left to take our clients to Athens to register. Charlayne's parents came along with us.

It was soon known that two black students would be coming to the university to register for the winter quarter. We arrived to face an angry throng of segregationists who wanted to show us just how

unwelcome we were. Hamilton and Charlayne were going to different departments in the school, so we split duties: Horace would attend to Hamilton, I would be responsible for Charlayne. We came
down to the university, parked our car, and got out. I escorted Charlayne through a howling mob, who saw this bright young woman
(and me) as their mortal enemies—no Southern hospitality, no
Christian spirit of brotherhood—just unbounded hatred and fear on
open display.

To a great extent, we were protected (and our position enhanced)
by the presence of the news media. The cameras captured for history
the tremendous ugliness of that scene. They caught something else,
too, that was just as important. As in other instances where blacks
have sought to exercise some of the basic rights of citizenship—
going unmolested to a lunch counter, enrolling in a state university
for which they were paying taxes, sitting where they wanted to on a
bus—there was always great dignity that stood in marked contrast
to the baseness of those who came out to jeer. Look at the old film
footage and newspaper pictures from those days: schoolchildren versus the mob, young adults trying to get an education versus the mob,
peaceful diners versus the mob. It comes through so clearly. There's
just no question who was out of moral line.

We spent the early part of the day going around campus with the
administration's complete cooperation. While those administrators
could not have been happy with the way things had turned out, they
never showed their displeasure directly to us. The students at the
university were another matter. They were quite vocal in their opposition. And of all of them, and this is an embarrassment to my profession to say it, the law students were the worst. When Hamilton
and Horace walked past the law school that day, those future
lawyers yelled the loudest and offered up the worst curses, furious at
the transformation we had brought to the world they lived in, as
well as the one they were about to enter. No students were better
suited to perceive, and lament, the ways in which successful civil
rights cases would change American attitudes toward law and the legal profession itself.

As we went about our affairs, the legal maneuvering continued at a breakneck pace. The university's application for a stay of the injunction ordering Hamilton and Charlayne to be admitted was granted while we were on campus. That meant, of course, that we had to leave. We got on the telephone with Mr. Hollowell. "What do we do now?" we asked. He knew a black businessman in the area, and he told us to go there and stay in a holding pattern until the issues could be resolved. It wasn't over yet. Ms. Motley asked the chief judge of the Fifth Circuit, Elbert P. Tuttle, to vacate the stay. He did, which meant that Hamilton and Charlayne could return.

It took more motions, more threats from the state, more action from the federal courts, but Hamilton and Charlayne finally took their place at the university, and they both graduated. Charlayne became a widely known journalist under the name Charlayne Hunter-Gault and Hamilton Holmes became a physician. It's amazing to think that a proposition so simple and right—that those two young Georgians should have been allowed to enter their state's university—provoked so much angst, energy, and opposition at the time. If I learned from *State v. Johnson* the limits of law in a society unwilling to do justice, *Holmes v. Danner* taught me that sustained social agitation, moral suasion, and political action can create an environment in which people in power feel compelled to do the right thing.

CHAPTER 7

MS. HURLEY AND
THE NAACP

I BEGAN MY CAREER during a special time in our country's history. Doors were opening for young black Americans on many fronts—in government, civil rights activities, and the not-for-profit sector (though not as much in the corporate world). In general, people were on the lookout for young, educated blacks. The civil rights movement needed people to fill the second and third rungs of the leadership ladder, some to be groomed for advancement. White organizations, to be progressive (or to be thought of as progressive), wanted to find a few blacks to join their ranks, too. If others in positions of power saw that a young person was serious about his or her work, they wanted that person to join them.

It was in this environment, around the time of my first-year anniversary working for Mr. Hollowell, that Ruby Hurley, the head of the Southeastern Regional Office of the NAACP, offered me a job as Georgia field director, a staff position for the national NAACP. At the time, I was truly preoccupied with managing my day-to-day existence: working for Mr. Hollowell full-time and for my mother, on occasion, and adjusting to the demands of family life. I barely had a moment to look up.

In the midst of all this, Ms. Hurley's offer came as a very welcome surprise. She knew me because her offices were on the same floor as Mr Hollowell's. In her position as an NAACP official, she was a conduit of cases to him. So we were very often in one another's presence from the time I started work. She'd had the chance to observe me on her own and, no doubt, got an additional perspective on me from Mr. Hollowell. This was the perfect way to be"discovered," which was in a sense what happened. Being a field director for the NAACP was my first real turn as a leader in the civil rights movement. Much of what came afterward was a direct result of having worked in that job.

The job paid $5,700 a year, a lot of money in 1961. Even though Mr. Hollowell had raised my pay from $35 to $50 a week, as a field director I'd be making more than twice my present salary. Then there was also the title, and the actual substance of the job: I would be in charge of something—which I had always wanted. The Georgia field director was the organizer, the advocate, the program person in the state, with responsibility for organizing new NAACP branches and increasing the membership of existing branches. It was a big job—Georgia is one of the largest states in the South—and I would be the youngest of the field directors working for Ms. Hurley. It was a great and unique opportunity.

There was something else on my mind as well. A contributing factor to my decision to leave was that I had flunked the Georgia bar exam. That in itself wasn't the end of the world. Just as many people do, I could have retaken the exam. Mr. Hollowell had no problem with that at all. There was more than enough work for me to do just as a law clerk.

But a disturbing thing had happened. During the University of Georgia case, I had had a strange conversation with Eugene Cook, who was then the attorney general of Georgia. Cook knew I had just graduated from law school and had recently taken the bar exam He promised me right there that I was not going to pass. He mentioned that I had been going around town serving subpoenas on the top officials of the university, a necessary part of any lawsuit, but Cook was particularly offended by this. "You need to be taught a lesson," he said.

I didn't take him very seriously at the time. But when the results came out and I found that I had not passed, I was deeply rattled. Was I really marked? If so, what was the point of taking the test again? If I hadn't been marked in some way and had just failed, I could just do it over. I was not sure what, if anything, had happened.

Ms. Hurley's offer really saved me from having to confront the issue head-on, or, more accurately, it postponed the matter. In the middle of pondering whether I should chance retaking the bar exam in that climate, a good job in my field, paying over twice as much as I was currently making, had come my way. Responsibility melded very nicely with self-interest. In June, exactly a year after I started work with Mr. Hollowell, I resigned.

It wasn't easy for me to leave. While my time in the office had been short, it was very intensely lived. Mr. Hollowell had become a mentor, if not a father figure, to me, and I worried about being thought of as having betrayed that relationship. A part of me strongly looked forward to developing as a lawyer under his guidance. In addition, the image of myself as a civil rights lawyer was very strong as well. After all, I'd been thinking about this as my most likely career from the time I was about fifteen. Now that I had gotten what I'd wished for, I had some ambivalence about walking away from it.

When I considered the implications of the offer more fully, I realized there couldn't have been a better situation for me at that time. I would have the chance to move (up) to another phase of my career while maintaining the ties to my old job that meant so much. Ms. Hurley's offices were still right next door, and we would continue to work with Mr. Hollowell's firm. I would see him, and I would see Horace, who had become not only a colleague but a friend. He and his wife socialized with Shirley and me. Howard Moore, another young lawyer, had recently joined the firm. Howard and I had gone to high school together and were old friends. I wasn't leaving Mr.

Hollowell behind just yet. We would just come to know each other in a different capacity.

TALL, ATTRACTIVE, POISED, ELEGANT, and well-dressed, Ruby Hurley was what you could call a true believer in the work of the NAACP. She brought a missionary-like intensity to her task, working hard to build the membership, zealously defending the organization against outright enemies and, as things developed, against those whom she felt would intrude upon its turf. With great courage, she'd been the first NAACP official in the South, setting up shop in Birmingham, Alabama. When Governor George Wallace and the state of Alabama effectively shut down the state's chapter, she moved her operations to Atlanta. There is no doubt in my mind that if she had been a man, Ms. Hurley would have been a natural to ascend to the top spot in the NAACP. But she was a woman and, therefore, ineligible to be considered a viable head of that organization, or of any other major civil rights group. It was a paradox: A movement designed to bring about human rights for all citizens was as much hobbled by sexism as the society at large. Even though she worked hard and was greatly respected, Ruby Hurley never got her due.

I started with the NAACP at the 1961 National Convention in Philadelphia, which turned out to be quite an experience for a young man just a year out of law school. No longer a law clerk, I was participating as one of the officials of the organization. The leading lights of the NAACP, people whom I'd admired from afar for years, were there, and I got to meet them. And this was very important to me—I was meeting them as a colleague very early on in my career. My head was filled with all the possibilities that lay before me.

There was Leon Higginbotham, at the time the president of the local branch in Philadelphia, along with Clarence Mitchell, Spotswood Robinson, Jack Greenberg, Wiley Branton, John Morsell, and Daisy Bates. Thurgood Marshall, Constance Baker Motley, Robert Ming, and Robert Carter were there. I'd met them before, as a Howard student hanging around after their moot-court arguments as they prepped for their Supreme Court appearances. This was also where I formally met Roy Wilkins, the executive director of the NAACP, which was a great thrill. I'm sure he didn't pay much attention to me—I was just a staff person, and a new one at that—but I was happy to be in the room at the staff meeting where he was presiding. Instead of being on the outside looking in, I was truly among all of these people—and part of the action—for the first time, even though I was just a beginner. I felt even more a part of the movement than when I was working for Mr. Hollowell. Lawyers are supposed to be somewhat detached, or to affect an air of detachment. Now there was no reason to check my partisan passion. It was part of the job.

Ruby Hurley took me around the meeting, proudly introducing me as the new field director in Georgia. I was not yet twenty-six years old and full of vitality. And I met all the leadership of the regional office, which covered North and South Carolina, Georgia, Florida, Alabama, Mississippi, and Tennessee. I met the heads of the state conferences of branches, the volunteers, the staff people, the other field directors. I could sense immediately the strong feeling of organization, family, and commitment.

Medgar Evers was also at the convention, and I met him there for the first time. He was the NAACP field director in Mississippi, already well into doing there what I was about to try to do in Georgia. I liked him from the very beginning and genuinely looked forward to working with him in the years to come. Smart, charismatic, with an ego as healthy as was required by the job, Medgar was one of the most impressive men I've ever met. Over the next two years we would become closer, talking over the telephone, meeting at conferences and hanging out together, traveling together in Mississippi and Georgia, and comparing notes on the highs and lows of our respective and parallel jobs.

I had a sense of closing yet another circle in my life. I'd played in the band during the NAACP Convention in Atlanta ten years before. Ralph Bunche gave the big speech that year. As a tuba player I was at the back of the band, furthest away from the audience but closest to the speaker's platform. I was so happy to be able to get a close-up view of someone who was such a hero to black Americans, and I imagined myself in a position like that. Ten years later, in Philadelphia, I had an even greater inkling that one day that might be possible.

In August, the month after the convention, I went to Frogmore, South Carolina, to attend a Southeastern Regional Office retreat. All of Ruby Hurley's field directors met at the Penn Community Center there to discuss our strategies for the coming year. The Penn Community Center was a Quaker institution, continuing the Friends' long tradition of progressive involvement in the affairs of blacks. Its head, a white man named Courtney Sislaw, was a very dedicated Quaker who had created a little interracial oasis right there in South Carolina.

The only problem was that along with the Quaker commitment to progressivism and equality came Quaker-type meals. In keeping with the will to simplicity, the center's menu was spare, and we only got two meals a day: breakfast early in the morning and supper at about four o'clock. This was nowhere near enough for a young man of my size or, as it turned out, for any of my colleagues. By around seven o'clock, we were all starved.

Something had to be done. Ms. Hurley had rented a big station wagon, so we piled into it to find food. As the youngest, I took my usual position as driver, and we set off. Naturally, we went first to find the black café. It was closed. We kept driving until we got into Beaufort, the largest town in the area. As we entered town, we saw a big blinking neon sign with the words "Steaks," "Chops," "Fish." It was a truck stop. So I turned into the parking lot, and Ms. Hurley immediately said, "Vernon, where are you going?" In those days black people didn't go to truck stops to get food.

And I said, "I have a friend in here; I'm going to stop and have a word with him." I continued driving around to the back.

When I started to slow down to find a place to park, she asked, now with a little more of an edge in her voice, "What are you doing?"

"I just want to see something."

She'd read my mind. She said, "You cannot go into this back door. You are an NAACP official." NAACP policy was to enter establishments only through the front door.

I said, "I know that, Ms. Hurley."

"I order you not to go in there." She was stern.

I kept driving slowly, and from the back Reverend I. D. Quincy Newman, the South Carolina field director—a much older man—said, "Vernon, Ruby has given you an order."

I said, "Don't worry about it." I stopped the car, jumped out holding the keys, and headed for the back entrance. When I opened the door, there was a busboy standing nearby.

"Where's the chef?" I asked.

The busboy walked to another part of the kitchen and called out for the chef. The chef, an imposing-looking black man, came over to me in his white uniform and a tall white chef's hat.

I introduced myself. "I'm Vernon Jordan. I'm the Georgia field director of the NAACP. We're meeting over at the Penn Center."

He said, "Oh yeah, we know you all are over there. How's it going?"

I said, "Well, fine, except the food is really bad, and we're hungry. We've been driving around trying to find something to eat. I want to know if you can do something about it."

"How many are you?"

I told him.

"Give me fifteen minutes."

By that time I could hear the car horn blowing. When I didn't come out, Medgar came inside and said, "Vernon, you're violating the policy of the NAACP. Ruby is really upset with you. You'd better come on out of here."

I said, "Medgar, tell her that I'm crazy or something—that you can't get me out of here. Something. Anything. I won't be long."

He said, "You're making a mistake. You're new. She doesn't like this."

"Look. Don't worry."

He went back out. Fifteen minutes after that, the chef came back with a huge flat bread box. In that box were eight T-bone steaks, lettuce, tomatoes, fried onion rings, french fries, and rolls. The dinners were on paper plates, and he'd put another plate over each one and stuck a toothpick through the center. When I asked the chef what the charge was, he said, "There's no charge. The white man is going to pay for dinner tonight."

I thanked him, carried the box outside waiter-style, just like the old days for me, and put the food in the back of the station wagon. As soon as I got in the car, Ms. Hurley lit into me like a blowtorch.

"You're young, you're stupid, and you violated NAACP policy," she said, going on and on like that at full tilt, accusing me of misfeasance, malfeasance, and nonfeasance. I knew enough to be passive in the face of this onslaught. A word from me would have been like gasoline on a fire, and it wouldn't have changed how she felt. She was totally outraged. I just took it; hands on the wheel, eyes on the road, telling her with my silence that I knew she was the boss.

As Ms. Hurley talked on, the aroma from the food—steaks, onions, hot rolls—began to fill the car. At a point when she paused in the middle of her tirade, probably to think of additional ways to browbeat me, Reverend Newman broke the silence from his seat in the back. Newman, who had a deep, deep voice and a wit to match it, said with his slow Southern drawl, "Ruby, I don't know what Vernon has, but it sure smells good." As much as we wanted to, no one—least of all me—dared to laugh. That would come later.

We got back to the center and went to the kitchen to have our feast. By this time, the aroma, along with the relaxed attitude of the field directors, had softened Ruby a little. She always had a bottle of scotch in her room, and she brought it out as her contribution to the evening's fare. So we ate and drank and had a good time that night. Ms. Hurley just dismissed me as a nut, and we were very soon able to laugh about what had happened.

I understood why Ms. Hurley was upset, but I always felt a little proud of what happened that night. Our objective was to have a decent meal. And I had worked that out and done so within the confines of the South that I'd always known and grown up in, along with a few things I'd learned as an adult. It isn't clear to me that I would have attempted something like that without the benefit of the experiences I had gained during my year with Mr. Hollowell. Most likely I would have followed the prescription of the days of my childhood, which was to avoid going to places like that at all. Instead, I had a growing sense of confidence (foolhardiness, Ms Hurley would say) that if given the chance, I could deal with any situation in a way that was ultimately satisfactory to all concerned. That was a big step forward for me.

THE BASIC JOB of an NAACP field director was to build the membership of local chapters, help them organize events, respond whenever there were allegations of discrimination and, in an era of protest and demonstrations, to decide when and if those activities were warranted. We were there to say to people that if the sheriff beat up someone in their town, they could protest. They could participate in voter registration programs. They could set up oratorical contests for young people, create a youth council, and conduct mass meetings. Any activities that could get people to come together for a common purpose, we would support. This was a large mandate in what was the heyday of the organization, especially for a person who had been a law clerk for just a year. I could be as creative as I wanted to be, within the confines of the structure of the NAACP. I also got to work with Mr. Hollowell from time to time. It was a formidable challenge, and I loved it.

I traveled throughout the state, to cities large and small. Our records were not always up-to-date, so I'd go into places like Hartwell, Georgia, find a filling station or a grocery store, and say to a black person there, "Do you know who the NAACP person is in town?"

Most of the time they knew, and they'd tell me. Often the exchange would take place in whispers if whites were within earshot. It was usually the undertaker, the county agent, a doctor, or a minister. It was almost always someone who wasn't dependent on the white community for his or her livelihood, so it was seldom a schoolteacher or a school principal. The chapter might not have met for years, but people knew who was, or had been, involved, whether they personally were members or not.

I'd go meet the designated person, introduce myself, and offer my ideas about how to revive the organization if it was inactive or, for those that already showed signs of life, how to get more members. For example, in 1961 the Brunswick, Georgia, chapter of the NAACP was just a social club, basically defunct. The head of it was a retired minister. Mrs. Lide, a beautiful woman with lots of children, was the secretary. When I went to see her, she said, "Well, we meet once a month at a member's house. We have a prayer and a song. We serve ice cream and cake." And I said, "I think we can do more than that."

I enlisted the help of a minister in town, Reverend Julius Caesar Hope, a pastor at the Zion Baptist Church. I stayed at his house and got to know him and other members of the community as we tried to build a strong organization in the area. All of this was at considerable risk. It may be hard for those not alive during those times to understand that at that time, the NAACP was considered, by most white Southerners, to be a subversive organization. We were asking people who didn't have much to put themselves at risk of losing everything to become involved. There was tremendous courage on display among people who had varying degrees of commitment to and fear about what we were trying to do.

When we did the membership campaign in many towns, instead of having the membership cards mailed individually to everyone, which could tip off white postal officials, who could be members of the Klan or otherwise just hostile to the NAACP, I would have Lucille Black, the membership secretary in New York, mail the membership cards in bulk to the Atlanta office. We'd then schedule a mass meeting where the names of new members would be called out. They'd come up front to get their NAACP cards. It was almost like graduation, a very proud moment.

I learned a lot about organizing in those days, especially from the people who were directly involved with the branches in the big cities—Atlanta, Savannah, Macon, Augusta—and from W. W. Law, a postal clerk from Savannah who was the president of the Georgia State Conference of NAACP Branches. He was my "lay boss," so to speak, the voice of the membership. He often appeared with me when we gave out new membership cards or when there was an important meeting. It was from Law and the heads of the major branches that I learned about running mass meetings. One of the most important rules, I learned, is that you never hold mass meetings at the largest church in town. It's better, they told me, to have a medium-sized church that is packed than the biggest church that is full but not packed. That way, you could say that you had an "overflowing crowd," and if people were sitting on windowsills or standing in the aisles, that would generate a sense of excitement. And the word would spread, reinforcing the sense of community support and involvement with the NAACP.

By the end of my first year as Georgia field director, we had exceeded all the other states in the South in recruiting new members. I was so young and inexperienced, yet so excited about my job, that I worked almost obsessively. I wanted to see those numbers rise. That would not have been possible without the help of people in dozens of Georgia towns who fed me and housed me on my many trips across the state. Our members were extremely gracious, and I relied very much on their generosity. Often I'd have to sleep on a pallet on the floor or share a bed. They gave what they had.

Sometimes I had to stay in those terrible little motels when people were afraid to house an NAACP official. One, in Tipton, Georgia, was so bad that I slept in my hat, suit, overcoat, socks, and shoes. For the ostensible purpose of washing up, the room came equipped with a bowl and a pitcher of soiled water, but no towel. The pitcher was dirty. The bedding was unclean and unkempt. I didn't want to touch anything. I just sat there huddled up in a chair the whole night waiting, endlessly it seemed, for the sun to rise so that I could get out of there.

Once I drove to Savannah and checked into a motel that cost about five dollars a night. I paid my bill up front, had dinner at a little café, then went to my room and collapsed in bed because after a full day's work—I'd driven from Atlanta, about 175 miles—I was exhausted. I couldn't have been in the room for more than about two hours when through the fog of deep sleep, I heard someone rapping hard on the door.

"Yeah, what's the matter?" I called out.

"Your time is up! Your time is up!" came the reply.

"My time is up? What are you talking about? I already paid you for the night."

The motel manager was totally disgusted. "Oh, hell, you're one of them," he said, stomping away.

This place was largely devoted to renting out rooms for assignations in two hour shifts. A couple would come in for their two hours and leave. That's how the motel made real money. The management was losing hard cash every extra hour I slept.

In addition to making connections in faraway towns, I was often invited to speak. In McCrae, Georgia, home of the former governors Gene and Herman Talmadge, it was the foreman of the Talmadge family farm, Alex Horne (probably unbeknownst to them), who was president of the local chapter of the NAACP. Mr. Horne called me and insisted that I come down to speak on New Year's Day for the town's annual Emancipation Proclamation program. Shirley and I had been invited to the Alpha Phi Alpha New Year's Ball in Atlanta on December 31, so afterward, I took her home and then drove to Macon to stay the rest of the night. The next day I drove down to McCrae to give my talk. It was a long haul. When I got to Mr. Horne's house, dinner was waiting and we sat down to eat. He showed me the program, which consisted of multiple choirs, multiple preachers bringing greetings from the surrounding area, and I was the keynote speaker. By all indications, this was going to be a very long evening.

The program was set for six o'clock, and we arrived at the church to find about ten people sitting in the audience. That was it. As the evening progressed, we picked up maybe one or two others. From the urgency of Mr. Horne's tone when he'd called, and from the description of the program, I assumed all along that this was going to be a big event. None of the ministers or choirs listed in the program showed up. The church itself was freezing, despite the feeble efforts of the wood-burning stove. I delivered the Emancipation Day speech wearing my overcoat.

This was very early in my career, and every appearance counted. I addressed those ten people as if they were ten thousand. The way I saw it was that those individuals, few in number but deeply faithful to the cause of the NAACP, had come out to make their witness for freedom and justice. And I gave them all I had, which at that stage of my career was probably not much. The word, however, would go forth that the new NAACP field director kept his commitments.

Just from the standpoint of my own personal growth and development, it was a lesson in leadership. It was also another opportunity to sharpen my skills as a speaker, figuring out what worked and what didn't. Applying a strict cost-benefit analysis, on paper, the evening might have seemed a waste. The collection plate yielded less than the cost of printing the program and paying my expenses.

There was so much to do in those days, things were moving so quickly, that I really did not have time to dwell on these events or on whether they turned out well or badly. I was constantly moving on to the next thing. I cannot even begin to estimate the number of late-night trips I made on those little two-lane highways in Georgia. I remember several times waking up driving on the wrong side of the road, but I knew I couldn't stop. I'd get out and shake my head, or if there was a filling station open, I'd stop and get a Coke and a candy bar to keep myself awake. And I'd go to the bathroom in the colored toilet—which was always dirty—and know that I had to press on.

A lot of the complaints we dealt with at the NAACP had to do with public accommodations, including the bathrooms at gas stations, which were labeled "Men" and "Women" for white people but had just one bathroom labeled "Colored" for black people. I remember one complaint from a soldier who had been driving from Tuskegee, Alabama, to South Carolina with his wife, who was several months pregnant. At a Texaco service station in Montezuma, Georgia, the soldier asked the white attendant to fill up the tank, while his pregnant wife got out to use the bathroom. The colored toilet was so filthy that she couldn't bear to go in, so she decided to use the bathroom for white women instead. When the attendant saw this, he stopped pumping the gas, went into the ladies' room, and literally pulled this pregnant black woman off the seat. There was no altercation—the soldier knew how exposed he and his expectant wife were there in rural Georgia—but he filed a complaint with the

NAACP. We wrote to Texaco and to the Justice Department and to any newspapers that might publicize the story.

Sometimes we got results, sometimes we didn't, but people in the outside world—all over the world in fact—were becoming more aware of the injustices that black people had to endure every day in the Jim Crow South.

SHIRLEY AND I were settling into our lives as a young couple, mixing two careers and coping with parenthood. Our first apartment was in a complex owned by Herman J. Russell, whose business acumen would lead him to a successful career as a major contractor and real-estate developer in Atlanta. Our friendship, which began in high school, has lasted through the years. Shirley and I had a second-hand Plymouth that her father bought for us. Each morning we'd take Vickee to a nearby nursery school and Shirley would drop me off at work, on the way to her job at the Fulton County Welfare Department. We would reverse the process at the end of the workday.

We were like many other young couples, struggling but happy, with so little money that sometimes the thirteen-dollar check for the diaper service would bounce. The man who delivered the diapers, an older white guy, was very good about it. He could see we were trying to make it, and he wanted to help. "I'll just wait a few days and run it back through," he'd say. We had excellent support from our parents. Shirley's mother was a strong, dependable babysitter for Vickee on weekdays when necessary and every weekend. My mother, as always, was going full bore with her catering. Although she was available in a crisis, she had little time or interest in babysitting.

Our goal was to stop renting and buy a house. After a time in Herman Russell's apartment complex, we moved into a larger duplex. When we were within striking distance of buying a home, we put our furniture in storage and moved in with Shirley's parents for a few months to save on rent. I didn't like that very much, but it was a means to an end. By the spring of 1964, we purchased our first home, a three-bedroom ranch-style house on the West Side of Atlanta, which was becoming home to Atlanta's growing black middle class. At that early stage of our life together, we established a pattern of entertaining at our home. It was not always elaborate. We just had friends over to play cards or to have dinner.

You couldn't say we were a "movement family" during this period. I did my job and Shirley did hers. She didn't involve herself directly in my work. Still, like all black people, she was often forced to deal with problems that arose because of racism, on her job and in our lives in general. For a time she was one of the few black caseworkers in Fulton County and lunched daily in the state-supported segregated black cafeteria on the grounds of the state capitol. When Fulton County finally allowed black caseworkers to take some white welfare cases, Shirley was assigned to deliver an emergency check to a white family. She went to their home and knocked on the door. When the man of the house came to the door, she explained who she was and why she was there. He told her to bring the check to the back door.

Here she was, a professional social worker from the county welfare department, bringing this white man an emergency check from the government to help him feed and house his family and he asked her to make the delivery to the back door. Nothing better captures how thoroughly poor whites had been brainwashed out of seeing their true position in Southern society. Despite being utterly downtrodden, he was convinced that he was better than Shirley just by virtue of being white.

She told him, "If you want this check, I'm delivering it through the front door or there will be no check." He opened the door and let her in. In those days, being black and doing your job the right way made you a part of the movement.

Then there were the other hassles that black families had to deal with during those times. In June 1962, we went to DePauw for my fifth-year reunion. On the way back, we decided to stop in Nashville because we'd heard that the Holiday Inn had finally desegregated. We drove along, bypassing the small towns that could have been trouble for two black people, until we got to Nashville. As soon as we walked to the front desk, the clerk said, "I know what you've heard, but we're not taking colored people yet."

Traveling was such a problem for black people. Things that whites could take for granted—finding a nice, clean, safe place to rest when you're taking long trips—were just out of the question for us.

O F COURSE, the NAACP was not alone in agitating for civil rights during this period. There was the Southern Christian Leadership Conference (SCLC), the Congress of Racial Equality (CORE), and the Student Nonviolent Coordinating Committee (SNCC), among other groups. Even the National Urban League was moving out of its traditional focus on social work and employment to a more activist role. It wasn't the intention of these groups to work at cross-purposes, but rather, each had its own focus as well as differing views about the best way to effect change. The NAACP, the oldest and most established of the groups, certainly had its own way of doing things, and there was some difficulty in adapting to the changed atmosphere brought on by the new civil rights groups.

The NAACP's focus was primarily on the law, taking action through the courts and promoting voter education and registration with the aim of electing officials who would then write and support legislation beneficial to black advancement. In short, the NAACP favored process-oriented action geared toward evolution, rather than revolution. The other groups were much more into direct action: sit-ins, boycotts, freedom rides. Those activities appealed to students, who, because of their youth, were impatient with talk, negotiation, and the slow machinery of the law. And, it should be said, young people had the energy and creativity to pull off the kind of dramatic action that drew the eyes of the nation and the world to the cause.

It was likewise the case that the leaders of the civil rights movement assumed separate but complementary roles. Martin Luther King, Jr., the head of the SCLC, was in the streets. Roy Wilkins of the NAACP was in the courts, along with Thurgood Marshall. And

Whitney Young of the National Urban League was in the board-rooms explaining it all to the country's business leaders. Each leader supplemented the others' efforts, and none could have succeeded without the others. But the younger activists at SNCC often had less patience than the leaders of the older organizations and wanted to engage in as much direct action as possible. They sought to confront and challenge the system with demonstrations and civil disobedi-ence. This would sometimes lead to tensions within the movement itself.

My position was interesting, in that I was a young person, but I was operating within the parameters of an older, traditional organi-zation. I was also trained as a lawyer, the only one among all the NAACP field directors in the South. My instinctive preference was for the law as the best vehicle for achieving lasting social change. I appreciated what the leaders of CORE, SNCC, and SCLC were do-ing, and tried to do some of it myself, although it was hard to com-pete with the public-relations efforts of SNCC and others who were really on the cutting edge. I also understood that drama was fine, but at the end of the day, the people who marched and participated in sit-ins would need lawyers to deal with the legal cases that grew out of their activities. Moreover, the examples of injustice their direct ac-tions highlighted so brilliantly would be ameliorated only when the laws were changed and black Americans were free to exercise the full weight of their political and economic power.

However the national leadership of the NAACP felt about it, be-tween 1960 and 1963, direct action really became the order of the day. One of the largest and most contentious examples was the Al-bany movement, which began in the fall of 1961 when SNCC began demonstrating against the Jim Crow laws by organizing students to sit in at lunch counters and encouraging blacks to boycott white businesses in Albany, Georgia. As the NAACP field director, I was in the midst of the internal politics, even if my organization was not taking the leading role in the demonstrations. I saw how tensions be-gan to develop when Martin Luther King, Jr., came to Albany, which meant that SNCC now had to share the limelight with the SCLC. All the headlines soon focused on King, because he was much better known, a personality the public recognized from his leadership of the Montgomery bus boycott a few years earlier. The SNCC kids really didn't want King there, but they couldn't do anything about it once he'd arrived.

Matters came to a head in Albany when the courts issued an injunction to stop the SCLC and SNCC from marching through the downtown area to demand their rights. The big issue then became whether King was going to violate the injunction, and in the planning meetings, I saw him think, pray, and meditate about what course to take. In the end, he decided to break the injunction, lead the march, and go to jail if necessary.

King's arrest really sparked the Albany movement. Everyone started marching and getting arrested—every day, it seemed that two hundred people would be arrested after breakfast, three hundred more after lunch, and two hundred more after dinner. Then every night there would be a mass meeting, and I was just one among the many who got to speak. This was not the NAACP's initiative, so we were in the background. The best that I could do was to work behind the scenes to try to bridge the differences between the activists and the old-line NAACP people, including Ruby Hurley, who didn't much like direct action or the people running the demonstrations.

I was also subpoenaed to testify at King's hearing, because I was in the meeting when he and the others were planning to break the injunction. In a twist of fate, Mr. Hollowell was one of King's lawyers, and I was in the strange position of being cross-examined by my former boss and mentor. I told the truth about the meeting, about how King was hesitant about breaking the injunction and was asking all kinds of questions about what would happen if he went forward. And I got criticized for that, for not portraying King as the resolute single-minded activist. But I thought he was asking precisely the kind of questions a leader ought to ask, and I admired him for the seriousness with which he analyzed and judged the situation.

Many of the direct-action people, especially the younger ones, could have benefited from taking King's thoughtful and considered approach. I remember in 1962, a group of about sixty black high-school students in Rome, Georgia, decided they were going to have a sit-in. They didn't understand the discipline at the heart of the tactic, that direct action required planning and strategy. Participants decided in advance how they would act, whether they were going to be arrested and go to jail, and who would represent them. They made arrangements with local people to help bail them out if they went to jail. It was all very considered and well thought out.

These students, along with some of the local members of the NAACP, got together and just went and sat in at lunch counters. After they were, quite predictably, arrested and taken to jail, some of the NAACP members called me to get them out. As my friend Horace Ward put it, they had it in their heads that the NAACP was like an insurance company. Paying dues to the organization covered them for such contingencies as getting arrested while engaging in forms of protest activities. I had to explain that this was not the case, but I also had to find a way to help them out.

So I called Horace and said, "You've got to come to Rome. They've got sixty kids in jail there."

Horace said, "Well, Vernon, I just can't appear on the scene. I can't just go there and say I'm representing these folks." He was right, of course. It was the Preston Cobb issue all over again: Lawyers weren't supposed to directly solicit clients. They had to ask for representation. This was even more true because many of those arrested were minors.

When I went to Rome to meet with the students who had called, I explained that I couldn't help them alone. They needed to hire lawyers, which was absolutely true. I told them that the NAACP regularly worked with Mr. Hollowell's firm and that they were the premier civil rights attorneys in the state. So Horace was retained.

While their cases were tried, something like five at a time, I worked behind the scenes with Frances Pauley, the head of the Georgia Council on Human Relations, a nonprofit interracial organization. We set up meetings with the city fathers and various civic leaders of the town to try to make a deal to end the prosecutions. In the end, we were successful, and most of the charges were dropped.

T HE WRITING WAS VERY DEFINITELY ON THE WALL. Many black people in the South were anxious to become personally involved (and not just as plaintiffs) in the struggle. If the NAACP wanted to remain relevant, we couldn't afford to let that energy dissipate or let others appear more willing to work with it. Ms. Hurley, and others in the national leadership, may have had no use for the SNCC kids, but we all understood that we had to do some things the way they were doing them or risk becoming obsolete. From 1962 on, a good part of my time was spent trying to find ways to move the NAACP in Georgia toward direct action.

To that end, I took the lead in organizing a boycott of downtown Augusta, Georgia. None of the stores in town hired black personnel, except in low-paying jobs. Public accommodations there were segregated. The idea was to get blacks in the area, and anyone who sympathized, to refuse to shop in the stores downtown. Reverend C. S. Hamilton of the Tabernacle Baptist Church, who was president of the Augusta branch of the NAACP, and Father Turner W. Morris, the pastor of the black Episcopal church, were critical local leaders in this effort, preaching about the boycott from the pulpit, helping me organize mass meetings that helped publicize what we were doing and why. My law-school classmate Jack Ruffin was local counsel to the Augusta branch. I spent a lot of time in Augusta, making speeches all over town. For the most part, both middle class and poor black citizens stood together in support of the boycott, which lasted almost seven months.

Healthy competition with the other civil rights organizations pushed the NAACP into directions we would not have gone but for the rivalry. In 1963, a group of "Freedom Walkers," organized by CORE, set out from Chattanooga, Tennessee, to walk to Jackson, Mississippi. One Freedom Walker was killed just as the group crossed the Tennessee state line into Alabama. By this time, Roy Wilkins and the national leadership were fully behind efforts to involve the NAACP in more aggressive actions. We were, to a degree, still playing catch-up to the other groups. When Wilkins learned about the Freedom Walkers, he asked me to go to Chattanooga—there was no Tennessee field director—to try to find some way to get the NAACP involved.

After I had arrived and surveyed the situation with local NAACP officials, we thought of a way to do it. The NAACP would create a "Freedom Canteen." I found a group of volunteers, and a man with a truck. We painted the truck white, wrote the words "NAACP Freedom Canteen" on the side of it, and loaded it with first-aid kits, food, drink—all the things the walkers would need along the route. As they marched, the canteen followed along and stopped as required to dispense needed supplies and to allow the marchers and the media to eat the food cooked by all those wonderful ladies from the NAACP in Chattanooga. This was another moment that won many reporters over to the cause of civil rights. They went along with the marchers and frequented the canteen themselves. We got a lot of positive media coverage, and the enterprise was considered quite a success.

Then there were ways to participate in the less-public forms of direct action. Hugh Gibert was a white lawyer I knew in Atlanta. He was a liberal on race and had done a lot of work for the American Civil Liberties Union in Georgia, which was brought into cases on the same side as Mr. Hollowell. In December 1962, Hugh said to me, "Vernon, I'm having my annual Christmas cocktail party, and we've never invited any Negroes before. And I like you, you're my friend. I want you and your wife to come to my party."

I said, "Okay, but I have a suggestion. Why don't I bring another couple? That might make everyone feel a little better."

"That's a good idea," he said, and so I called my friend Bill Stanley, who was a school principal, and invited him and his wife, Ella, to Hugh's party. The four of us went to the party together, thinking that we would probably spend most of the evening talking to one another. But the reaction we got was hostile in a completely unexpected way.

All of Hugh's servants, of course, were black. That was to be expected in Atlanta in 1962, but one maid seemed to take particular offense at our very presence. As the evening wore on, we noticed something curious. Whenever she would come out of the kitchen with a plate of hors d'oeuvres, she would pass them to all the white guests, but never to the Stanleys or the Jordans. She just glared at us and moved on.

I knew from working at parties like this for my mother's catering business that the maids and butlers often helped themselves to the remnants of a guest's drink, rather than just pouring it down the sink. And I could tell, as the party progressed, that this particular maid was having as much of a good time as the guests. Finally, she got sufficiently lubricated that she walked up to us and said, "You know, you've got no business here."

I looked her straight in the eye and responded, "And you know, you've got no business not serving us those hors d'oeuvres."

She was intensely angry at our being there—our presence seemed to turn her whole world upside down—but she didn't know what to do about it, except to launch her own strange form of protest. On the question of race, there was a lot of work to be done all around.

CHAPTER 8

THE DOLLAR AND THE BALLOT

ONE OF MY GREAT FORTUNES in life is that I have had the chance to do work that fit well with my personal interests and goals. It is very difficult, if not impossible over a long period of time, to achieve excellence in any endeavor when one does not have a feel for or lacks interest in the job or role one has taken on. My mother's example was very instructive on this point. She was so comfortable with the demands of her chosen trade that she approached artistry in plying it. The attention to detail, the willingness to go the extra mile to make sure things were done the right way, evinced a soul that had found its true calling.

Later on in my life, after I had established myself, I was approached about the job of commissioner of the American Soccer League, a prestigious position that paid quite well. My signing on would have drawn lots of attention because of my race—I'd have been a "first." There was one problem: I had no interest in it. I wasn't even a soccer fan. It wasn't the right thing for me to do, no matter how attractive to others the proposition may have seemed.

Some asked how I could turn that down, thinking what it could have meant for me and, no doubt, for black people to have one of our own in that position. I knew myself well enough to know that I wouldn't have been able to give my all and, therefore, the chances were great that things wouldn't have worked. That wouldn't have done me, or certainly black people, any good at all.

There is no question that I was willing and able to give myself completely to my job as Georgia field director for the NAACP. The climate could not have been more perfect for my development. I had measured autonomy—definitely in charge of a domain—but with the luxury of supervision when I needed it. My speech-making skills improved. I learned how to organize events, spot talent, and find the right people to help me do jobs that needed to be done. Disputes within local branches required my efforts at mediation, which gave me valuable insights about when to leave people alone to work things out and when to intervene. As I worked and matured in the job, I was on display to others who had the ability and willingness to help me move from one level to another.

That's what happened in the spring of 1963 when Leslie Dunbar, the executive director of the Southern Regional Council, asked me to become his executive assistant. This put me in a real quandary. I was in the middle of doing a job that was very comfortable to me, and now along came an offer of another opportunity that seemed equally intriguing. Instead of being an organizer, I would be an executive, viewing the movement from a wholly different perspective.

The Southern Regional Council was the oldest continuing interracial organization in the South. It was founded with a mission to foster racial tolerance and social progress for blacks. To that end, it was heavily involved in trying to expand voting rights, supporting organized labor, and encouraging community activism. It was also a research organization that compiled facts and figures about the state of race relations in the South. The SRC produced numerous reports and studies on race and the effects of segregation, serving as a repository of information for journalists and academics. Given its origins, the SRC was radical only in the sense that the concept of interracialism was radical in the South, and that was no small thing. Still, like the NAACP, it was considered mainstream by the other, more activist groups.

The success of any social movement depends upon the contributions of diverse and unique elements. The SRC had its own important role to play in the struggle, and those who ran it were quite committed to changing the South for the better. Their goals and methods simply reflected the class origins and capabilities of its membership. This was the elite of Southern society, white and black. The board of directors included the president of Dillard University and the dean of students at Tuskegee University.

Leslie Dunbar, a white West Virginian with a very gentle and easy manner, was a political scientist by training and had a long commitment to working to end racism. He was familiar with all aspects of the civil rights movement, and knew most, if not all, its leadership. This was a very small community, and the SRC was right there in Atlanta. Leslie had heard my name from a number of people, including members of his own board who knew and liked me. One of my champions was Frances Pauley of the Georgia Council on Human Relations, with whom I had worked on the student protests in Rome, Georgia. Leslie also talked to Roy Wilkins and was particularly struck because Roy spoke very highly of me and, according to Leslie, said he hoped one day I might succeed him at the NAACP.

Whatever plans Roy may have had along those lines, Leslie pressed the case for my joining the SRC very forcefully. As he talked, and I mulled it over, I began to see the job as a step up. Because the SRC's base of operations covered the whole of the South, I would have a hand in promoting projects that covered the entire region. The broader mandate offered the chance for more varied experiences and, with that, even greater opportunities down the road.

I didn't feel comfortable making the decision on my own, and as I've always done before and since, I decided to speak with people whose judgment I trusted, to get their thoughts about what to do. Even when I have an idea or preference about the best course of action, I have found it useful to sound out others about any life-changing decision I might make. The advice can be accepted or rejected, but it doesn't hurt, and it often helps, to think through contingencies with other people who may challenge your assumptions and offer another perspective.

I decided to talk with members of the NAACP's executive committee. I spoke with John Morsell, Roy Wilkins's chief assistant, and Gloster Current, who was the director of the NAACP's branches. They had two different opinions. Morsell urged me to stay. Gloster Current urged me to go. Current was a very prickly character; imperious, short-tempered, and somewhat contemptuous of young people who expressed any degree of independence. We'd had our first blowup during that NAACP retreat at the Penn Community Center in Frogmore, South Carolina. Our group was discussing some issue, and I entered the fray. My view was contrary to Current's, and when he could see this, he interrupted me with more exasperation than was warranted: "Where did you come from? What do you know about it? I've been in this organization since 1946."

I stood my ground. "Well, Mr. Current, this is what I think," I said. "It doesn't matter how long you've been here. I'm entitled to have an opinion." Even that mild statement was more than he could take. From that moment on, he was suspicious of me.

There were other moments between us. On one occasion, I was standing with him and Medgar Evers at the airport in Jackson, Mississippi, after an NAACP meeting. He had backed Medgar up against the fence and was berating him because his membership numbers were down. Mississippi occupied a place all its own in the modern civil rights struggle—as it has in the black consciousness from slavery until modern times. No place was harder or meaner. I knew what Medgar was up against, because things were tough enough for me in Georgia. Current should have known, too. Even more important, Medgar was my comrade, in a way that Current could never be.

In the middle of this harangue, I said to Current, "Look, you know, you're about to get on this airplane and go back up to Hollis, New York. In Hollis you don't have to deal with these mean Mississippi crackers down here. Medgar has to deal with them every single day. And you're telling him about his membership. You ought to leave him alone. Any membership he gets, he's lucky. Just leave him alone."

Current turned to me and said, "You're just a smart-ass."

"Leave him alone," I repeated.

Given the precarious nature of our relationship, I wasn't very hopeful about meeting with Current to discuss my future. He was such a staunch NAACP man, zealously defending the organization against anyone or anything he perceived as a threat, even if no real threat existed. His response to my predicament was true to form.

"Go ahead and leave if you want," he told me. He didn't say, "Good riddance!" but he might as well have.

Robert Carter was the general counsel of the NAACP, and I went to see him at his home in Harlem to talk about what I should do. Carter had been the lawyer for many plaintiffs in the desegregation cases in the 1950s, and like Morsell, he urged me to stay. He thought that there was much more to be done at the NAACP, that the organization still had things to offer me and that I still had things to offer it.

Then there was Roy Wilkins himself. I spent the longest time talking to him. We'd gotten to know each other during my time as a field director. When he'd come to Georgia, I'd pick him up at the airport. If he had speaking engagements in the state I'd drive him there. Sitting and listening to Roy was just like going to school. I liked to talk, but this was really my time to be silent. Riding with Roy on the highways of Georgia was where I got my graduate degree in black leadership and organization. Even when I wasn't sure I agreed with certain positions he took, I learned a great deal from just listening to Roy's point of view. We had established a rapport by this time, and he sensed (and appreciated) my ambition. Sometimes, he'd send me on special missions, like the one in Tennessee to get the NAACP involved with the Freedom Walkers. As any young person attentive to the preferences of an older, much admired figure, I knew he liked me. And I liked him.

Roy was prepared, he said, to offer me Ruby Hurley's job as head of the Southeastern Regional Office, just to get me to stay. I saw that not as a serious offer, but rather as a gesture to let me know that there were genuine opportunities for me to rise through the ranks at the NAACP. Medgar Evers was the star among all the field directors. If anyone could take Ruby's place, it was he. The fact is I didn't think there was anyone among us who could take Ruby's place. She was a very strong figure within the NAACP, and she always delivered the votes of the southeastern region to Roy at the national conventions. I could never deliver those votes the way she did, because I didn't have the relationships that she had with the presidents of the state conferences and the local branch leadership.

I had deep respect and affection for Roy, and I really did believe I could go places within the NAACP. In the end, though, Leslie's offer was just too tempting. My innate restlessness had taken hold. The pull of playing a different role, working in an interracial context, was just too strong. And if I was destined to lead a civil rights organization, that could come to pass even if I spent time (perhaps because I had spent time) at the SRC.

This had happened before, and it would happen again: I'd come to a point where a challenge that seemed just right for me had been put in my path. Taking it would mean frustrating others' expectations. Not taking it would leave me with a sense of regret about what might have been. I opted for change, my choice made easier by my knowledge that I had worked hard and done the very best I could at the NAACP. Even more important, my superiors and co-workers knew this as well. Leaving is always easier under those circumstances.

Ms. Hurley was disappointed and extremely angry when I told her my decision. Like Gloster Current, she was fanatically loyal to the NAACP. "I cannot believe you're doing this," she said. She would not speak to me for several months after my announcement. Even when the lines of communication opened up, relations between us continued to be strained. It would take a few years before the air was cleared and we could become friends again.

I called Medgar Evers in May 1963 to tell him that I was leaving. He was disappointed, but he accepted my explanation of why it was time for me to move on. He was such a great man. As we talked I thought back to the first time we'd met, at the Philadelphia National Convention. His reputation had preceded him, and I was so proud then (as I remain) to be able to say I had the same job in Georgia that Medgar Evers had in Mississippi.

We talked about my plans, about how mad Ms. Hurley was at me. He said he couldn't leave yet; his work was unfinished. We said our farewells, and I went off to my new job at the Southern Regional Council. The next month, Medgar was dead, killed by an assassin's bullet in front of his house. His wife and children were inside at the time.

Like the rest of the nation throughout the 1960s, I was deeply affected by the murders of the Kennedys, Dr. King, the four young girls in the Birmingham church, and all the other lesser-known individuals who died as martyrs for the cause. But because he was my friend and colleague, no death in that violent decade wounded me more deeply than Medgar's. For any black person in the South, and certainly any black man, danger was a constant companion—the threat of violence lurked behind even the most innocuous circumstances. Medgar's activities were the very opposite of innocuous to the white supremacists who ran his home state, and there he was—out in the open, exposed. He was, I believe, the most courageous man in the movement because he dared to stand tall in Mississippi.

That's what had made me so angry at Gloster Current for his airport tirade about membership numbers. How trivial that was compared to what Medgar had actually taken on! The unspoken fear of losing him, of losing my own life, was part of the job. We managed it by remembering what it was we were trying to do, by keeping a healthy attitude about the limits of what could be accomplished, by supporting one another, and by accepting that, to a real degree, it was all out of our hands. And now, the very worst had happened.

Even though I was well into my new job, Roy called Leslie Dunbar and asked if I could go to Mississippi during the period of adjustment after Medgar's murder. Of course Leslie agreed, and I went immediately to Jackson to help out.

First there was the funeral, followed by a march in honor of

Medgar and his family. That day was like hell in every respect—hot, humid, souls in total agony. This was the first time I had experienced the true hatefulness of a Southern police force of that era. The officers were standing, dripping with sweat, not only with their hands on their guns but with their fingers on the triggers. If there had been the slightest hint of trouble, I have no doubt they would have emptied their weapons on us.

Earlier, Roy and I had gone together to the funeral home to view Medgar's body. As we stood over him, Roy noticed the cardboard cutout of a handkerchief put in his breast pocket by the laundry service. Roy murmured, "We can't have that." He removed the cardboard, took out his own handkerchief, and arranged it very neatly in Medgar's pocket. Totally helpless in the face of death, as we all are, Roy's very human impulse was to do what he could. I've never forgotten the sight, a general performing a last duty to his fallen soldier.

What I also remember about that time is that even as I stood there wanting desperately to cry (I've never been afraid of tears), I could not do it. Even when I was alone, thinking of what had happened, my eyes stayed dry. My anger was such that it wouldn't yield to tears. I've often thought it would have been better if I had been able to shed tears for my friend, but I just couldn't.

THE SRC WAS THE PERFECT LEARNING EXPERIENCE for me. Leslie Dunbar, a friend and adviser to me to this day, was an excellent mentor for one who wanted very much to be a public man. "You have to write," he told me at the very beginning of my tenure. It was crucial, he said, to get my thoughts and ideas out into circulation beyond my own organization. People could agree or disagree, but most important, they would get the chance to know something about me and my ideas. In addition, the process of writing is helpful. Putting things on paper pushes the mind toward clarity, and that would make me better able to defend my ideas if I ever had to. I took what he said to heart, publishing my first article for the *Nation* magazine in 1964.

There was also plenty of writing to be done in-house. I wrote reports for the SRC board, including, much to my initial dismay, financial reports, about which I knew really nothing. I had to become familiar with budgets and balance sheets because part of my job was standing before the board making presentations based upon them. Leslie also sent me up to New York to fund-raise for the SRC. I brought proposals to the Ford Foundation at its old offices on Madison Avenue, made my presentations, and brought home the money. All this was new territory, very far away from my days as a law clerk and movement organizer.

It was also while I was at the SRC that I finally passed the bar exam. Though I had moved in a different direction from practicing trial law like Mr. Hollowell, it still mattered to me that I didn't have my license, and I agonized about that. I hadn't retaken the bar exam in Georgia, because I still took Attorney General Cook's words to heart and wondered whether I was a marked man. So I made arrangements, with Leslie Dunbar's approval, to go to Arkansas to take the bar exam there.

One of the advantages of taking the Arkansas bar exam in those days was that the results were available within a week after the test was given, in marked contrast to the months it took in other states. This was possible because the examiners graded each section of the examination as it was finished. They must have worked around the clock, holed up on a mountain somewhere until they got it done.

So the week after the exam was given—the following Monday morning—you could call the clerk and find out whether you had passed. That year I was first in line. I called Little Rock early Monday to find out my results. I had passed. It felt so good to hear that I waited a minute and called the clerk right back and said, "I want you to tell me that one more time." Five years later, in 1969, even though I was no longer practicing law, I "waived in" to the Georgia bar, and there was nothing anybody could do to stop me. I was sworn in by Superior Court Judge Luther Alverson, a good friend. With that behind me, I felt even more free to concentrate on my work.

There was a lot to keep my attention. The SRC was involved in so many diverse efforts during those days. One program that was of particular interest to me was the Voter Education Project (VEP), run by Wiley A. Branton, the distinguished Arkansas lawyer who had represented the "Little Rock Nine," the teenagers who had integrated Central High School in 1957. The VEP was a research project designed to study the causes of low black voter registration in the South. To do this, the VEP funded national and local groups that were trying to register black voters. Those groups would then report back to us on their efforts; how many people were successfully registered, how many tried and were thwarted, and why and how they were turned away. Interestingly enough from today's perspective, when the Republican Party seems so out of touch with the black electorate, the VEP, a tax-exempt organization, had the support of the Democratic and Republican National Committees. During those years, each party thought it could compete strongly for black votes.

In many cities and towns across the South, blacks were legally permitted to register to vote, but the white establishment made it almost impossible for them to exercise the franchise or to do so in an unfettered way. A variety of roadblocks were raised to deny black access to the polls—some of them harkening back to the days of Reconstruction and its aftermath—poll taxes, literacy tests. Black citizens would go to register and be asked how many bubbles there were in a bar of soap. Added to these quasi-legal tactics, was a general pattern of intimidation by state registrars and local police—not to mention acts of violence, intimidation, and economic coercion by private citizens within the white community.

One of my personal heroes in the civil rights movement was a little-known, unheralded, itinerant Baptist preacher in Columbus, Georgia, Reverend Primus King, who ran his own barbershop during the week and preached on Sundays. Reverend King was a plaintiff in the 1944 case challenging the white primary in Georgia, and he filed suit after going to the Muscogee County courthouse to register to vote in the white primary. He was told by the registrar that "colored people" were not allowed to vote. His local counsel were two white lawyers, one from Columbus and one from Macon. His other counsel was Thurgood Marshall of the NAACP Legal Defense Fund. After the lawsuit was filed, Primus King was summoned to a meeting with the white establishment, where he was told that he had, by his lawsuit, disturbed "the peace and tranquility among the races," and the establishment asked that he withdraw the suit.

Reverend King responded, "I am a good citizen, I own property, I pay my taxes, I can read and write, and I have not committed a crime of moral turpitude. I have a right to vote in the white primary." And at the suggestion that if he did not withdraw the suit, he could end up in the Chattahoochee River, King replied, "Well, if I get thrown in the river, at least I will be thrown in for something, because all those other colored people were thrown in for nothing." Primus King was a courageous man who never got his due, yet I can still hear him from the pulpits of rural churches, preaching, "Shout on Sunday, register on Monday!"

Because I had grown up in Atlanta, the biggest city in the South, I had not personally faced the kind of intimidation that rural blacks faced, and in fact, I had been voting regularly since I was eighteen. I knew, however, from my travels around Georgia as the NAACP field director that the black citizens of the South desperately needed help in their quest for unhampered access to the voting booth. Primus King was a wonderful example as one who stood alone, and made a difference. But southern blacks were up against a system, and it would take no less than a systematic effort on the part of the Federal government to solve the problem of black disenfranchisement.

In the summer of 1964, Wiley Branton became executive director of Welfare Education Legal Defense Fund, which coordinated activities with the national civil rights organizations, though he remained director of the VEP. I became acting director of the VEP, while still keeping my position working for Leslie. It was a critical time, because the Republican presidential candidate that year, Senator Barry Goldwater, had taken a stand against civil rights, while most Democrats under President Lyndon Johnson, were in favor. To this day, the attitude that the Republicans are against civil rights hasn't changed much among blacks.

With the help of grants from several foundations, the VEP became the primary vehicle for channeling money to organizations that supported voting rights. During Branton's tenure, that goal seemed illu-

sory. For a time, the VEP stopped making grants in some areas because the desired result—increased black voter registration—just
wasn't materializing. We'd make a grant, for example, to a group
from SNCC to register voters. Group members would do all the legwork, making the necessary contacts and encouraging people to sign
up, and when they'd go to pick up the person to register, the
prospective registrant would be hiding in the house or outside in the
backyard, so afraid were they of white officials who threatened
reprisals. On a strict cost-benefit analysis, we were burning through
cash quickly and fruitlessly—spending far too much money to register too small a number of individuals.

Despite the faltering of our efforts to support voter registration,
my job at the SRC continued to contribute to my professional development. I got to know people who would, over the years, come to
play important roles in the advancement of my career. One such person was John Hervey Wheeler, the president of the Mechanics and
Farmers Bank of Durham, North Carolina, and the first black president of the SRC. He mentored me and often sent me to represent
him on the national commissions on which he sat. He would be an
adviser and confidant to me for many years, and he was a blessing in
my life.

It was also crucial for me that I came to the attention of Louis
Martin, the vice chairman of the Democratic National Committee,
one of the great unsung black heroes of that era. Martin, an aide to
President Johnson, preferred to keep himself as much in the background as was possible, but he was always very active in pressing the
cause of black advancement. Unlike more public figures like Martin
Luther King, Jr. or Thurgood Marshall, he fought and won his battles for black advancement in the back rooms rather than in the
streets. Louis Martin pointed me out to Sargent Shriver as someone
who was up and coming and should be considered for a position in
the administration. Early in 1965, Shriver called me up to Washington to interview for a job at the Office of Economic Opportunity,
which was part of President Johnson's War on Poverty. Johnson,
with characteristic stubbornness, had bulldozed a reluctant Shriver
(then head of the Peace Corps) into taking the top spot at OEO.

When I went to see him, he was running the Peace Corps and OEO. Everyone was in a hurry in those days, and Shriver interviewed and hired me while he shaved in the rest room at the OEO building, then on Nineteenth and M Streets.

The job didn't require relocating, as I worked in the Southeast Regional Office in Atlanta. It was exhilarating to be a part of the youth culture in government at that time. President John F. Kennedy had called many young people to service during his presidency. His martyrdom only increased the sense of urgency about using government to help solve some of the pressing problems of the day, especially poverty and civil rights. There was a certain glamour to being involved in government in those days.

I was an attorney consultant for the OEO, and my primary job was to review grants for the Community Action Program. In practice, that meant that I had to deal with the state governments, which had the legal authority to incorporate the local CAP boards and wanted to put their own people—that is, white people—in leadership positions. It was my responsibility to assure that there was diverse representation—that is, black people—on those boards.

In Mississippi, I had a particularly difficult task, because the governor himself, Paul Johnson, was the official responsible for approving all incorporations. (In most states, the secretary of state performs this function.) Johnson wouldn't approve a CAP application if it didn't include his people, and as the representative of OEO, I wouldn't approve his application if it didn't include my people. But politics is all about working things out with people who do not necessarily agree with you. Because we had to work together, I became Paul Johnson's man in the federal government, and he became my man in the state government. And it worked. As strange as it seemed, in the summer of 1965, I found myself in Johnson's hometown, Hattiesburg, Mississippi, drinking corn whiskey in the back of a warehouse with all these white guys who were his political cronies. They may not have been my first choice of drinking companions, but with their cooperation I hoped to fight poverty in their state and have a real impact on people's lives.

As much as I enjoyed what I was doing, my mind was still very much on what was going on at the SRC. While I was at the OEO, Leslie Dunbar had gone to head the Field Foundation in New York, and he was succeeded by Paul Anthony, a Virginian with a long tenure at the SRC. Wiley Branton had taken a high position in the Johnson administration. The VEP was still without a permanent director, and in fact was dormant. But the passage of the Voting Rights Act in August 1965 changed the entire landscape. For the first time, federal registrars came to the South to make sure that local officials did not thwart the enforcement of the law. From my office at the OEO, I understood immediately what this might mean: The VEP could now do better at the job it had been designed to do. With the help and protection of the federal government, money from this not-for-profit entity could be used to transform the Southern electorate and, along with it, the South.

I thought back to Ms. Hurley's statement about white people wanting to keep blacks away from the dollar and the ballot. She was never more right. Economic development and voting rights—participating in democracy—are central to black advancement. As for voting rights, there was no part of the movement that seemed more critical to me than ensuring black access to this country's electoral process, as voters and as elected officials. In a democracy, voting is the most elemental form of direct action. Denying black people the vote cut us off from the power that flows from exercising that fundamental right, which said more forcefully than anything else that we were not full citizens of this country. Now, the VEP had a fighting chance to alter the calculus. I wanted very badly to return to the SRC and run what I fully expected would be a newly invigorated VEP. This time there was no equivocation on my part, no long deliberative process. I resigned from the OEO and went to do just that.

MY FATHER-IN-LAW, Shedrick Yarbrough, was worried. I'd been married to his daughter for seven years (two while I was in law school), and since graduation, he had watched me take and then leave a total of four jobs. They were all good jobs, ones that set the stage for opportunities beyond any of our wildest dreams at the time. Yet he could only make judgments on the basis of the present, and in that present he had a son-in-law who seemed to move with alarming (to him) frequency from one position to the next.

In those days, success in a career was measured by longevity. The general expectation was that you would get a job—choose a profession—and stay with it, rising through the ranks as high as you could go. The desire for stability and a sense of loyalty combined to make people stay put. Blacks felt this impulse even more strongly, especially members of the old guard like my father-in-law. Our lives, jobs, and career opportunities were always much more tenuous than whites'. Whatever was gained was to be held on to ferociously.

What led my father-in-law to speak openly about my employment strategy to date was that I had just left the OEO after having worked there just eight months. Besides a brief stint at the post office when I was in college, the OEO was my longest, and last, turn working for any government.

Mr. Yarbrough was incredulous. Of all the jobs to walk away from. Government work was long thought in the black community to be a relatively safe haven—and they were not far wrong in this view. Although there was discrimination in the public sector, it was less severe than in the private sector. Getting and keeping a good job there was out of reach for all but a handful of black people.

"You're crazy! How could you quit a job like that? If you work for the government you get a steady paycheck. You have some protection against being fired." Perhaps from his perspective, a job at OEO, or some similar position, was what I'd been preparing for all along.

It was not. I was in more peculiar circumstances, riding a wave powered by history as much as anything else. Not that I had a firm handle on this at the time, but I did sense that the situation for me and those like me was different—it was extremely dynamic. We really were, just as President Kennedy had said, facing a "New Frontier" that seemed wide open for individuals who were prepared and eager to roam across it. In that world, free agency and flexibility

were the orders of the day. Nothing was planned or thought out besides making myself ready to take (if I wanted to) whatever interesting opportunity came along. That's how I'd become a field director
for the NAACP, that's how I'd ended up leaving that job to work
with Leslie Dunbar at the Southern Regional Council. Then it was
on to the OEO and, to Mr. Yarbrough's chagrin, back to another job
at SRC. This career path seemed capricious to him, and he feared
this wandering might come to a crashing halt. It never did.

WHEN I CAME BACK TO THE VEP IN OCTOBER 1965, I found
that the problems that Wiley Branton had experienced trying to increase black registration and voting had virtually disappeared when
the federal registrars came down to monitor the process. The transformation worked by this partnership of government and private effort was astonishing and almost immediate, unleashing the creativity
of dozens of groups and hundreds of individuals who had ideas
about the best ways to promote greater black participation in political life. And there I was, right in the middle of it, observing, participating, in what I consider to be the most important and most
personally gratifying job I've ever held.

What made the VEP so great for me was that there was a clearly
defined mission, a goal to be reached, with a process in place to help
us get where we wanted to go. The country's major philanthropic
foundations—the Ford Foundation, the Rockefeller Brothers Fund,
the Field Foundation, the Stern Family Foundation, and others—
were relying on the VEP to distribute their money where it could do
the most good. Success and failure could be measured with precision, and the concrete nature of this appealed to me. A local voters'
league or civil rights group would submit a plan to us, saying how
they were going to increase registration in a particular place following a particular time schedule. They had to present a budget, tell us
how many people they needed to hire, what their jobs would be, just
how it would all work. Then we made a judgment about it, yes or
no. All the major civil rights organizations came to us for funding

voter-related projects, and my colleagues and I disbursed money to the SCLC, CORE, SNCC, and the NAACP, among others. That made me a kind of chancellor of the exchequer. This was a heavy responsibility, and I took it very seriously.

Because I controlled the disbursement of so much money, I felt under scrutiny at all times. I remember taking a trip to Alabama for the VEP, where I was invited to the home of a local doctor for dinner. We were joined by the local dentist, the high-school principal, a teacher or two, the undertaker—sort of a gathering of the local "talented tenth." We had steaks on the grill, drinks in our hands, and were having a good time, unwinding together. Then the host came out with a cigar box, full of marijuana that he had grown in his backyard. This was all very much of that time. They didn't care that I was a stranger to them; they were just going to carry on the way they liked to carry on. But I couldn't. I have never smoked a joint in my life, and I didn't smoke that night, either. The last thing I needed were news stories that the head of the VEP was at some party in Alabama smoking pot. I was the custodian of all this foundation money, and I wasn't going to give the opponents of black voting a reason to undercut support for what we were trying to do.

Weldon Rougeau was my field director and aide-de-camp in this enterprise. He was truly a battle-scarred veteran of the movement. Weldon had been expelled from Southern University for his activities on behalf of CORE. At one of the group's demonstrations, he was arrested and put in solitary confinement for ninety days. After leaving Southern, he went to Loyola University in Chicago on a CORE scholarship. When he returned to the South, he came to work with us. When a grant proposal would come into the office, it was Weldon's job to go out into the field to meet with the prospective grantees to discuss their submission, offering ways to strengthen it if that could be done. At the same time, Weldon was also evaluating the applicants to make sure they were the right people for the job they'd set out to do. He would come back with a very precise report that often painted a very moving portrait of people who were working, at some risk to themselves (as was Weldon), to increase voter registration. Time would pass, and those who were given grants would report to us on the results of their efforts: how many people they'd registered, how much money they'd spent, the problems they'd encountered.

Through the efforts of one of our grantees, a county in Alabama or Mississippi would go from having a pool of twenty registered voters to having 1,000 within six weeks. This kind of thing happened over and over, and it brought us a form of instant gratification that was much more than personal. There was never any doubt in our minds that we were doing some of the most vital work in the South. Those newly registered and voting black people would change Southern politics forever.

This transformation of the electoral landscape—enfranchised black voters who could put in office one of their own or a sympathetic white person—struck deep into many Southern communities. Our studies showed, for example, that police brutality went down when black voter registration went up. As time passed, all those town officials, sheriffs, mayors, and city managers were forced to rethink their operations with the arrival of a new power base to be reckoned with. "Out-niggering" an opponent wasn't as viable an option as it had been before. As time passed, the most sensible politicians soon fell into doing what comes naturally: currying favor with potential constituents, black and white.

Things didn't always happen as planned. A voter registration drive would fail, or things would take much longer than we expected. Sometimes we had to cut off a local organization because there were problems with the way it handled money, or there was local feuding that detracted from our mission. But these events were valuable in their own way, too. The successes and failures taught me how to distinguish between ideas that would work and those that would not. I also came to discern qualities in individuals that indicated whether they would be able to pull off whatever plan they brought before us. These were no small matters. A good amount of money was involved, and choices had to be made about how it was spent. I was accountable to the institutions and people who were funding us for every dollar.

All this set off a very valuable trickle-down effect. Local voters' leagues, the direct action groups such as CORE, SCLC, SNCC, and the NAACP, benefited from the marriage of increased accountability and successful voter-registration drives. The competition for the money was intense, and as it tends to do in other contexts, the competition put all these groups a little more on their toes. Everyone soon learned that it wasn't enough to just have a good heart and good intentions; they had to present a viable plan to get the funds and they had to successfully execute the plan if they wanted more to undertake other projects.

Although the core of the VEP's mission was registration and voting, it seemed to me that wasn't really going to be enough. Having never been a part of the process and because of the South's poor record of educating the masses of blacks, the people we were signing up as voters were not as familiar with the political system as they should have been. Many did not even see voting as relevant to their lives. I knew if we wanted to make the most of this opportunity, we had to do more than just register people and encourage them to vote. An all-out effort was required. So we put together a "citizenship training" program, somewhat akin to what is provided to immigrants seeking U.S. citizenship. Some of these materials were written by Julian Bond, who had been elected to the Georgia legislature but was expelled from his seat by members who objected to his political views. We explained the structure of the U.S. government—the three branches, the role and function of each—along with providing other basic information we thought all citizens should know about their government. I saw very quickly that having the right to vote just got black people in the door; knowing how to vote gave them the wherewithal to walk through the next door and out into the world.

Getting more black elected officials was also a primary goal. So we encouraged blacks who had promise to stand for office, holding training sessions, in conjunction with the NAACP Legal Defense Fund, to give suggestions about how to do it. Our first meeting was at Reverend Fred Gray's church in Montgomery, Alabama, where we brought together all the black candidates for office in Alabama to explain what the requirements were for their candidacies and how to conform to the state statutes. I remember one man who wanted to run

This is the earliest photograph of me, as a baby on my mother's lap.
(Courtesy of the author.)

My father is holding my younger brother, Windsor, as I stand at his side.
(Courtesy of the author.)

My paternal grandparents,
Charlie and Annie Jordan.
(Courtesy of the author.)

My older half-brother, Warren Griggs,
served in the Army during World War
II, and his visits home were among the
highlights of my childhood.
(Courtesy of the author.)

My mother with Windsor and me,
all dressed up for an important occasion.
(Courtesy of the author.)

Keeping my eye on the larger world during my time at David T. Howard High School, I attended the National Conference on Citizenship in Washington, D.C., reported on it for my school newspaper, and won honors in the State Negro Voters League Oratorical Contest for speaking on "The Negro in America." (From the Papers of Vernon E. Jordan, Jr., Moorland-Spingarn Research Center, Howard University.)

The Howard Rambler

VOL. XVIII—No. 1   November, 1952   David T. Howard High School, Atlanta, Ga.   Price Ten Cents

National Conference On Citizenship

By VERNON E. JORDAN, JR.,

The Seventh National Conference of Citizenship convened Sept. 17-19 at the Statler Hotel, Washington, D. C.

Approximately 1,000 delegates representing 600 public and private agencies throughout the nation were in attendance at the three-day conference, co-sponsored by the United States Department of Justice and the National Education Association.

The Conference theme was "The Constitution and the Citizen." Its sub-topic was "The Rights and Responsibilities of the Citizen Under the Constitution."

Objectives of the conference were to re-examine the functions and duties of American Citizenship in today's world, to assist in the development of more dynamic procedures for making citizenship more effective, to indicate the ways and means by which various organizations may contribute concretely to the development of a more active, alert, enlightened, conscientious, and progressive citizenry in our country. It can be said very truthfully that all three objectives were carried out to their fullest extent.

The opening session proved to be the most interesting. It was presided over by the Honorable Justin Miller, Chairman of the conference. Colors were advanced by the American Legion National Guard of Honor.

Welcome addresses were delivered by the Honorable James P. McGranery, Attorney General of the United States and Mrs. Sarah G. Caldwell, President, National Educational Association.

The purpose of the conference was given by Dr. Richard B. Kennon, Executive Secretary, NEA Commission for the Defense of Democracy through Education.

The highlight of the opening session was the speech delivered by the Honorable Harry S. Truman, President of the United States. The President's address was part of the first official observance of Citizenship Day, new annual patriotic day by act of Congress. In it the President told the delegates that it is their job to make the ideals and principles of Americanism clear to all citizens and particularly to young people.

Another highlight of the opening session was the naturalization of fifty-two men and women from the Washington area who were special guests of the conference and had the special distinction of being welcomed into American citizenship by President Truman. He urged them to put aside their old nationalistic or racial feuds and to become a part of

VERNON E. JORDAN, JR.

a great community based on a set of universal ideals.

These fifty-two persons were naturalized in a special session of the U. S. District Court for the District of Columbia held in the Statler Hotel's Presidential Room. The court was presided over by the Honorable F. Dickinson Letts.

On Wednesday afternoon a Wreath Laying Ceremony was given in honor of the thirteen original states that signed the Constitution. The program was held in the Sylvan Theatre on Washington Monument grounds. Wreaths sent from each of the thirteen original states were placed at the foot of Washington Monument. Guest Speaker for the occasion was Atty. Gen'l. James P. McGranery.

The Wednesday evening session in the Presidential Room of the Statler was an event that all delegates had looked forward to with much anticipation. The keynote address was the Constitution and the Citizen, given by the conference chairman, Justin Miller. After the keynote was sounded, an Adult and Youth Panel on Citizenship was held with high school students from all over the United States participating. The youth panel members were very much distribed over the fact that in some states 18-year-olds were not allowed to vote. The panel felt that if at 18 we can fight and maybe die for our country, then certainly we should be able to vote. The invocation for this program was given by Miss Carolyn Denton, a Negro and senior at the College of Liberal Arts, Howard University.

(Continued Next Issue)

CONTEST WINNER — David T. Howard High School announces another winner in a State Oratorical Contest. Vernon Jordan a 10th grade student recently in Macon, Georgia, won honors in the State Negro Voters League Oratorical Contest. Going against the best young speakers from every section of the state, this was quite an achievement for this young man. His coach, Professor Frederick D. Browne expressed the feeling that David T. Howard along with other schools in the state should support the Negro Voters League and encourage more pupils to take an active part in its program. The ballot he pointed out is our strongest weapon and our youth must be taught nothing unAmerican about encouraging people to use the ballot and gaining recognition, since these are the basis of our American way of life.

Jordans' subject was "The Negro In America." He pointed to our gains in the various fields of endeavor but also cited losses in many more. There is yet a great need for closer coordination of our efforts if we are to take our places in the many new areas now opening up to youth. He stated that preparation, perspiration, and perseverance are the three things most needed by the Negro Youth today. This states coach Browne is the right season for our youth to take a lesson from Jordan's speech — during commencement season.

Crisis in 'Backwater'

VERN JORDAN (right) as Jefferson Gray in "Backwater" threatens Pat Clithero (center) and Bill McLuckey. The drama concerning the racial problem, written by Frank Staroba and Art Beer, will be given in Speech hall Thursday and Friday evenings. Curtain time is 8:15.

As a sophomore at DePauw University in Greencastle, Indiana, I collaborated on a play called "Backwater," which confronted the racial issues of the time. I also performed on stage in the lead role. (From the Papers of Vernon E. Jordan, Jr., Moorland-Spingarn Research Center, Howard University.)

During my time at DePauw, I worked as the head waiter at the Longden Hall dining room. When Vice President Richard Nixon came to DePauw in 1956 to dedicate the new library, there was a luncheon afterward, and I was chosen to be a waiter at the head table. In 1971, when I visited President Nixon at the White House as executive director of the National Urban League, I brought this picture with me, and Nixon inscribed it. (Courtesy of the author.)

This is the home of Robert F. Maddox, the president of the First National Bank of Atlanta, for whom I worked as a chauffeur during summers at college and law school. The property was later sold to the state of Georgia, which is where the governor's mansion now stands. (Courtesy of the Atlanta History Center.)

While at Howard University, I met Shirley Yarbrough, who was a senior during my first year of law school. Here we are in the living room of her parents' house during our courtship. (Courtesy of the author.)

My first job out of law school, in 1960, was to work for Donald Hollowell, a leading civil rights attorney in Atlanta. Our most prominent case was *Holmes v. Danner*, which desegregated the University of Georgia, and I was enlisted to escort Charlayne Hunter, one of the victorious plaintiffs, as she registered for classes on January 9, 1961. (Associated Press.)

In October 1995, Hamilton Holmes, the other plaintiff in the University of Georgia case, died of a heart attack, and joining me at his funeral were Mr. Hollowell (*third from left*), his associate, Judge Horace Ward (*third from right*), and Charlayne Hunter-Gault (*center, with shawl*). (Photograph by Harmon Perry.)

Ruby Hurley was the head of the NAACP's Southeastern Regional Office and hired me in 1961 to be the Georgia field director of the NAACP. She was talented enough, I thought, to run the whole organization if she had been given the chance. (Library of Congress.)

During my time with the NAACP in Georgia, my counterpart in Mississippi was Medgar Evers, who was the star among all the field directors. On June 1, 1963, he and Roy Wilkins, the executive director of the NAACP, were arrested for picketing outside a Woolworth's in Jackson. Eleven days later, Medgar was shot dead in front of his home. (© Bettman/CORBIS.)

Leslie Dunbar ran the Southern Regional Council, the oldest interracial organization in the South. As his executive assistant from 1963 to 1965, I broadened my horizons, began publishing articles on current issues, and learned how to manage the financial aspects of a large organization. (Courtesy of Leslie Dunbar.)

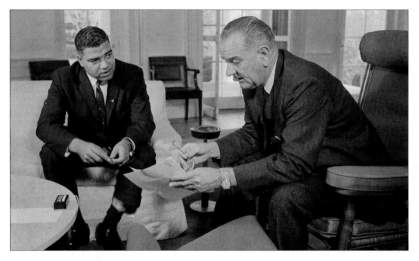

Whitney Young, the executive director of the National Urban League, shown here at a meeting with President Lyndon Johnson at the White House. After I moved to New York to be the executive director of the United Negro College Fund, Whitney took me under his wing, making introductions and showing me the ropes about fundraising.
(© Bettman/CORBIS.)

Here I am with Lyndon Johnson in the early 1970s, after he had left the White House.
(Lyndon Baines Johnson Library photo by Frank Wolfe.)

In early 1967, I was about to embark on my first overseas trip, to Israel, on a program sponsored by the American Jewish Committee. Shirley and our daughter, Vickee, are looking over a tourist map in anticipation of that trip. (Courtesy of the author.)

In 1971, after the death of Whitney Young, I was named executive director of the National Urban League. My work at the league brought me in contact with business leaders, top government officials, and major philanthropic organizations.

It also brought me into the public eye as a spokesman and advocate for the black community in America.

In the early 1970s, corporate boardrooms were nearly exclusively white, and I (along with others) led the way to integrate them. I was invited to be a director of several firms, including the Celanese Corporation, Xerox, J. C. Penney, and American Express. This photograph, from the 1980s, shows the American Express board. (Courtesy of American Express.)

Jesse Jackson and I played different roles within the civil rights movement, but we also worked together on many occasions, as at this event in the 1970s. (Courtesy of the author.)

My work at the Urban League involved me increasingly in national politics. Here I am with Senator Birch Bayh of Indiana, Representative Barbara Jordan of Texas, and Roy Wilkins, the longtime head of the NAACP.
(Courtesy of the author.)

At the National Urban League's 67th Annual Conference in July 1977, I gave a speech that was very critical of the Carter administration's record on race. President Carter addressed the conference the next day, and this photograph captured the tension between us.
(Photograph by Diana Walker.)

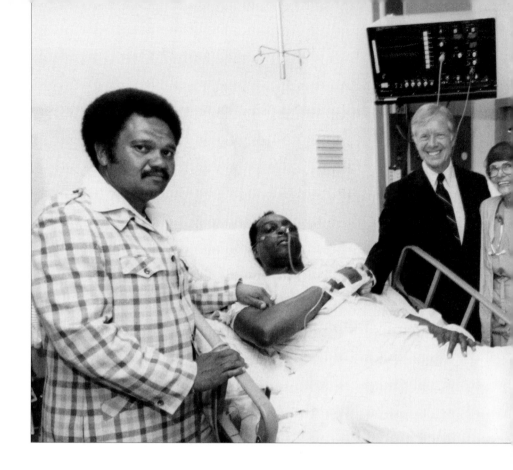

By the fall of 1980, I was back at work. In December I attended a meeting of civil rights leaders at the White House. As I shook hands with President Carter, Coretta Scott King conversed with Dorothy Height, the president of the National Council of Negro Women. At the right edge of the photo, out of the limelight, is Louis Martin, the president's special assistant for minority affairs and a leading player in the national Democratic Party.
(White House photo.)

On May 29, 1980, I was the target of an assassination attempt in Fort Wayne, Indiana, where I had traveled to speak at an Urban League dinner. When President Carter visited me in Parkview Hospital three days later, it was the first story ever reported on a new cable network called CNN. Standing at left is Dr. Robert Stovall, a member of the board of the Fort Wayne Urban League, who insisted that I get the best medical care possible, and at the far right is Dr. Jeffrey Towles, who operated on me and saved my life. (White House photo.)

Here I am with Justice Thurgood Marshall, whose work at the NAACP Legal Defense and Education Fund helped inspire me to become a lawyer. At right is Wiley A. Branton, who had been lead counsel to the Little Rock Nine and was my predecessor at the Voter Education Project.
(Courtesy of the author.)

I have attended many university commencements over the years, but none was more special to me than the 1981 commencement at the University of Pennsylvania, at which Vickee received her bachelor's degree. Among my fellow honorees that day was the historian John Hope Franklin. (Courtesy of the author.)

Rev. Gardner Taylor has been present at the most significant moments (both sad and joyous) of my life. He has performed eulogies, weddings, and christenings for the Jordan family, and when the NAACP bestowed upon me its highest award, the Springarn Medal, in July 2001, he presented it to me at the formal ceremony. (Courtesy Scurlock Studio Collection, Archives Center, National Museum of American History.)

For over thirty years, Franklin Thomas has been my closest friend, and we were among the first blacks to serve as corporate directors. Frank was for many years the president of the Ford Foundation, and today he continues to serve on many corporate and nonprofit boards.
(Courtesy of the author.)

In 1981, Robert Strauss recruited me to join his law firm, Akin, Gump, Strauss, Hauer & Feld. Strauss, the former chairman of the Democratic National Committee, is one of the great "wise men" of Washington whose counsel has been sought by presidents of both parties.
(Courtesy of the author.)

In November 1992, President-elect Bill Clinton asked me to serve as chairman of his transition team, the first (and, to date, only) black person ever to hold such a position. Clinton and Vice President-elect Al Gore posed for this photograph in the transition offices. (Courtesy of the author.)

To Vernon~ from the only WASP who knows the lyrics — Bill Clinton 8-93

At a party at Katharine Graham's house on Martha's Vineyard, Bill Clinton and I launched into an impromptu rendition of the black national anthem, "Lift Ev'ry Voice and Sing." Afterward, Clinton inscribed this photograph, "To Vernon, from the only WASP who knows the lyrics." (White House photo.)

My daughter Vickee's wedding in 1988 was a joyous occasion for our family. Clockwise from lower left are my wife, Ann; her daughter Toni; her son, Mercer; Vickee's husband, Barry; Vickee; myself; and Ann's daughter Janice.
(Courtesy of the author.)

This is one of my favorite photos of Vickee and me.
(© Mariana Cook, 1992.)

for office but who had never registered to vote. He wouldn't have been able to vote for himself in his own election. We tried to run interference on errors like that, and I think we were very helpful to them.

We didn't stop there. In 1968, when a significant number of blacks got elected to positions throughout the South, we convened education conferences to discuss, among other things, what was required to be a good elected official. At one point, we brought all the members of the school boards throughout the South to Clark College for a three-day session. After that, it was the legislators. All the black officials who were the "first" since Reconstruction in their respective states came, people like Barbara Jordan and my old friend and law-school roommate, Joe Lockeridge. There was never a more hopeful time. We were on the threshold of something very momentous, and so conscious of that fact. Given my background, interests, and capabilities, I was exactly where I wanted to be, doing exactly what I wanted to do at the time.

WHILE THE VEP WAS MY PRIME FOCUS during that era, I began to have experiences that broadened my horizons and altered the trajectory of my life in, at first, imperceptible, but very significant ways. Not long after I had returned to the VEP, President Johnson, at the suggestion of Louis Martin once again, put me on his newly created White House Council to Fulfill These Rights. All the leading lights of the civil rights movement were involved. The co-chairs were A. Philip Randolph, William T. Coleman, Jr., Morris Abram, Bob Heineman, and Stephen Currier. When we'd meet in the Indian Treaty Room at the White House, sitting around the council table would be Roy Wilkins, Martin Luther King, Whitney Young, Dorothy Height, John Lewis, and, to my slight amazement and great delight, me. It was a heady experience, going to the White House for meetings with people like that. Mostly I just listened—taking care to pick the right time to say something, making sure that whatever I said made sense.

One of the best parts of this assignment was that it brought me back in touch with Roy Wilkins, the first chance I'd gotten to spend any extensive time with him since leaving the NAACP. Roy loved pound cake. After our meetings, we'd walk over to a little diner on Fifteenth and K Street and sit at the counter and have pound cake— he'd drink tea, I'd drink milk. In that informal setting we talked seriously, gossiped, bounced off ideas about my future. Once again, it was like going to school.

Not long after that, LBJ appointed me (again, it was Louis Martin's doing) to the Presidential Advisory Commission on Selective Service. Burke Marshall was the chair and Charles Rangel was the general counsel, my first introduction to both men. Since I had not reached thirty-six years of age, I was still eligible for the draft, a fact noted with some humor in a *Washington Post* article on the day the paper covered our first meeting. (I had had student deferments through college and law school, and even though I had been classified 1-A since then, my number had never been called.) Louis Hershey, the commissioner of the Selective Service, appeared before us, and at one point during the course of his opening statement, he turned to me and said, "I'm going to get you."

What was notable about my appointment was not just that I was among people like Marshall, Dr. Jean Noble, Kingman Brewster of Yale, and Thomas Gates of J. P. Morgan, but that this was my first opportunity to deal in an area other than civil rights. To be blunt, the experience was very good for my self-confidence, suggesting as it did that I had a larger arena in which to play.

Aside from the excitement of being in such illustrious company, I learned a valuable lesson from my time on these commissions: If I had stayed in the government, at OEO, I would never have been asked to serve on either one, and that would have been a tremendous forgone opportunity. Although public service is an honor, one gives up many things by working for the government, and the chance to serve on boards and commissions is one of them. Doing that was a tremendous boost to my career. I was catapulted into circles of influential and powerful people well beyond my age and with résumés far more impressive than mine.

During these years, I also went abroad for the first time. My first trip out of the country was to Israel, just before the 1967 Six-Day

War. The American Jewish Committee had set up a program to send a group of black Americans to learn about the Jewish nation. Charles Wittenstein, the AJC's southern regional director, suggested that I be put on the list. Wittenstein knew me largely through the VEP, and he'd asked me to speak at various events around town. It was a great window on the world, forcing me again to think about issues beyond the South and civil rights. All these new experiences were stimulating. Up until those times, my life's work and interests had been fairly narrowly focused. As my vision of the world broadened, my visions of what I could do in the world followed suit. The restlessness rose in me again.

ALL WAS NOT WELL. The problem seemed small at the beginning. I'd first noticed it while I watched Shirley dancing sometime in 1963. She loved to dance, and she was quite good at it. We were out one evening and Shirley was on the floor with others doing a popular line dance of the day called the Madison. I was sitting it out, watching her from a table off to the side. She kept missing steps, something she never did. There were other things, sudden stiffness, loss of muscle control. We put it down to nerves or fatigue, in the way of young people who just can't imagine that anything could be seriously wrong with their young bodies. But in 1965, Shirley was struck with sudden paralysis. I took her to the hospital, where she underwent a battery of tests. Things were inconclusive. Then we went to the neurologist for more tests, and we got the results: multiple sclerosis.

Multiple sclerosis? I didn't even know what that was. Where did it come from? What was the normal course of the illness? Was it curable? The doctor explained it to us. No one knew exactly why it struck some people, and there was no "normal course." It was a progressive disease, not immediately fatal, but each individual had his or her own pattern of responses to the illness. And no, there was no cure.

We were both stunned by this, not having had any experience with serious illness. Shirley was twenty-eight years old. We had a little girl. We had a life and a set of expectations about how that life together would proceed. This was our beginning, and now this illness had set itself down among us seemingly from nowhere. Why?

We left the doctor's office and went back to the car. Once inside, we attempted conversation but never got beyond a few syllables. Instead, we sat in our car in that parking lot for almost three hours and cried, I much longer and harder than Shirley, who, as I think of it, was probably in a form of shock. For my part, the sense of helplessness overwhelmed me, a very difficult thing for one used to the notion that any problem can be solved if you work hard enough and long enough at it. I would have done anything in the world, but I knew there was nothing I could do to change this, absolutely nothing.

The next day, after I had pulled myself together, I went, as I always did in moments of crisis, to see my mother. I sat in the living room, at the lowest point of my life, and told her what we'd just found out. I asked her, mixing sorrow, rage, and self-pity, "Why did this have to happen to Shirley? Why did this have to happen to Vickee?" And then, "Why did this happen to me?"

She said, "Son, the Lord doesn't give you more of a load than you can tote. That's your load. Now, tote it. Is there anything else you want to talk about?"

"No ma'am." There was nothing more to be said—"That's your load. Now, tote it." I was still sad, so sorry for my young wife, but my mother's words stiffened my spine and resolve. On the way there, everything looked dim. I couldn't see my way clear to a future. How could we possibly regain ourselves and go on? Upon leaving my mother and the house I'd grown up in, I knew we would have to do just that, to make a new future with the particular hand that life had dealt us. I went home to my wife and daughter.

O N THE EVENING OF APRIL 4, 1968, I was at home, dressing to go to a local branch of the YWCA to speak at the kickoff of the NAACP membership campaign, when the news came over the radio that Martin Luther King, Jr., had been shot in Memphis. The announcer did not know what his condition was, but I had a sense that the news was going to be bad.

I thought back to the day four and a half years earlier when the news came that President Kennedy had been shot in Dallas. What I remembered most was that the day had exposed the divisions in the South, as I heard white children cheering at the news—"They got Kennedy!"—inspired, I believe, by parents who had expressed scorn at the president's efforts to enforce the laws and court decisions against segregation. This was quite a contrast to my childhood memory of being taken by my mother in 1945 to see Franklin Roosevelt's funeral train as it passed through Atlanta on its way north from Warm Springs. That was a death that seemed to have brought the country together, not torn it apart.

I sensed that Dr. King's death, if it came, would be more like Kennedy's—divisive along racial lines and discouraging to those who had invested such hope in their young and charismatic leader. I left the house and went to my office, where I looked up a poem that had immediately come into my mind, about fearlessness in death. I found the poem, copied it out, put it in my pocket, and went to the meeting.

Before I rose to speak, the word came that Dr. King had died, but I spoke anyway. I talked about how we had to keep moving forward, how we couldn't let this terrible event stop us from marching forward to our goal. The leader had fallen, but we were still standing.

I did not speak for more than a few minutes—it was not the time to make a long speech—but I did read the poem, Claude McKay's *If We Must Die,* which I remember to this day:

> If we must die, let it not be like hogs
> Hunted and penned in an inglorious spot,
> While round us bark the mad and hungry dogs,
> Making their mock at our accursed lot.
> If we must die, O let us nobly die,
> So that our precious blood may not be shed

In vain; then even the monsters we defy
Shall be constrained to honor us though dead!
O kinsmen! we must meet the common foe!
Though far outnumbered let us show us brave,
And for their thousand blows deal one death-blow!
What though before us lies the open grave?
Like men we'll face the murderous, cowardly pack,
Pressed to the wall, dying, but fighting back!

And then, five days later, was the funeral. I remember that it was my job to meet Nelson Rockefeller's private plane, to bring him and the dignitaries who came with him—McGeorge Bundy and Fred Friendly, among others—to the church. Though the service was packed with people, I made sure that the guests from up North got in. I stood outside with the crowd and heard the service from there, and then we walked with the hundreds of other mourners behind King's coffin to the burial site.

Dr. King's death was a turning point for the civil rights movement, because there was no one prominent enough or charismatic enough to replace him as the public face of the movement. We were in for a long period of transition as blacks sought to take advantage of the gains made in the courts and legislatures in the area of civil rights. I had seen the shift in the VEP's work before and after the Voting Rights Act, and I was now starting to think of strategies to fight the new battles that were just over the horizon. We were in a new world.

CHAPTER 9

A WORLD OPENED WIDE

A TELEPHONE CALL interrupted my afternoon nap one Sunday in the winter of 1968. The man on the other end of the line introduced himself as Jack Wofford. I'd never heard of him. Wofford explained that he was with the Institute of Politics at the John F. Kennedy School of Government at Harvard, then came quickly to the point. "I'm calling to ask if you would consider becoming a Fellow at the Kennedy School."

Of course I had heard of Harvard and instinctively understood that anything associated with it would be considered prestigious. I had no idea, however, what being a Fellow meant, whether it was something I really wanted to do, or could do consistent with my commitment to the VEP. Receiving the call was extremely flattering but also a bit mystifying, coming as it did out of the blue. There was no way to answer definitively at that moment.

With uncertainty running through my head, I said, "I'll think about it."

Wofford pressed on. "Before you make up your mind, come up and talk to us."

I agreed to do that much.

Not long after our conversation, I was in Cambridge, Massachusetts, meeting with Wofford, Professor Richard Neustadt, and Donald Price, the dean of the Kennedy School. It was clear that they were very interested in having me—I would be the first black Fellow ever—and they stressed how important this could be to the development of my career. I could take classes and teach a seminar, too, something I had never thought of doing.

As I listened, it became clear that going to Harvard was yet another opportunity that had come my way just at the right time, very much like Ms. Hurley's offer to join the NAACP. I'd been at the VEP three and a half years, my longest tenure in any job up until then. Things had reached the point where I was beginning to wonder if I had not come to the end of the road there—an inner warning signal that should never be ignored in any job or career. When you feel it's time to go, then you should go if you have the means to do that. While I knew the job of ensuring that blacks had fair access to the vote was of critical importance, whether I had to keep doing it, and for how long, was another matter. I'd given everything I had. From its initially slow start in 1962, through the years immediately following the passage of the Voting Rights Act, the VEP had helped to register almost 2 million new voters. There was more to be done, but the project was running smoothly. Couldn't someone else take the reins?

Along with the honor of being chosen for the position, the beauty of the Kennedy School Fellowship was that it was temporary, six months from January to June. That would give me much-needed time away from the daily demands of the VEP, time that I could use to sort out just what direction I wanted to go next.

Harvard was everything I had hoped it would be. Being back in an academic setting after nine years, without the pressure of grades or worrying about getting a job, gave me the freedom to explore new ideas and think about the world in an unfettered way. Like my trip overseas to Israel and my time on the National Advisory Commission on Selective Service, this was a taste of life beyond civil rights, and I liked it very much. Not that the subject of race was left out of the ongoing conversation. It was very much a part of it. But my colleagues and I discussed a wide range of topics during our many lunches and dinners together. Coming off of 1968, one of the most politically charged years of the century, we had a lot to talk about: the assassinations of Martin Luther King, Jr., and Robert F. Kennedy, the war in Vietnam, the explosion of black ghettos, the student movements that had sprouted up simultaneously on almost every continent. Considering all these things, I began to see myself not solely as a black American citizen but as a citizen of the world.

Even with that added sensibility, I understood that as the first black Fellow, I was blazing a trail in some fashion and therefore had a special charge to keep. I couldn't let down the side, not unlike my time at DePauw University. I had some feeling of being on display, that everything I did—the way I dressed, my conversation, the way I presented my ideas—could set a precedent in the minds of those who would choose how many blacks would follow in my footsteps in the program. Whether we want to or not, all blacks end up representing the entire race wherever we are, and given the racial landscape, the bad things we do are taken as more generally representative than the good things. It's unfair, but it is very real.

The seminar I taught, "Blacks and the Southern Political Process," was an exception to the general rule that there was no pressure. It stands as one of the most frightening things I have ever done. No matter how hard I prepared for class, there was the ever-present threat that one or more of my students (all very bright) could ask questions I didn't know how to answer. That was a great incentive for intense and extensive preparation, but I never had any sense that I had safely covered all bases. The class worked out, but a high level of tension (hidden, I hoped) was always there.

For the most part, my work at the VEP continued on an even keel, even as I was spending most of my time in Cambridge. The exception was one week when I returned to Atlanta to find a small number of protesters picketing outside our offices with signs saying things like "Vernon Jordan doesn't care" and "Jordan—Keeper of White People's Money." I stood out on the sidewalk among them for a while—they didn't know who I was—just to find out where they were from. It turned out that the picketers had been sent by Hosea Williams, who was very active in voter registration drives in Georgia. Williams, a deeply committed man, had achieved great success in past registration efforts and would do so again very famously in his work with the SCLC. However, the proposal he had recently sent to the VEP asking for support to fund another drive had been wholly inadequate, and so we had turned him down. The picket line was his way of voicing his displeasure with our decision—going public in a way calculated to cause the VEP, and me, maximum embarrassment.

I went upstairs to my office, fished out his proposal, and sent it right away to *The Atlanta Constitution*, which printed it in its entirety. The problems with the document—its budgeted expenditures, for instance, were outrageously high—were obvious to any impartial observer. After the proposal ran in the paper, the picketers vanished. I never heard another word about it, and I was never picketed again. In the end, Hosea Williams resubmitted his application and got a voter registration grant for less than one-third of his original request.

NOT LONG BEFORE Jack Wofford had called to ask me to come to Harvard, I had actually had another out-of-the-blue experience. In the fall of 1968, a woman who worked at Dillard University had visited me at the VEP. She told me that the university, a historically black college located in New Orleans, was in the process of searching for a new president. Would I be interested in the job? she asked. Of all the possible careers I had turned over in my head up until that point, being the president of a college or university had never entered my mind. I was surprised and, because I didn't think matters would get much beyond our initial discussion, fairly irreverent (but polite) in my responses. No, I did not want to be the president of Dillard University, I told her. She went away, and I thought that that would be the end. It was not.

While I was in Cambridge, David Hunter, the executive director of the Stern Family Fund, called me on behalf of himself and Mrs. Edgar Stern, who took a hands-on interest in the workings of her family's foundation. The fund was not only one of the original supporters of the VEP but the Stern family—and especially Mrs. Stern, who lived in New Orleans—contributed to Dillard. The intersection between the two led Hunter to call me to press the case for my interviewing in the first round of the search.

"Why don't you come and talk to me and Mrs. Stern about this," Hunter suggested.

I went to New York and met with them. During the course of the interview, I told them again that I wasn't interested.

"Well, why," Mrs. Stern asked, "did you come to this interview if you don't want the job?"

I was direct. "Because I have sense enough to know that if you summon me I ought to come," I replied. There was no need to say it explicitly, but they were, after all, partly paying for my current job. How could I say no? That was not the end of it. Even as I confessed my lack of interest, I had the feeling that I was going to be seeing Dillard fairly soon, anyway.

Through my time at the Southern Regional Council, I had gotten to know a few presidents of historically black colleges. I was especially close to Herman Long, the president of Talladega College, Vivian Henderson of Clark College, Jim Lawson of Fisk University, and Norman Francis of Xavier University, Dillard's crosstown rival. I spoke to them all about the Dillard search. They were unanimous in their enthusiasm for their profession: The water's wonderful, they said, come on in.

Although impressed by their reaction, deep down I knew I wasn't prepared at the age of thirty-three to take on a college presidency. I was not a scholar. I did not have a Ph.D. Surely it would have been better to have someone who had dedicated at least a part of his or her life to scholarship and academia take on such an important task. It was also clear to me that in 1969, trustee boards were not looking for college presidents so much as they were looking for truant officers. Campuses all over the country were sites of protests, sometimes violent, or just lower-level obstructionist tactics. Some people thrive in an atmosphere of chaos and disorder. I do not.

Still, my curiosity was piqued. What would an interview for a future college president involve? What was the process? I was most interested in hearing exactly why they thought I might be the right man for the job. So Shirley and I went to New Orleans in June 1969 to see what it was all about.

Dinner with the search committee that first evening went well. The next day, Shirley, weary from travel and burdened with symptoms of multiple sclerosis, stayed behind in the very nice hotel in the French Quarter, where they'd put us up, while I made the rounds talking to members of the administration and meeting students. The campus was visually stunning, an impressive array of gleaming white buildings surrounding a grove of magnificent oak trees. Closed off from the surrounding neighborhood, it was a small world unto itself, sedate but infused with the youthful energy of young women and men who represented the hopes of our race, many of whom had been sent there by parents struggling to pay for their education.

Dillard's president, Dr. Albert Dent, was one of a long line of Morehouse graduates who had served in that office. His coming retirement promised a major transformation in the school's administration, as he had been president for twenty-seven years. I knew Dr. Dent; he was on the board of trustees of the Southern Regional Council. He was very happy to have me in the running to succeed him and talked me up quite a bit to his faculty and staff. So much so that at that afternoon's reception, it was almost as if the decision had already been made. They seemed to welcome me, not as a candidate, but as the new president. It made me uncomfortable to have men and women who were much older, whom I'd admired from afar for their academic achievements, act in a far too obsequious manner to me—"Dr. Jordan," they'd say, or even "Mr. President." I didn't like it at all.

Not everyone was happy to see me. As it turned out, the dean of the faculty desperately wanted to be president and was very upset that it looked as if I would be chosen. That evening, I went to a party hosted by what could be called the radical wing of the faculty. They wanted to get me alone to see what I thought about various issues so they could figure out whether I'd be friend or foe in whatever faculty battles were undoubtedly going on at the time. We were in the middle of some mild verbal jousting when the dean arrived, as drunk as he could be.

We had met earlier in the day, and he had actually showed me the list of candidates who were being considered for the job. I found that inappropriate and told him so, although it was interesting to learn that the first two candidates had turned down the job and I was third on the list. Despite his lapse in judgment on that matter, I was more than a little shocked when he came to the party in that state. We had some strained, aimless conversation, the kind you have with people when they've had way too much to drink. His colleagues were mortified by his behavior, and I felt bad for all of them. It was as if he'd sucked all the oxygen out of the room just by stepping into it. Pretty soon, people began to drift away. I said farewell and went back to the hotel to report to Shirley on the events of the day and evening.

We were fast asleep when the telephone rang. It was three o'clock in the morning.

"Mr. President."

"Who is this?"

It was the dean, exhausted, and judging from what he said next, near the absolute end of his rope. He was the rightful successor to Dent, he proclaimed bitterly, but he knew now that that wasn't going to happen. Then he switched gears, pulled himself together a bit, and began to pledge his fealty. "If you keep me as dean, I just want you to know that I am going to serve you as I would want to be served. I promise I'll be loyal and faithful. You won't have any problem with me."

"Well, I appreciate that very much," I said. "But it's too early in the morning for this. I'll see you tomorrow."

As jarring as that was (not at all what I expected to come up in the interview process for a college presidency), I felt a little sorry for him. He was disappointed about not getting the job. The sad irony, of course, was that I did not really want the job and was anxious to end this whole charade as soon as possible.

The next morning, Shirley and I went to campus to look at the president's house. As soon as we got there, we realized that this wasn't going to work. By then, Shirley was regularly using a cane, and the house had two stories. Getting up and down those stairs would be too difficult and possibly dangerous for her. I pointed this out. The chairman of the search committee was not deterred. "We'll build you a new house, and put everything on one floor," he said airily. They were not going to be shaken from the view that I was going to be the next president of Dillard University.

As the final part of the interview process, I was supposed to attend the commencement exercises that afternoon. It was more of a special occasion than usual, because 1969 was Dillard's centennial year. Thurgood Marshall was set to speak, and I believe to this day that the administration had planned to use the ceremony to announce that they had found Dr. Dent's successor: me.

A driver took us back to the hotel after we'd seen the house and indicated that he'd be back to pick us to go to the commencement. By this time, I was in a minor panic because things seemed to be heading in a direction that I did not want to go. Riding through the streets of New Orleans, one thing became very clear to me: I had to avoid the commencement exercises at all cost. There was just no way I could show up. Attending would have amounted to an acceptance of their determination that I was going to be the new president. By the time we got back to the hotel, I had made a decision.

As soon as we walked into our room, I told Shirley we should begin packing because I was going to make plane reservations and we were going to get out of town as soon as possible. That's just what we did. By one o'clock that afternoon, we were on our way back to Atlanta.

After dropping Shirley off at home, I went even deeper under cover. Luckily, Dick Neustadt at Harvard had arranged for me to attend my first Bilderberg meeting, in Elsinore, Denmark. Bilderberg is an organization that started in 1954 in Bilderberg, Holland, founded by a group of prominent European and American business executives and government officials to have informative and informal discussions, primarily about Cold War issues and the Soviet threat to democratic institutions in Europe and the United States. When I went that year, it was presided over by Prince Bernhard of the Netherlands and was attended by such notables as David Rockefeller, Cyrus Vance, Sir Eric Roll, and Ernst van der Buegel. I was excited to be attending because it would be a window on the world and would broaden my perspective. I was scheduled to leave right after my interview at Dillard, which was very convenient, given the way things had turned out. Of course, I hadn't told anyone at Dillard that I was leaving the country. I simply disappeared. There are some things you just have to run away from. So I ran away to Denmark and was hiding out there when an official at Dillard tracked me down and asked what had happened. I explained that I simply did not want to be president of a college. What had started as a gesture of respect to my benefactors and a way to satisfy my curiosity (and perhaps, my vanity) had taken on a life of its own and gotten completely out of hand. I was sorry, but there was nothing to be done.

P OLITICS SEEMED A MORE NATURAL FIT with my interests and abilities—a logical extension of everything I'd been involved in from the time of my youth: making speeches, debating policy issues, thinking about ways to change the political situation for black people. My early forays into "politics," running for president of the student body in high school and for class treasurer in college, were attempts to bring all those things together in the only way available to me at the time. I was operating on a much bigger stage now, in a world that was opening up for young blacks like me. Who could have known that better than I, having spent four years heading up a project designed to help open up that world? After all that time supporting voter registration drives to get blacks to the polls, training black candidates for office, and putting on conferences for black elected officials, maybe it was time for me to jump into those waters myself.

The thought had been running through my mind for some time— well before I became a Fellow at the Kennedy School. Sometime near the end of my stay at Harvard, the idea of running for Congress in 1970 from the Fifth District of Georgia emerged as my most likely next step. As I wrapped things up in Cambridge—Shirley and Vickee came to spend the last days with me and we drove back to Atlanta together—I knew my mission had been generally accomplished. The fellowship itself was amazing, introducing me to people who would remain lifelong friends. Although I hadn't lined up a definite new career, at least I'd narrowed it down to a plausible alternative.

Settling back in Atlanta gave me a better view on the run for Congress, and in retrospect it seems that my head was more in it than my heart, which is just death to any campaign effort. You must have the heart to run. I did not. Evidence of that was my failure to do the kinds of things necessary to run for office: I made no attempt to raise funds and I hadn't planned any strategy, nor had I made any serious efforts to line up support. For the most part I was just talking aloud about it to various people.

The truth is, I really didn't believe that I—or any other black candidate in 1970—could win running against Fletcher Thompson, the white Republican incumbent. After 1972, when the lines of the district were to be redrawn and include more black voters, things would be different. There was, however, a solid reason to run in 1970. Were I to win the Democratic primary, even an inevitable loss to Thompson would put me in the forefront of the minds of the voters. There was a good chance of that happening. Atlanta was my hometown, my mother was very well known there, and I had developed a fairly high visibility as a result of my work at the NAACP, the SRC, and the VEP.

I went to a cocktail party in the fall of 1969, a gathering of white liberals and a few blacks. At one point during the evening, Jimmy Carter, then a young state senator from Plains who had lost the 1966 race for governor in the Democratic primary, announced that he was going to run for governor again in 1970. Literally, on the spur of the moment, I demanded equal time to say that I was going to be a candidate for the Fifth District congressional seat. Everyone in the room was quite surprised, including Shirley, who knew I was thinking about running but had no idea that things had gotten to the point that I would make an announcement. Actually, I didn't either. This was more a spontaneous eruption—"Me, too!"—than anything else. It just seemed like the right thing to do at that time. Of course the newspapers picked up on it, because of Carter's statement, and once again, almost like the Dillard experience, I was off to the races on a horse I wasn't firmly committed to riding.

I'd met Carter once before, soon after he had lost that gubernatorial race to the segregationist candidate, Lester Maddox. David Gambrell, a young lawyer who was very supportive of Carter's political career, brought him by my office at the VEP and said he thought the two of us were going places and that we should know one another. We were two ambitious young Georgians anxious to make our mark in the world, and over the course of the years, our paths would cross both in our home state and on the national stage—in good times and in bad.

News of my candidacy reached my friend in Greensboro, North Carolina, Ann Forsyth. I had met Ann and her husband, Frank, while I worked at the Southern Regional Council. Ann is what newspaper columnists would refer to as a "tobacco heiress," a granddaughter of R. J. Reynolds and a member of the Cannon and Stouffer families. It was through that last connection that our paths first crossed. Ann conceived the Stouffer Family Foundation's Scholars Program, which sought out talented black youngsters in the South and paid for their tuition at formerly all-white preparatory schools in the South—places like St. Albans in Washington, D.C.; Woodberry Forest in Virginia; and Indian Springs in Alabama. It was a unique, quietly implemented educational venture that reached some 100 black boys and girls.

In those days, anyone who was working seriously on behalf of black advancement would know about or come into contact with people who were of the same mind on the subject. That's how Ann found me. She, Frank, and John Ealy, the noted North Carolina writer, visited me at the Southern Regional Council to enlist my help in finding future Stouffer scholars. I signed on to the project with great enthusiasm.

Ann and I became good friends. She loved Shirley, and always took a great interest in Vickee. We would visit her at her home in Winston-Salem, and we established a beautiful friendship that has lasted throughout the years. When Ann heard that I was going to run for Congress, she and Frank came down to Atlanta to discuss my plans, a lovely gesture in itself; but what was even more amazing was what they brought with them—a large brown paper bag full of cash. I don't remember exactly how much it was, but it was enough to make anyone who couldn't be called a "tobacco heiress" stop dead in their tracks.

They were worried, she said, about Shirley and what would happen to our family if I ran for Congress. I'd have to give up my job. Shirley was no longer working, there were medical expenses related to her illness, and we had hired a full-time housekeeper.

"This will help you take care of Shirley and Vickee," Ann said as she handed over the bag.

Shirley and I were both touched, and not a little stunned, by this show of love and support. Ann and Frank simply refused to leave with the money, and so it sat in our closet until events very soon overtook us and I could return it without seeming ungracious or ungrateful.

ALBERT DENT FORGAVE ME for the debacle at Dillard. Two weeks after I'd announced for Congress, he came to Atlanta to see me about another job prospect. The executive committee of the United Negro College Fund, of which he was a member, wanted to know if I would be interested in becoming the College Fund's executive director. I didn't have to think much about it. Of course I was interested. Between a surefire losing run for Congress that I wasn't certain I wanted to make and the executive directorship of a historic black institution where I would get to do all the things I wanted to do and thought I did well, there was no contest.

So I made yet another trip up to New York in November 1969 to talk with a group of people who would help me set my course in life. I met at the University Club with the executive committee, which included Dr. Dent; Frederick D. Patterson, founder of the College Fund and the third president of the Tuskegee Institute; Mrs. Edward M. M. Warburg of the Warburg banking family; Chauncey Waddell of the financial firm Waddell & Reed; and Dudley Dowell, the president of New York Life.

We talked. They told me why they wanted me for the position. I conveyed my sincere interest, and then they mentioned the salary: $25,000 a year. My heart fell. Although that wasn't bad for 1969, it was a problem for me. I was making about $22,000 at the VEP in Atlanta, where the cost of living was much lower than in New York. In addition, I had expenses, planned and unplanned, because of Shirley's special needs—a housekeeper, medical care—the very things that had propelled Ann Forsyth to my doorstep with her offer of financial support. No matter how attractive the job title, I simply had to have a salary that would take care of our basic needs, and $25,000 in New York just wouldn't do that.

I wanted the job very badly but I had to say, "I really want to do this, but I can't come up here for $25,000."

They were shocked. "Why not?" they asked.

I explained that I was already making nearly the same amount and would end up losing money in the transition from Atlanta to New York, which I simply could not do.

They looked at one another and then asked me to step outside. After a moment, Chauncey Wardell came out and said, "Well, we can lend you money to help you buy a house and that should help you a bit."

"No, no, no," I said. "You don't have to lend me anything. Just pay me a solid salary, and I can buy my own house."

He went back inside. They called me in after quite a while and offered me $42,500 a year, which I thought was all the money in the world at that time. I accepted their offer.

Dr. Patterson walked out with me when I left the meeting. As we strolled down the street, he said, "Young man, you drive a tough bargain."

I said, "Dr. Patterson, these are tough times."

Before I left New York, I stopped in to talk to Whitney Young, the executive director of the National Urban League, whom I had known for some time. We had spoken before about the possibility of my coming to the Urban League as his deputy.

Nothing came of it, and he wrote me a letter saying that there was only one job at the Urban League for me and that was his job, and he wasn't ready to leave. As for the United Negro College Fund, he said, by all means take it. "There's no place like New York," he told me. "You'll like it. It will be good for your family and you can do some good for black people."

What a feeling. I barely needed the plane to get back to Atlanta. When I got home, I said, "Shirley, we're moving to New York. I'm going to take the United Negro College Fund job."

Without a second thought, she smiled and asked, "When do we leave?"

That was the end of my run for Congress, and my last even semi-serious thought of running for any office. I've never regretted not choosing politics as a career. In some ways, I've had the best of all worlds. I've had constituencies, influenced social policy, gotten to do a lot of things elected officials do without the almost inhumane demands of running for office. As much as they seemed right for me on the surface, neither the ministry nor electoral politics are suitable careers for congenitally private and independent people.

Andrew Young, known mainly at the time as having been one of Martin Luther King, Jr.'s lieutenants, came by to see me not long after I returned from New York. He'd heard about the United Negro College Fund offer and wanted to know if I was going to take it, because he too was thinking of running for the Fifth District seat. With me out of the race, there would be one less person to worry about, and he would be more inclined to make the run.

I told him that I was moving to New York and that he should run for office, even though I was sure that he, like any black challenger to Thompson, would lose this time around but would win in 1972. That's exactly what happened. On his second attempt, Andy went to Washington to represent the Fifth District of Georgia.

SHIRLEY WAS HAPPY. My parents were excited. My mother saw this as part of a divine plan. "You have to do this," she said, even though it meant that we would be moving to New York. The black newspapers, which had always followed my career and had been very kind to me, made the story headline news. There was great pride in black Atlanta that another one of our own had been chosen to head a major black institution. Whitney Young had come from Atlanta to run the National Urban League, and now I was following in his footsteps. It was race pride and hometown pride all rolled up into one.

The enthusiasm was not universal. Once again, my father-in-law was nonplussed. Here I was with a nice house, a good job that I'd held onto for four years—longer than he'd ever seen. We were managing with Shirley's illness very well. Why was I going to change jobs yet again? This was just a gap in our understanding of the world that wouldn't be bridged until he finally realized that there was no need to fear: I was going to make it, and I would always take good care of his daughter.

There were other negative responses as well. Some people, mostly white businessmen, tried to talk me out of doing it. The most vociferous was my friend Billy Stern, who was chairman of the Trust Company of Georgia. We had become friends when we were involved in a fund-raising campaign for the Atlanta Arts Center to commemorate the deaths of a group of Atlantans who had recently been killed in an airplane accident at Orly Airport in Paris. In Billy's view, and that of several friendly white business leaders, it was almost my sacred duty to stay and run for office—to remain tied to Atlanta in some fashion. "We need people like you here," he said.

"Billy, if I stay, will you put me on the board of the Trust Company of Georgia?" I asked.

He was silent a moment, and then he said, "Well, you know I can't do that."

That said it all. Billy was a good and decent man, the son of a suffragette who had passed on her sound values to him. Later on, after he retired from the Trust Company, he worked as the dean of Atlanta University's School of Business for one dollar a year. But he was asking me to stay in a place where positions that would come easily, as a matter of right, to white men with my training and credentials would be totally off-limits to me. I did not want to live that way any more.

Several years later, after I became head of the National Urban League, Billy hosted fund-raisers for the Urban League in Atlanta. Whenever he was in New York, we'd go out for dinner. By this time, I was on several corporate boards, including Bankers Trust. One day over lunch, having seen the way the world had opened up to me since the day he had tried to persuade me to stay in Atlanta, Billy said, "Vernon, I understand why you left."

THE EXECUTIVE COMMITTEE PUT IT IN WRITING. A letter arrived at my office formally offering me the College Fund job. Beyond ecstatic, on the way home from work that day I decided to stop by to see one of my best buddies, Bill Stanley, to show him the letter. I had known Bill for many years, and he and his wife, Ella, had accompanied Shirley and me to Hugh Gibert's Christmas party back in 1962. As soon as I saw him reading it, I knew I had made an error. He didn't say a word, didn't congratulate me, didn't say it was a mistake for me to take the job or anything else. There was nothing but awkward silence between us. Then it hit me: He thought I was bragging or showing off, while I thought I was sharing a marvelous moment with a close friend.

Friendship can be a tricky business to manage. Affection often exists alongside competitiveness, and it's a tremendous loss whenever the will to compete comes to dominate. One of life's greatest pleasures is to have the chance to exult in the good fortunes of people you care about, and I really expected better from my friend. From my end, there was no basis for competition between us. We were in different fields (he was a school principal), and we had our own separate territory. Even if we had worked in the same area, weren't we friends? Bill's reaction simply floored me, and that was the one truly down note during the whole period. There was little left for us to say. Feeling a mixture of embarrassment and hurt as I sat there in his home, where I'd been so comfortable before, I changed the subject.

We talked a while about inconsequential things, and then I went home. Bill and Ella did come to my going-away party, and they visited Shirley and me in New York once, but our friendship was never the same.

The scene of our departure from Atlanta was also something less than auspicious. Vickee had broken her ankle and was in a cast and a wheelchair. Shirley was in a wheelchair, which we always used in airports. Both had to be put on lifts in order to get onto the plane. Mrs. Gaines, our housekeeper, had decided to come to New York with us. She was there, all dressed up and excited about her first airplane ride, seemingly oblivious to the pain of separation about to be visited upon the weeping grandparents who acted as if we were riding off into the sunset forever. Like so many moments in life, it was happy and sad.

I had never thought I'd leave the South. Billy Stern knew what he was doing when he tried to appeal to my sense of commitment to and love for that region, and Atlanta in particular. We are all a tangle of personal ambition and impulses toward altruism. Given the opportunity, there was no question I wanted out, to enter and compete in a bigger arena that just happened to be north of the Mason-Dixon line. There was also no doubt that I had long defined myself as a warrior on Southern turf. What helped ease my vague sense that I was, in some way, betraying the cause was that the United Negro College Fund was fundamentally about the South: Southern colleges, in the main, and Southern students. It was a rationalization, but I needed something—besides satisfying my own personal yearnings— to justify leaving the place I had thought would always be my home.

CHAPTER 10

BUILDING BLOCKS

I N BECOMING THE EXECUTIVE DIRECTOR of the United Negro College Fund in March 1970, I was taking a job that not a lot of people wanted. The College Fund had hit a turbulent patch, and its troubles were something of an open secret. Because of disputes about its overall management, several key members of the board of trustees had abruptly resigned, including the philanthropist John D. Rockefeller III, the advertising executive David Ogilvy, and Andrew Heiskell, the chairman of Time Inc. No organization—especially one that depended heavily upon its ties to the corporate world—could lose people like that all at once without suffering a devastating blow.

There were other problems. The president of the College Fund, Dr. Stephen H. Wright, had recently departed, and morale was low throughout the organization. When Dr. Harry V. Richardson, who had come from Gammon Theological Seminary to serve as an interim, part-time executive director, found out that I was being considered for the position, he pleaded, "Vernon, you've got to take this job so I can go home!"

On the one hand, it wasn't good to hear that I was stepping onto a ship that seemed in such peril. On the other hand, the circumstances presented the perfect opportunity to step in as rescuer. From my view (maybe a naive one—I was only thirty-four years old), the situation was clearly salvageable and could be put right. In point of fact, it had to be put right. This was one of those moments in life when too much was on the line to worry about all the ways to fail, because the consequences of failure were simply too awful to contemplate. This was a very high-profile position for me, a move from a regional stage to a national stage, and I had been entrusted with the fortunes of a well-established institution that represented, for many black Americans, a means of transforming their lives. Things just had to work.

Our problems were not solely internal. Many people in the country (black and white) had doubts about the utility of the historically black colleges that were supported by the United Negro College Fund. Were they really needed in an era in which all legal barriers to black entrance into white colleges had been destroyed? Wasn't it contradictory to call for the integration of higher education (my work to desegregate the University of Georgia) and, at the same time, fight to preserve historically black colleges?

If we had, in the five years since the passage of the Voting Rights Act and the six years since the passage of the Civil Rights Act, done away with the effects of 300 years of white supremacy and were operating on a level playing field, those concerns might be valid. But we had not, and have not yet. It made no sense to force young blacks, many of them from the poorest segment of society, to forgo opportunities in order to indulge some fantasy about a nonexistent "color-blind" society. The white colleges were opening up only to a limited number of black students each year; we had thousands of young people who needed an education if they were to make their own way in the world. I've never had a moment's doubt about the importance of historically black colleges, given how far this country has to go before all blacks are brought into full political, social, and economic citizenship. If these colleges didn't exist, we would have to invent them. My zeal on this point allowed me to plunge headlong into marketing the College Fund to those who had the resources to help support it.

And make no mistake, I was engaged in marketing. Fund-raising is essentially salesmanship, which requires knowing both your product and your target audience. It always helps to really believe in the value of your product, which I did very fervently. This was in my blood. Being at the College Fund reconnected me to my past, living in the University Homes projects near black colleges and attending a historically black law school. In my own mind, I saw myself as having forty colleges and 40,000 kids to market. I wasn't there to set academic policy or to make political statements; my clearly defined role was to raise as much money as possible to help as many black youngsters as possible get an education.

As deep a commitment as that was, the fact remained that I'd never been responsible for doing any serious fund-raising. I'd never had a fund-raising staff and knew nothing about direct mail. Our biggest contributions came from corporations, so corporate executives were naturally an important audience that had to be cultivated. I'd certainly never raised corporate money, nor had I ever been in a corporate boardroom, except as a waiter in my mother's business. Just as with any other subgroup, the corporate world has a culture of its own, with particular rules, expectations, and ways of communicating. That had not been my world, so there were some things to learn. Fortunately, the learning curve was not that steep, and I fairly quickly saw what I had to do.

More precisely, I discovered that the differences between the world I had inhabited and the one I was entering were not really so great. In significant ways, both cultures were doing the same things—managing and dealing with people—but calling them by different names. How to deal with rampaging egos and clashes of personality, how to move a staff or an individual toward the organization's goals, the best way to reward success and punish failure—these are questions that come up in every enterprise. The best answers often have similar properties no matter the field or discipline.

Very early on I found that I could draw on the skills sharpened as an NAACP field director, at the Southern Regional Council, and at the Voter Education Project—among them meeting and establishing a quick rapport with people, speaking the language of exhortation— "Please come along with us on this great mission"—dealing with rivalries among far-flung but connected groups, and, in general, taking on the role of the person in command whenever required. I made do with what I had at my disposal.

As with the VEP, there was a concreteness to the College Fund's objective that I found very attractive. We needed to raise a defined amount of money, and success was as precisely defined as a dollar amount. If we reached that goal, we would know. If we did not reach it, we would know that as well. There was a definite way to mark the value of an effort, and knowing that guided and comforted me.

All this was taking place as I had to fulfill responsibilities, and do so in a way suitable to one who was serving in a job national in scope. For the first time in my life, I gave a national press conference—my initiation into addressing the nation at large. The spirit of the times was very much in evidence in one of the first questions posed to me.

"Mr. Jordan, nobody uses the word 'Negro' anymore. Are you going to change the name to the 'United Black College Fund'?"

"No," I said. "It was founded as the United Negro College Fund."

"Have you discussed that with the board?"

"No, I haven't discussed it with the board."

By being very direct, and not equivocating, I think I prevented what was an irrelevancy from turning into a small media-manufactured "problem." I have followed that prescription ever since.

Then there was my first speech as the executive director, in Detroit. Up until that time, I had written all of my own speeches. That wasn't how it worked at the College Fund. As executive director, I had a speechwriter on staff, but in this case, he presented me with a draft not to my liking. I rewrote the speech, and my formal debut before the troops worked out well. Soon, however, I came to understand the value of a good speechwriter, as the demands on my time made it impractical for me to draft my own speeches.

Along with performing the initial ceremonial duties, an important order of business was to try to mend some fences. Dr. Patterson suggested that we had to make an effort to get John D. Rockefeller III back on the board. He set up the meeting and we walked over to 30 Rockefeller Plaza, my first time in that building, to try to persuade Mr. Rockefeller to return to the UNCF board of trustees.

He was not to be moved. As a matter of fact, he was extremely abrupt with us. When I got back to my office I found out why.

Datus Smith, one of Rockefeller's aides, called me and said, "Young man, you made a big mistake. You shouldn't have come here with Dr. Patterson. He's unhappy with Dr. Patterson."

I said, "Well, I didn't know that."

Mr. Smith said, "I'm going to arrange another meeting. This time you'll come alone."

That's exactly what I did.

No sooner had I sat down than Mr. Rockefeller said, "What are you doing here again? I told you I wasn't going to go back on that board."

I said, "Listen, Mr. Rockefeller, I just got to town. I barely know how to get here from Fifty-second Street. But I need your help. We need your help." And then—a blatant appeal to sentiment: "I know your mother wrote you and your brothers a letter saying that you were supposed to help people, and the United Negro College Fund needs your help."

He wasn't impressed by the gambit. "I know what my mother wrote," he replied. "But I'm not coming back on the board." That was the end.

I stood up and said, "Mr. Rockefeller, thank you for seeing me again. I will do it without you." We shook hands and I left.

Dealing with the board wasn't the only issue confronting me. I had to take control of managing the staff, many of whom had been there for a long time and were used to doing things according to their own plan and in their own time. These were in the main very dedicated people. But I was new and, from their perspective, green. As a result, I was tested in ways that I don't think I would have been had I been older. Once again, I dealt with it by being very direct, very early on, to establish that I was in charge, mistakes and all, and I wanted to be treated that way.

As I surveyed our operations, it was very apparent who was pulling their weight and who was not. It's never easy, but I had to fire a number of people who had been in their jobs for a long time and who simply were not doing them well or were just taking advantage of the organization. For example, there was one person who had an annual contract but only ran his fund-raising campaign three months out of the year. That would not do. I remember him so clearly, standing in the airport with tears in his eyes after I'd delivered the news. It was tough, but he just had to go.

In something of an irony, at that time, all of the fund-raisers for the UNCF throughout the country were white. There was a reason for this. For the most part, it was whites who had access to the sources of funding. Their classmates and friends controlled corporate and foundation purses. It struck me that we should still try to field a more diverse group of fund-raisers. The College Fund could be a training ground for Development Offices at member colleges. So in all the areas where I had to replace individuals who weren't performing well, I brought in young black people to work as fund-raisers. The diversity improved the quality of our efforts and lifted morale. Judging from the success we had that year, the strategy worked.

VERNON, WHAT ARE YOU DOING at six o'clock?" The voice on the phone was Whitney Young's. The UNCF was in the same office building as the National Urban League, a setup which had been arranged by the General Education Board, founded by Rockefeller interests many years before.

"I'm doing what I do every day—going to catch my train."

He said, "Don't do that. Come go with me to the Four Seasons. I'm going to show you how a cultivation [a fund-raiser] works."

I said, "Great. I'll meet you downstairs at a quarter to six."

As we walked the half block to the Four Seasons, I said, "Whitney, you're really good to do this for me."

His reply was a little surprising, somewhat sad, and very instructive.

"When I came to town in 1960, none of the established leadership"—he meant the black leadership—"lifted a hand to help me out, show me around. So, I made my own way. But I owe you better than I got, and so I want you to see this." There was no bitterness in his voice, just matter-of-fact resignation.

A moment before we went inside, Whitney continued, revealing what he thought had been behind their hands-off policy. "What most guys don't understand about fund-raising in New York is that there's enough money here for all of us. There's no need to be petty and competitive." His words were a great lesson to me that helped shape my outlook on how to go about doing my job at the UNCF and, later, at the Urban League. Whitney was absolutely right. There was enough money in New York so that we could all do well and work together at the same time. I went inside with him and learned things that night that would help me for years to come. First, I learned that to convene people for a fund-raising event, you had to have a host with sufficient influence and position that he (or she) could in fact convene such a group. Second, the host had to believe in what you were doing—had to have some passion for it. Third, the host had to be prepared to pay for the fund-raising event. Fourth, not only did the host have to be physically present, but he or she had to be willing to use his or her organization and influence to rally others. Fifth, the refreshments should be hors d'oeuvres and drinks, and brief fund-raising speeches were essential, because you had to remember that people were between work and home. And finally, you had to get the commitment for the money then and there.

Along with Whitney Young, a few others opened their arms and homes to me: William T. Trent, the first executive director of the College Fund; Dr. Kenneth Clark, a professor at City College; and Judge James D. Watson of the U.S. Court of Claims. For the most part, my experience with the established black leadership in New York City, which really meant Manhattan, was similar to Whitney's. It was a small, Harlem-based, largely closed world composed of longtime friends and family members—a difficult nut to crack. There was some resentment, I was told later, that in a period of nine years, two outsiders from Atlanta had come into the city and had taken two plum jobs: Whitney at the Urban League, me at the College Fund. But I didn't have time to concern myself with that, there was a job to do.

I threw myself into my work with all that I had. One of the lessons I had learned as Georgia field director for the NAACP was that people out in the field love to have the leader show up in their local area. That's exactly what I did. I visited and spoke to every local UNCF campaign—listening and remembering when people told me their names and the names of family members, showing interest in the work they were doing. I was everywhere, introducing myself, speaking, doing fund-raisers—generally showing the flag whenever and wherever, at untold numbers of fund-raising lunches and speaking engagements before alumni groups. In towns all over the country, there were little corps of supporters that needed energizing, and I was the energizer.

On a more intimate level, I sat down in offices and boardrooms with leaders of corporate America, made my case, and asked for their support. Following my policy, I was always very direct with them. "This is what I need you to do," I would tell them, and they, more often than not, responded positively.

While dealing with corporate leaders I found that it wasn't enough to be simply a supplicant; businessmen responded better when they had an interest in the cause I was presenting. So I made sure they knew that if they invested in our students, they would get good employees in return. Toward that end, I started a program to bring professors from our colleges up to New York so they could spend time at the big corporations to see how they worked. Once they understood the modus operandi of the companies, they could do a better job of counseling the students who wanted to go into business. This worked to everyone's advantage and encouraged the corporations to support us more enthusiastically.

The job was the perfect combination of personal gratification (it feels good to go places and have people say nice things about you) and the sense of doing something that was unquestionably a help to others. The more funds we raised, the more kids would get to go to college. It was as simple, and as crucial, as that.

MY RELATIVE YOUTH was a benefit and something of a small burden. It gave me the stamina to travel almost incessantly without too much strain and the optimism to banish any thought of failure. But just as some members of the executive staff had to get used to dealing with a boss who was much younger, the presidents of the various UNCF colleges had to adjust to the new young man in their midst upon whom they were relying to bring home the bacon. Many were skeptical. They saw me as a youngster, inexperienced and unknowledgeable. Then something happened that changed their view.

The College Fund had scheduled its annual meeting in Chicago that spring, where we were to pitch to members of a leading corporation in the city. A question arose: Who was going to speak? I piped up immediately, "I'm going to speak." As far as I was concerned, the matter was settled. There was some grumbling, but I was insistent. To my great relief, after the speech, on the bus as we returned to our hotel, all the presidents gave me a big round of applause. I had, apparently, exceeded their expectations, and they were satisfied that I could do well for the organization. That meant the world to me.

We solidified our relationship at what was a yearly retreat to Capahosic, Virginia, a resort built by R. R. Moten, the second president of Tuskegee University. Tuskegee students had made the bricks for the buildings and had helped erect the structures themselves. Each summer, after all their commencements were over, the presidents would meet at Capahosic to talk about the year's events and their plans for the future and to simply unwind after the pressures of the academic year. We discussed the College Fund's various projects and initiatives.

This was the equivalent of a black Bohemian Grove, a unique gathering of members of the "talented tenth." During my time at the College Fund, there were no female presidents of UNCF colleges. When we convened at Capahosic, the atmosphere was very male, with conversations over poker games or while sitting on the porch drinking. We played tennis, went on long walks, and ate great Southern cuisine. I loved every minute of it. Most of these men had been at their business for many years. Wisdom, experience, and just solid information about the way the world worked was on almost constant display. I took in as much as I could.

What we were working for was also on easy display. Over the

past three decades, I have attended college commencements by the dozen. I can honestly say that there is nothing like a commencement at a historically black college—nothing compares to it. There is such beauty and passion in a ceremony where all who participate know and believe that every name called represents an advancement, not just for the particular individual or his or her family, but for an entire race of people. Every degree conferred is a repudiation of all the ancient slurs against black people's humanity and justifies the faith of those who kept going when the future seemed hopeless. Of course, commencements at white colleges are important occasions as well, but white students in America do not carry the badges and incidents of slavery that black students do. As a result, I've observed over the years the difference in atmosphere—the culture, the music—between white and black commencements.

I remember well the commencement exercises I attended at predominately white schools in the late 1960s and early 1970s—the more prestigious the school, the less seriously the students seemed to take their graduation exercises. With all the nonchalance and assurance of future masters of the universe, they would show up in T-shirts, blue jeans, and sandals, sometimes wearing a cap and gown, often not. In all fairness, the student movement of the 1960s had taken a particular turn at white colleges and affected the students' attitude toward authority in a way that hadn't really taken hold as deeply among black students.

My first honorary degree was from Brandeis University in 1969. Things were so bad, the administration gave us our degrees the night before the exercises because they were unsure of what would happen. Max Murphy, a congressman from Buffalo, New York, had come to talk about the war in Vietnam; Alan Guttmacher, head of Planned Parenthood, was supposed to talk about birth control; and my speech was about race.

At the ceremony, as I looked out over a sea of casually dressed graduates, my eyes rested on the middle section, where a group of black students sat, conspicuous not only because of their skin color but as the only cluster of students wearing their caps and gowns. Had they appeared otherwise, their parents probably would not have believed they were graduating. Their understanding of where they stood in the march of history (black people had endured so much for them to be there), and the responsibility that flowed from that, was multiplied a dozen times over at black colleges. The feeling among students, faculty, and parents was almost religious in its intensity.

I particularly remember speaking at the commencement at Livingstone College, a UNCF member institution in North Carolina, with a graduating class of 125. After I finished, the graduates lined up to proceed across the stage as their names were individually called. One by one, they came up to get their diplomas. The moment arrived for one particular student. He walked across the stage, calm and poised, and as soon as his hand touched the diploma, his mother jumped up and shouted, "Thank you, Jesus! Thank you, Jesus!"

Most of that graduating class was on financial aid. A majority were the first in their families to earn a college degree, and but for Livingstone, the United Negro College Fund, or a student loan, college was an impossible dream. This single mother, a laundress by trade, could not contain her joy. The twelve bishops of the AME Zion Church seated on the stage joined the rest of us in tears of happiness and complete understanding.

I had witnessed this deep well of faith and emotion long before coming to the College Fund. While still at the VEP, I got a call early one spring Sunday morning from Dr. Lucius Pitt, the president of Miles College in Alabama.

"Vernon, it's Lucius Pitt."

"Lucius. It's six o'clock Sunday morning."

"You know, Vernon, it doesn't make sense to have a friend if you can't call on him in time of need."

Knowing full well what time of year it was, I asked, "Lucius, what time is your commencement?"

"Tomorrow at four o'clock."

"Okay, I'll be there."

The scheduled speaker had suffered a severe heart attack the evening before Lucius called. So the following morning, I was on my way.

Miles College sits on a hill in Fairfield, Alabama, on the outskirts of Birmingham. I arrived just ahead of what I thought was going to be a monstrous rainstorm. When we walked outside after lunch, on our way to put on our robes, clusters of storm clouds blotted out the sun in regular, ever shorter, intervals.

As we put on our robes, I suggested, "We're going to have move this inside, right, Lucius? It's going to rain."

"No, it's not," he said.

We got in line for the processional. I am especially fond of academic processions—the more pomp and circumstance, the better.

"It's going to rain," I repeated as we started out the door.

"Not to worry," Lucius said. "It's not going to rain today." He was adamant.

We sat on the platform. I looked up periodically at the heavy clouds that seemed to lower themselves to touch the treetops, but not a drop of rain fell. Lucius's faith was too strong to let it happen. He believed he had worked it out with the Lord not to let it rain that day.

At the end of the ceremony, there was another moment that seemed divinely inspired. Lucius called a student to the platform. As she came forward, the class stood in applause. When she got to his side, Lucius told the story of all the difficulties she had overcome—a cruel marriage, five years to complete her degree, bad credit, and little money. Yet she was graduating at the top of her class because of her faith, perseverance, and intelligence. Then he asked her to sing "You'll Never Walk Alone." It was a soul-wrenching, sublimely joyous moment. Everyone cried. That's what black college commencements meant to me. That's what the United Negro College Fund stood for. This was for me, "my charge to keep, my calling to fulfill."

TAKING THE JOB at the United Negro College Fund meant, of course, that Shirley, Vickee, and I had to adjust to life in the North. We bought a house in Hartsdale, New York, just north of the city in Westchester County, where we were the only black family in the neighborhood.

That didn't bother us, but it seemed to have a strange effect on the white people around us. It was autumn, and we hadn't put up curtains on the picture window in our dining room, so when the leaves fell, our neighbors in the houses behind ours could see inside our house. One day, Shirley was at the drugstore when a white lady who lived nearby saw her and said, "I was just so surprised the other day. I saw you and your husband and your daughter in the house, sitting down to the table having dinner. I did not know black people did that."

When Shirley told me this story, it was my turn to be surprised. It was incomprehensible to me that any family would not sit down to dinner together. What did this white woman think we did at dinnertime? Even though she was an upper-middle-class suburbanite in 1970, she was in many ways as ignorant about black people as my freshman roommates at DePauw had been in 1953. I would find that a lot of white people—even educated white people—were ignorant in this way, and I found it interesting to observe that the ignorance did not run in the other direction: Black people did not share this ignorance about whites. In part, this may have been because so many black people worked as household help, cleaning white people's houses, washing and ironing their clothes, that we didn't think of white people as mysterious. Different, perhaps—but not mysterious. We didn't have as much to learn about them as they, apparently, had to learn about us.

MARCH 1, 1971, was my first-year anniversary at the College Fund, and I had reason to be pleased with how things had gone. We raised $10 million, more than ever in the organization's history. I had settled nicely into my role and had grown very comfortable in New York City. The situation was perfect for thinking about the coming year and how to break our newly minted fund-raising record.

Then on March 9, Whitney Young drowned while in Lagos, Nigeria. This was yet another devastating blow to the civil rights movement and to me personally. Once again I'd lost a comrade in the struggle and a close friend. Whitney's body was flown back to the United States by Chappie James, the first black general in the air force. Waiting in the airport with the Young family and the Urban League family were a number of Whitney's friends and admirers, including Ann and Ted Kneel, Reverend Jesse Jackson, Bayard Rustin, Jackie Robinson, and others, including me.

The funeral was held in Riverside Chapel. Dr. Benjamin Mays and Dr. Howard Thurman gave eulogies before a church filled to capacity. There was a great public outpouring of emotion as the funeral cortege wound its way through Harlem before the final trip to Kentucky for burial.

The speculation about Whitney's successor had started even as his body was being lifted onto the plane. In the air, Bayard Rustin passed me a note. It read, "If you want to succeed Whitney, nod your head or shake your head, yes or no."

I looked over at Rustin and shook my head slowly. Not so much in answer to his query but because I thought it was an inappropriate question at an inappropriate time. The thought had not entered my mind. In the first place, I'd just gotten to the College Fund and was still wrapped up in the thrill of having had such a successful first year. Second, there had been no time to think of it. The tradition in the Urban League was that no one stepped down just as a matter of course. Whitney was a young, vibrant, energetic, and forceful leader who had showed no signs of going anywhere for a long time. His death at the age of forty-nine was a turn of events that no one would have contemplated, and therefore there was really no point before the tragedy to even dream of the possibility. Certainly the few days between the announcement of his death and his funeral were not conducive to any considerations along those lines. Besides, Sterling Tucker, the head of the Washington Urban League, was known to be very close to Whitney and instantly seemed the most natural man to take his place. I simply chose not to deal with the issue or with Rustin. Later that day, he said to me, "You're making a big mistake."

I went back to work.

JOHN D. ROCKEFELLER III invited me to visit him at 30 Rockefeller Plaza. It had been a little over a year since I'd come there to
ask him to reconsider his decision to leave the board of the United
Negro College Fund. When I arrived, Douglas Dillon, the chairman
of the Rockefeller Foundation and a former secretary of the treasury,
was also present. Mr. Rockefeller said, "Mr. Jordan, you were in
here a year ago and you told me you would do it without me, and
you did. You've done a very good job. Now, I want to ask you to do
something for me."

"What is that?"

"I want you to become a Rockefeller Foundation trustee."

"Mr. Rockefeller, I've got better judgment than you. The answer
is yes."

There are some opportunities in life that do not demand study
and consultation. This was one of them.

A FEW WEEKS AFTER WHITNEY'S DEATH, Enid Baird asked me
out to lunch. Enid had been with the Urban League a very long time,
working as Whitney's executive assistant, and before that as secretary to Lester Granger, who was Whitney's predecessor. In the wake
of Whitney's death, Enid had been chosen to be the executive assistant to the search committee, which, as things turned out, was
headed up my friend and mentor, Louis Martin.

When Enid asked if we could meet for lunch, I had a pretty good
idea what would be the general topic of conversation. "Of course," I
said.

We met. "I'm going to do something that's very unprofessional
and maybe unethical," she said. "But I have to tell you that you're
the man to succeed Whitney."

Although I was pleased by her compliment, I played it down,
though I knew with Louis Martin in charge, the possibility that I

might be chosen wasn't entirely far-fetched, even if it seemed clear that Sterling Tucker was the front-runner.

"You're kidding me."

Enid said, "No, I promise you. They're going to have this search, but they're going to end up with you, Vernon. Mark my words."

Over the next few weeks, I had the sense that people were talking behind my back, because they were. At a glittering dinner for the National Committee Against Discrimination in Housing, at which the beautiful Myrna Loy was the star attraction, David Rockefeller put his hand on my shoulder and said, apropos of nothing, "You're the right candidate."

I knew, but I asked him what he was talking about, hoping to draw him out a bit.

He said, "Never mind. You'll see."

Later, the call came from Louis Martin sometime in the beginning of May, asking if I'd come to the Waldorf-Astoria to talk to the search committee. He mentioned a specific date and time.

"I can't do that," I said.

"Why not?"

"I've got to speak at a College Fund lunch in Rochester." That community had strongly supported the UNCF over the years.

"Cancel it," Louie demanded.

"I can't just cancel," I said.

"We want to talk to you about the most important job in America," he said.

"Louie, I already have the most important job in America. I cannot cancel this."

Louie laughed and said, "Give me a moment." Then he hung up.

He called me back a few minutes later. "All right, you son of a bitch, what time is your speech?"

"It's exactly at noon."

"Well, can you arrange to speak and then leave, let them have lunch without you?"

I said yes.

"Do that, and we'll send a plane to Rochester to get you." Then

he used one of his favorite phrases—part serious, part sardonic—
"You're a great American."

I went to Rochester, gave my speech, made my apologies, and flew
back to New York. Whitney's driver, Carl Payne, a former New
York City police officer, picked me up at the airport. When I got settled in the car, he said, "I just want you to know that I know what's
going on."

"What do you mean, you know what's going on?"

"I know what this is about. And I hope you're going to say yes."

The search committee consisted of Louis Martin, Dan Collins,
Wendell Freeman, Charles Hamilton, Ronald Davenport, Esa Pos-
ton, James Linen, and Lindsey Kimball from the Rockefeller Brothers Fund. They began by talking about the Urban League, what
Whitney had meant to the organization, and what they were looking for in his successor. After a while, someone, I don't remember
who, asked point-blank if I wanted to run the National Urban
League.

"How can I say I want something that hasn't been offered to
me?" I asked, hoping to make them come to the point.

They asked me to talk about one of the most meaningful events in
my life. My thoughts immediately went to my grandfather, whose
only wish was to be able to go to the bathroom inside before he
died. We talked a little more, and finally Louie became exasperated.
"Let's just cut this out," he said. "You know why you're here. We're
offering you the Urban League job."

"I accept."

I had no idea about salary or benefits, had never seen a job description, knew nothing of a personal nature about the job. But I
knew in my soul that if I didn't say yes, I would regret it the rest of
my life. This was very much like the circumstance I faced when
choosing between staying at the NAACP or going to the Southern
Regional Council. My current position gave me great satisfaction,
and I was doing the job well. There was every indication that things
would continue in that vein.

As I viewed the Southern Regional Council position as a step up, I
viewed the National Urban League in the same way, not in terms of

fundamental importance but in the breadth of subject areas upon which I could have an effect. The College Fund job was primarily fund-raising, marketing, and public relations, with several program-related activities. The Urban League, however, was advocacy—which meant action—constituency-based services to black people.

Whitney, whom I believe has never gotten his due as a significant figure in black history, had moved the Urban League into new and uncharted waters. I was anxious to pick up where he had left off. Before his time, the Urban League really was an organization of social workers rendering crucial social services at the local level. It wasn't viewed as a civil rights organization. Whitney was one of the organizers and speakers at the March on Washington in 1963, speaking out on the issues of the day and joining forces with other civil rights leaders whenever the need arose. He galvanized the Urban League constituency and made them believe they were a natural and vital element in the drive for black progress.

Here was my ready-made constituency, concerned not with one narrow issue, but with the health, welfare, education, legal status—literally every aspect—of black American life. Everything I had worked for, all that I wanted to do up until that point, the lessons learned from my restless moves from one job to another could be used in service of the Urban League. I simply had to say yes. "No" was not an option.

After accepting the job, I stayed a while with the search committee and had a drink to celebrate. Then I walked out of the Waldorf and down Park Avenue to Grand Central Terminal to catch my train home. By then the adrenaline powering my day had worn off, and I was suddenly very hungry. There was time enough before my train for a quick beer and sandwich at a place right there in the station. And whom did I see leaving the restaurant but Roy and Minnie Wilkins. It was providential.

Roy said, "Vernon, I hear you're the leading candidate for Whitney's job."

"Well, I don't know about that," I said, not revealing what had just happened.

Roy went on, "I want to tell two things. First, you're really an

NAACP man and you should succeed me. Second, I'm not ready to go, yet."

We had a few more words, and I took the train to Hartsdale.

THE BOARD OF TRUSTEES of the National Urban League had to approve the search committee's selection. There was a gap between the day I accepted the job and when my appointment would be official. In that time, the committee asked that I remain silent about our proceedings, which was a tricky proposition because word of what had happened, or some version of it, spread quickly.

The weekend before the vote, I got a call from Sterling Tucker, who had heard about my interview with the search committee. "I understand you've got the Urban League job. But I want to hear it from you, because if it's true, I'll withdraw from contention." I stayed silent.

Then there was John Cashin, from Huntsville, Alabama, an activist in the civil rights movement. He called me up and said, "I need to know something from you right now. I have some other people on the line who want to know whether you want the Urban League job," implying that they could somehow deliver it to me if I wanted it.

Later on, at a College Fund event in Washington, Belford Lawson, a prominent attorney there, asked, "Well, Vernon, who do you think is going to succeed Whitney?"

Of course I couldn't say anything.

Belford went on, "I promise you one thing. Whoever it is will be an Alpha man," meaning a member of the Alpha Phi Alpha fraternity. "It's always been an Alpha man. George Edmund Haines was an Alpha. Eugene Kinkle Jones was an Alpha, Lester Granger and Whitney were Alphas."

The day of the board of trustees' vote, I waited for the call in my office, one floor below what had been Whitney's office. They called me that afternoon, and I walked from Fifty-second Street between Park and Madison over to the Time Inc. building on Sixth Avenue— on that day a very long walk indeed. So much had happened in my life in such a short time, and I turned that over in my head as I went along. I also thought of Butler T. Henderson, whom I'd just recruited from Atlanta to serve as my new deputy at the College Fund. How would he fare? What could I do to make his transition easier? There was no fear about my coming position, just an underlying concern about the one I was leaving behind. But the matter had been settled, and I was going to go forward. Once at my destination, I stepped into a room full of smiling and clapping trustees.

They had arranged a press conference and a cocktail party right there in the Time Inc. building. As we had drinks, I got the first congratulatory call from Clifford J. Alexander, Jr., who had been head of the Equal Opportunity Commission under Lyndon Johnson and would go on to become the first black secretary of the army in Jimmy Carter's administration.

And about a week after the announcement, I saw Belford Lawson, who said, "You son of bitch! You knew all along." I recalled his comment about his fraternity, and I was proud that for the first time, Omega Psi Phi, my fraternity, had one of its members as executive director of the National Urban League.

Very often we think a particular turn of events is about one thing when it is really about something else. The College Fund, as important as it was, turned out to have been a scrimmage for the Urban League job. I am convinced that if I had not been executive director of the United Negro College Fund, I would never have been executive director, and then president, of the National Urban League. There was no way I could have gone from the VEP to being Whitney Young's successor. What seemed in 1970 to be a steady platform to stand on for a while turned out to have been a door that opened into a world that would take me far beyond anything I could have imagined.

CHAPTER 11

BUILDING BRIDGES

DURING ONE OF OUR MANY CONVERSATIONS, Whitney Young spoke of the loneliness of his position as head of the National Urban League. In the midst of the endless fund-raising events, the countless speeches before supporters, the camaraderie of like-minded individuals, he was a man alone at the end of the day. It is a cliché, which like all clichés carries a fundamental truth: Leadership is a lonely business.

Being at the helm means dealing with outside expectations, reasonable and not, while at the same time placing enough distance between yourself and others to be able to keep your own counsel. Given my nature, the basic solitude of that posture was not a problem. I would have carved out a private sphere for myself no matter what, as I've always tried to do wherever I've been. Still, at times the isolation can make for some difficult moments.

In Whitney's case, the loneliness may have been even more pronounced, given the course he set during his time at the Urban League—attempting to move the organization beyond its social-service orientation into the more generalized arena of civil rights. When Whitney began that process, he was taking on decades of institutional traditions built since the League's formation in 1911. He had to contend not only with the "foot soldiers" within the group who, by the time he arrived, had a well-developed sense of the League's mission and how they fit into the program but also with the League's white patrons, an even more delicate operation.

It's always a tricky business when black organizations manage to garner white support. Many have foundered on the rocks of submerged conflicts between blacks and whites who, on the surface, are working for the same goal but whose interests and deeply felt needs may be fundamentally opposed. Whites of goodwill join the groups, but sometimes blacks, after gaining power and confidence, feel they must assert authority by demanding leadership positions or fashioning agendas that may alienate their white supporters. The cultures often clash.

A leader of an interracial organization must walk a fine line. If he or she is black, leaning too far in one direction risks the charge of being called an "Uncle Tom" or "Aunt Sally" by blacks within the group and those who are outside observers. If one goes in the other direction, one risks being labeled insensitive or ungrateful by whites. The dilemma isn't really surprising. Given our history, blacks and whites have not had many opportunities to work together as equals. We are still, even now, trying to find a way to do that in schools, in the workplace, in local and national institutions—in all arenas of American life. This will be the work of the twenty-first century.

All experiences must be viewed in the context of their times. Whitney had his, and I had mine. The defining influence on my tenure at the Urban League was that it spanned a difficult period of adjustment for the civil rights movement. To put it in terms of metaphor, the civil rights movement of the 1950s and 1960s was about defining and conferring the right to check into the hotel. The movement of the 1970s was about obtaining the wherewithal to check out—to have the resources to pay the bill. Many people thought (and more whites than blacks thought this way) that defining the right was sufficient. But blacks had been so left out of, so excluded from equal participation in the economic bounty of American society that affirmative steps had to be taken to bring us into the mainstream. It would not happen without concerted activity, and without that effort all the gains we had made on paper would be more symbolic than real.

Even as the emphasis of the movement shifted—without some people noticing the change—there was a perceived vacuum of leadership. When I arrived at the Urban League, Martin Luther King, Jr., had been dead for three years and the young Reverend Jesse Jackson, his most natural successor, was just coming into his own as a leading figure in the black community. The NAACP had lost some of its clout, taking a back seat to the strident tone of the Black Power movement as the debate between the militant and accommodationist stance within the black community played itself out in everything from politics to the Ali-Frazier boxing match.

Ironically, despite the militancy of rhetoric during the early 1970s, the true intensity of the civil rights movement of the 1960s had all but evaporated. Leadership by the dramatic act, so crucial and effective against very specific racist laws, met very different prospects in a world where legalized discrimination no longer existed. If the target was a law that prevented blacks from eating in a certain place, one could demonstrate the unfairness of that by showing up, trying to order food, and being turned away or beaten. It was the same with voting: Show up to register and be turned away or threatened. In that context, direct action was not mere symbolism. This was the real thing.

With "written down," de jure white supremacy out of the law books but de facto advantages continuing in the culture, the question of how to respond to it became much harder. In some ways, we have been grappling with this new situation since the 1970s. What does black leadership mean, and how does it express itself in a society where the remaining barriers are very real, though amorphous, ever-shifting, and still dangerous to black aspirations?

In 1971, the old view of black leadership was still very much in evidence. First, there was the notion that there had to be a "leader" of the black community. What single individual would step up and take the mantle of Martin Luther King, Jr.? This was very much the mindset of the times. Certainly, members of the media fostered the concept, anxious as they were (as they are now) to anoint one black person as the leader of all black people. The media took a great interest in me from the very first press conference announcing my succession to Whitney Young. This was nothing for me to complain about. The initial coverage was extremely favorable, and it went a long way toward strengthening my hand in the beginning stages of my stewardship.

It seemed clear that what could be called "the establishment" in American life wanted to treat me as a "leader" of black America. Not long after my appointment, President Richard Nixon very publicly invited me to the White House for a one-on-one chat. Two years into his presidency, he was still mistrusted by black Americans for having ridden into office on the so-called "Southern strategy" that had played to conservative whites' anxieties about the rise of black power and influence. Any outreach to blacks could only have done him good at that point.

When I received his invitation, my main thought was that I had been invited by the president of the United States to come to the White House because I was Whitney Young's successor at the Urban League, and I knew that Nixon had had great respect for Whitney. I knew before going in that I had to convey to him as strongly and respectfully as I could that Whitney and I were not the same person and that any good working relationship between us would have to take that into account.

For me to delve into Richard Nixon's complex nature at this point would be to explore already well-mapped territory. It is worth pointing out, however, that unlike other prominent members of the Republican Party, Nixon had been an early supporter of civil rights. In 1960, when he first ran for president, there had not been much difference between him and John F. Kennedy on this score. In fact, Nixon's record of speaking out when it was not politically expedient may even have been a little better. He was rewarded for this in the 1960 election with a sizable proportion of the black vote. Nixon actually carried the black vote in Fulton County, Georgia, during that election despite Martin Luther King, Sr.'s endorsement of John Kennedy.

The political landscape had changed over the decade of the 1960s, and Nixon, astute politician that he was, adjusted to the demands of the new era, particularly at campaign time in 1968 when he talked about "law and order" (a code phrase for keeping blacks in line) and the "silent majority" (his nod to lower- and middle-class white resentment of the changes brought by the various social revolutions of the 1960s). Even with that, perhaps because of his Quaker background, Nixon was much better on civil rights for blacks than many members of his party during his time and since. In any case, in my mind, my job was not to make a judgment.

I walked into the Oval Office to find the president, at the last moment, reading a copy of the "Man in the News" article that had recently run about me in the New York Times. When he saw me come in, he hurriedly stuffed the clipping into his pocket and stuck out his hand in greeting.

I returned the gesture, and we sat down on either side of the fireplace. After he welcomed me, I pulled out the photograph from the day of his visit to DePauw during my senior year. The picture showed a much younger Nixon with just the beginning of what would become the famous receding hairline, and a much younger, thinner Vernon Jordan with a head full of hair.

He looked at it and said, "That's me!"

"That's you," I confirmed.

"Where is this?"

"Mr. President, this is DePauw University. This is where I went to college. You came there in 1956 to help dedicate the new library. I was the headwaiter at Longden Hall. That's me, and my fellow headwaiter at Mason Hall, Pat Sharpe."

Nixon had no memory of this whatsoever, which was not a surprise, given the thousands of events of that sort he had attended over the course of his political life.

"Mr. President," I said, "This photograph was taken when both of us were on our way up."

Nixon loved it. It made him think back to his youth. He was not a rich kid, and he was very proud of the fact that he had worked all his life. We were alike in that sense, and he appreciated the similarity.

After I'd thanked him for speaking at Whitney's burial in Kentucky and for the federal dollars the Urban League had received, we got down to the message I wanted to deliver. It was important, I said, for him to understand that Whitney and I were different. We had different backgrounds, different orientations. We were at different stages in our lives—Whitney was almost fifty when he died. I was thirty-five. I said, "Mr. President, if there are policies of yours with which I disagree, they will be addressed. From time to time you may not like what I say, or how or where I say it. I hope we can work through our differences when those occasions arise."

Nixon was very receptive, though there was never any real chemistry between us. From the outset, it was clear that he was a man who would accommodate me and my requests only if he found it to his political advantage. I don't think Nixon personalized the relationships that grew out of his political life. In this he was very different from Lyndon Johnson, for whom everything was personal. With Nixon, it was all about "the deal," which was fine with me because I felt the same way about him.

We talked on, and the president said at one point, "If there is anything you want from this administration, John Ehrlichman is your man." In the Nixon White House, Ehrlichman sat at the left hand of the president and H. R. Haldeman sat at the right. So I was off, I thought, to a very good start.

And I was. The Urban League did have generally favorable experiences with the Nixon administration, although my open association with Ehrlichman raised eyebrows in some quarters. The press took note of our tennis dates. One day, on my way to work, I was confronted in the elevator at the League office by a young black man with a big Afro, dressed in a dashiki.

"Good morning," I said.

"Mr. Jordan, I'm glad to see you because I want to say something to you."

"Yes?"

"You can't be my leader playing tennis at the White House with John Ehrlichman."

"Which federal program are you on?" I asked.

"The Labor Education Advancement Program."

"How much do you make?"

"Twenty thousand a year."

I said, "I'm playing tennis with John Ehrlichman so you can continue to be a $20,000-a-year militant. Do you understand that?"

He completely misapprehended the demands of leadership and the nature of politics in general. For him, my playing tennis with Ehrlichman meant that I adhered to the tenets of whatever he believed was Ehrlichman's philosophy, or that I simply—or simplemindedly—didn't recognize our points of difference. This wasn't true, and I knew it, but my exchange with the young man in the elevator was exasperating. If he felt that way, there must have been multiples of others with a similar view. In the end, I couldn't let that get in the way of my doing what I believed was in the best interests of the Urban League and its constituents.

It is possible, and sometimes absolutely imperative, to work with people with whom you have fundamental disagreements. Very little would be accomplished in the world—in government, business, family, anywhere—if this were not true. On the importance of the Urban League's mission, there was common ground, and the president of the United States had designated Ehrlichman as the person to go to for the sake of helping to fulfill that mission. So I went, and I had no qualms about going.

The end of this story came in 1981 and shows the truth of the saying "Things could always be worse." Ronald Reagan had taken office and began slashing every federal program he could find, even ones like the Labor Education Advancement Program, which actually made money for the government. For every dollar put into that program, the government got back four dollars as otherwise unemployed individuals were turned into working and taxpaying citizens. Its success did not matter; under Reagan, it had to go.

With less federal money at my disposal, I took on the task of going through the various Urban League programs and making the cuts. My friend on the elevator was on the list. He came to see me.

"What do you want?" I asked.

"I want to ask a question. You know I'm on the list to be cut."

"Yes, I know that."

"Well," he said, "do you think you can get a tennis game at the White House?"

I have never doubted that it was right for me to have worked with the Nixon administration to maintain the viability of the National Urban League. Over the coming years, not all decisions would be so clear-cut. I remember vividly one particular moment on a fundraising tour in Seattle, Washington. We were all set for an event at the Rainier Club, high on a hill overlooking the city—just a spectacular presentation of Seattle's physical beauty. This was a "cultivation" for the National Urban League, and as was my usual practice, I had invited the chairmen and executives of the local chapters—in this case, Seattle, Tacoma, and Portland—so that they could gain exposure and knowledge of the process. There was every prospect of a successful day when Gary Bloom, my director of development, rushed down the stairs of the club just before noon to tell me that Margaret Anderson, a white woman who was the treasurer and a founding member of the Tacoma Urban League, would not be allowed at the lunch.

"Why not?" I asked. Gary explained that the Rainier Club, like many of its counterparts in cities across the country, did not allow women into the club. This was a contingency that perhaps should have been, but was not, foreseen. Recrimination was pointless at that moment. Instead, a decision had to be made, and very quickly.

"So what are you going to do, Mister Equal Opportunity?" Anderson asked. My mind raced as I weighed various responses. I could refuse to go through with the fund-raiser, in protest of the discriminatory rule and say that if Anderson were not allowed in, I would not speak or eat there. Certainly that stance would have drawn the attention of the media, and, in some quarters I may have been a hero. Of course, other observers might cast me as a demagogue, using our mistake—we could have known of their policy beforehand—to garner publicity for myself.

What about League members? Our credo was nondiscrimination, but I knew there were many among my constituents who didn't view gender exclusion as being on a par with racial discrimination. Black churches all across America had separate Bible study classes for men and women. There were single-sex institutions among the historically black colleges, such as Morehouse (all male) and Spelman (all female). Did I have the right, without discussion, to unilaterally decide to forgo the benefits of this fund-raiser? I decided to go ahead with the event as planned, without Anderson.

"Margaret," I said, "I'd like you to go shopping."

Tom Dixon, the executive director of the Tacoma Urban League, spoke up to say, "If my treasurer can't go, I'm not going."

Anderson then said, "Tom, what's going on at this luncheon is more important to the League than whether or not I'm there. Go to the luncheon." And he did.

At the beginning of my speech, I talked about Anderson's exclusion, hoping it might one day serve as an item of evidence as to why the club should change its policy. Later on, the club did make the change. Whether this episode figured in the discussion, I don't know. It seemed to me at the time that I had split the difference just the right way, but the decision haunts me even now. It is entirely possible that today, having gone through the 1970s, 1980s, and 1990s with the change in sensibilities about discrimination against women, if I were the head of an organization like the Urban League, I would have responded differently. Nothing is certain except my present uncertainty about the way I decided to resolve that situation.

GOING TO THE URBAN LEAGUE was the second time I had responsibility for a national organization. But the situations at the Urban League and the United Negro College Fund could not have been more different. Upon coming to the College Fund, I found a good deal of chaos and some evidence of a bad atmosphere. Though reeling from the sudden loss of a beloved leader, the Urban League was very much intact and functional. We had a good board, which had been brought closer together by the trauma of Whitney's death and the search for a successor. All down the line, things were running smoothly. My initial task was to get to know the people, to assess their strengths and weaknesses, and to reassure them that the ship would still sail smoothly.

In a way, I symbolized the shift in emphasis that Whitney had set in motion. Until my appointment, every leader of the Urban League had been a professional social worker, largely leading other professional social workers. I was a lawyer. From that perspective alone, there was ample reason for the rank and file to view me with some degree of skepticism. What did this lawyer have in mind for the future?

Along with my background in law, I began my time at the Urban League with different arrows in my quiver. Because of my previous jobs, I was reasonably known in the foundation community and the corporate world. These were my ready-made bases from which to build upon the work that Whitney had started.

The one important place where I was not widely experienced or known was in government circles. I'd been on two presidential advisory commissions, and I had spent a few months at the Office of Economic Opportunity in 1965, but that didn't approach the intensity of my exposure to the world of foundations and corporate America. What few contacts I had in government were important and helpful at the start.

Early on I received a valuable piece of advice from Lyndon Johnson, whom I'd known since my days serving on the White House Council to Fulfill These Rights. Now out of office, he hosted a conference on civil rights in Austin, Texas, and I was invited to give the keynote address. Johnson was near the end of his life. And here he was, the hated figure of a huge segment of the youth of that day, sporting that generation's badge of rebellion: long hair falling down over the back of his shirt collar. After my speech, Johnson took me aside. "I had a real reason for asking you to come here and speak. You and I have a lot in common. I grew up poor and white in the South. You grew up poor and black in the South." He went on, going into territory that I knew affected him deeply. "We were both doing all right with our careers, and then both of us succeeded great men under tragic circumstances. Kennedy was assassinated, and that put me right on the spot. Nobody had great expectations of me. Except for Vietnam, I was a pretty good president."

I agreed with him, and he continued.

"You can be one hell of a leader at the Urban League. And that's another reason I invited you here—to help you get started. But I've got some advice for you, and I'm giving you advice that I couldn't have taken myself: Get your own people! I couldn't get rid of Bobby, and I couldn't get rid of Mac Bundy, and I couldn't get rid of McNamara because the nation was in mourning for this young president. But you can get rid of anybody and get your own people in there."

He was right. The eyes of the world were on Johnson in November 1963, and he had deferred to those sensibilities at some cost to himself, which left him to govern for a time with people whose primary loyalties were to another—actually to the memory of another who would remain forever young and attractive, forever martyred and mourned. "I could not get my people in there right away; you ought to," he insisted.

Not long after that conference, I had another Johnson moment. I was in my office when I was told that President Johnson was on the telephone.

I picked up my phone. "Good morning, Mr. President," I said.

"Vernon?"

"Yes, Mr. President."

"I did a lot for your people."

"Yes, Mr. President."

"Well, I did a lot for your people, didn't I?"

"Yes, sir."

"Goddammit, Vernon, I did a lot for your people."

"Of course, you did, Mr. President. But why are you calling me?"

He said, "I'm calling you because my boy Chuck"—his son-in-law, Charles Robb—"is the head of that forum that damn fool Kennedy boy started at the University of Virginia Law School. And he's having his first forum, and I want you to speak for him, you hear? I did a lot for your people."

"Mr. President, I'll go."

That was very much Lyndon Johnson's way.

I also got some useful advice from another legendary politician, Mayor Richard J. Daley of Chicago. During my first appearance at the traditional Equal Opportunity Day luncheon at the Chicago Urban League, I was seated next to Mayor Daley on the dais. He inquired as to how I was doing in my new job. I said, "Well, Mr.

Mayor, I'm trying to find out where the bodies are buried and trying to get control of the situation."

Daley said, "Control is the word, son. Control is the word." Mayor Daley was right.

One complication to my settling in quickly at the Urban League was that I was still the executive director of the United Negro College Fund even after I had technically become the executive director of the Urban League. When I accepted the job, the Urban League search committee members said that they had planned to have me start right away. That was not possible. I felt uncomfortable enough about departing from the College Fund after just one year, and there was no way I could leave it totally in the lurch by walking out with the equivalent of two weeks' notice. As much as the search committee did not like it, we worked out a deal in which Harold Sims, Whitney's deputy, would continue to serve as acting executive director for seven months, until the end of the year. My tenure would officially begin on January 1, 1972.

This was a somewhat awkward arrangement because Harold had also been considered for the job. As the months wore on and he became more accustomed to running the Urban League, even as an interim measure, I could sense him holding onto the reins. At one point, he floated the notion that we might run the Urban League together. "We could make the greatest civil rights team in history!" he said.

I had no interest in that idea.

While I was shuttling back and forth between these two organizations, that August the Urban League held its annual conference in Detroit. As the acting executive director, Harold was to make the keynote address. Well before my appointment, the actor Ossie Davis had signed on to speak at the closing dinner. Now that there was a designated successor to Whitney, many Urban League members wanted to hear the new guy, and I was more than happy to be added to the program.

Ossie Davis spoke first, and he was his usual entertaining and insightful self. The audience was very much taken with him. But throughout the course of his remarks, he kept referring to me as Vernon "Jerden," a pronunciation common in some parts of the South. I decided to have a little fun with it. So when I got up to speak, I began by saying, "Ossie Davis comes from Waycross, Georgia. That's in Ware County. Down in Ware County, they pronounce it 'Jerden.' I'm from the city, and where I come from we pronounce it 'Jordan,' not 'Jerden.'" We all had a good laugh. And then as to my succession, keeping with the notion that I wanted them to be clear about who I was, I quoted a line from a popular television comedian of the day, Flip Wilson: "What you see is what you get." The audience laughed again, but I was serious.

I knew what I had to do that night, standing there in the place of a man so many of them had known and loved, and who had been taken from them in such a cruel way. My speech included a tribute to Whitney that was an acknowledgment of their pain and my own. It carried promises that I would try to live up to the very best of what he stood for and to help the Urban League realize the dreams I knew he had for the organization.

Earlier in the week, in the Urban League's General Assembly, some of the more militant members had challenged me, demanding to know what I was going to do about their concerns. Some of their questions I answered, some I didn't, trying to establish that I wasn't going to be driven by any faction. Between that session and the speech, I believe I managed to convey what I knew was the most important message: The ship was going to sail, and all would be well.

Given the undertow of resistance that naturally occurs whenever there is a change of leadership at an organization, the board empowered me to begin my duties three months earlier than we had originally planned. There was a lot on our agenda, and one major item in particular—an Equal Opportunity Day Dinner to honor Whitney posthumously. That event would take place in the fall. Then there was the next general conference in St. Louis the following spring, well into my tenure. I'd been to Urban League conferences before, but I knew nothing about how to run one. So for the last three months of 1971, I was actually running two national organizations, helping the College Fund raise money and planning for the reorganization of the Urban League.

I had a lot of help making the transition. Before I took over the Urban League, the board arranged for me to go to a conference, which turned out to be very valuable, run by the American Management Association. The attendees were mostly corporate executives who had been promoted to management positions. Even though we were a not-for-profit entity, the basic issues of effective management were very much the same as they would have been in a large corporation. It is a terrible mistake to assume that charitable organizations should be held to a lesser standard of professionalism and competence because their primary focus is nonprofit. The board and I were on the same wavelength on this issue, and my attendance at the management conference sent an important message to all members of the general staff.

Then there was the support from an informal network of friends. Dr. Kenneth B. Clark, whom I'd known since my time at the VEP, and Jean Fairfax of the Legal Defense Fund convened a meeting at Clark's home. Andrew Young, Carl Holman, Dorothy Height, Jimmie Booker, Lisle Carter, and Highland Lewis came, and over a two-day period we discussed the challenges confronting me as my tenure began.

This was a very generous gesture that showed me that they wanted to be helpful to the Urban League and to me. This was a tough time for the civil rights movement, and they wanted to ensure that the League would continue its momentum. Their interest and magnanimity meant a lot to me, and much of what they told me was thought-provoking. There was, however, a problem. Intelligent and earnest as they were, none of them had actually seen the League from the inside. Kenneth Clark had provided an ear for Whitney Young during his time at the League, and I'm sure this gave him an idea of what running the organization was like in theory. The fact is that I found the actual practice of running the Urban League very different from any theories.

In the first place, like plugging a different variable into an equation, my presence altered the final answer about the best way to proceed. Naturally, League staffers responded to me in a different way than they had to Whitney. And when they didn't, adjustments had to be made. Betty Whaley, a prominent and important staff member who had worked very closely with Whitney, gave me problems from the beginning. She had supported Sterling Tucker, the head of the Washington Urban League, to succeed Whitney. I anticipated that there might be some difficulties because of that, especially when she assured me that Whitney had consulted her about everything.

Once, she came to tell me about a developing problem and presented several choices for a resolution. "You can do 'A,' 'B,' or 'C,'" she said after laying out everything.

"I think we'll do 'B,'" I said.

"Whitney would have done 'C,'" Betty announced.

Nothing that had been said in our conclave at Kenneth Clark's place or at the American Management Association meeting told me how to deal with a move like that. She was acting out of her pain at the loss of a valued friend and boss and not a little resentment at the appearance of his successor. That was understandable, but this type of thing couldn't continue if we wanted to do our jobs effectively. Something had to give.

"I want to tell you two things," I said to her. "First, Whitney is not here. Second, the sooner you find that out, the longer you can stay here." Betty never fully adjusted to my arrival, and within a year's time, she had resigned.

There was nothing pathological about any of this. Complex currents of grief, apprehension, and hope erupt whenever any institution suddenly loses a leader. Under the circumstances, I used my working group's suggestions whenever I was able, but for the most part I had to figure things out as I went along. Later on I would learn of the complaint among some of my advisers that I wasn't checking in with them as often as they had expected. Ken was apparently the most unhappy. I was sorry for that, but once I started to run the League, I knew very deeply that it was, in fact, my job—and my duty—to run it as I saw best.

Enid Baird, Whitney's longtime secretary and assistant, gave me my most frightening moment during those early months. She sent me a letter of resignation, based on her view that it was my right to choose my own person to serve in that capacity. This was characteristic of Enid, who was without a doubt one of the best and most professional people with whom I've ever worked. She thought she was helping me, but I was extremely alarmed at the prospect of losing her because I knew she would be an essential component of any success I would have at the League.

As soon as I received the letter, I dashed to her office and explained that while I appreciated the professionalism of the gesture, she would not be doing me a favor by leaving. In fact, it would be disastrous.

"You can't do that," I said. "You have to stay and help me get through this."

Enid was near tears. "If you hadn't come up here and said that, I would have died," she said.

My instincts about Enid were on target. Over the years, she was beyond marvelous. She knew everyone who had anything to do with the Urban League, what they were doing, and why. A very good, solid writer, when she brought me the morning mail, she would have already drafted the responses because she knew exactly what to say and how to say it. It would be impossible to calculate the value to one in my position of having a person like that as a colleague.

Once I was fully in the position to take Lyndon Johnson's advice, staff reorganization became a major priority. Where Whitney had one deputy director, I had two: one for administration, Alexander Allen, a longtime Urban Leaguer; and another for programs, Adolph Holmes, a retired military officer who was already on the program staff. Next, it occurred to me that the League should have a full-time general counsel, something it had never had before. My dealings with corporate America heavily influenced me on this score. When all was said and done, we were, in fact, a corporation with some of the same needs, problems, and potential areas of exposure as other corporations. We were in contract negotiations with governments, and there were many other legal issues that needed attention as well. Could we afford not to have our own lawyer in house? Ronald H. Brown, an Urban League staffer who had recently finished law school, more than fit the bill. Brown would in later years go on to become the head of the Democratic National Committee and then the first black secretary of commerce in our country's history. This was, I thought, the perfect set: Allen, the longtime member, represented the old Urban League; Holmes represented the new Urban League; and Ron Brown represented youth.

Dan Davis, a gifted speechwriter on staff, who had performed brilliantly for Whitney, continued in this crucial role, and along with Jimmy Williams, director of communications, rounded out the senior management. With my executive staff in order, we were now ready to go full-speed ahead.

M Y FAMILY MOVED FORWARD AS WELL. Shirley, who never lost her taste for adventure, had been very excited about moving to New York, even though it was a major change that left us without an extended family network to help smooth out the difficulties caused by her illness. While I settled into the Urban League, she and Vickee were adjusting to life in Westchester County. As things turned out, the two of them were spending a good deal of time without me.

None of us could have known it when we first moved to New York, but my days at the College Fund were the start of a professional career with almost constant travel at its core. Things reached epic proportions at the Urban League, where I was on the road almost 180 days out of a year. I loved it, although it was burdensome at times. Moving from one place to the next, one project to the next, fit well with my innate restlessness. Then there was the inevitable longing for home and respite from strangers, however friendly and supportive.

On one of my trips to Little Rock, Arkansas, in 1973, I met an up-and-coming young politician named Bill Clinton. We sat and talked after my speech at an Urban League dinner. Clinton struck me as very intelligent and ambitious, and I knew even then that one day he was going to be president of the United States. I could see that he was aggressive, sure of himself, and genuine. It was clear that he had a deep, caring concern about race, and so there was an immediate affinity between us. We were both lawyers who had returned to the South because we wanted to do something about the issue of race.

He was, of course, less directly involved in that effort than I was, but his interest was obvious—and that is why he had shown up at the Urban League dinner.

Clinton's interest in, and empathy for, racial issues often came forward, even in light moments. I recall one such incident from a party, years later, at Katharine Graham's house on Martha's Vineyard. The singer Carly Simon was there, and she had entertained the other guests with a few songs, which I guess served as inspiration for what followed. After she finished, Clinton and I began to sing, a capella, the black national anthem, "Lift Ev'ry Voice and Sing." We sang the whole song, just the two of us. Someone took a photograph of us singing, which Clinton later inscribed, "To Vernon, from the only WASP who knows the lyrics."

I had met Clinton's wife, Hillary Rodham, in 1969 at a League of Women Voters event at Colorado State University in Fort Collins, Colorado. I was still at the Voter Education Project at the time and had come there to give a speech. She came up to me afterward and introduced herself. We liked each other at once. So it was very good to re-establish the connection with her as well.

Of course my prediction that Bill Clinton was going to be a major figure in American politics turned out to be correct. I followed his career as he rose to the governorship of his state in 1978. When he lost his bid for re-election in 1980, I went down to Little Rock to see him and Hillary. Their daughter, Chelsea, was still a crawling baby. Hillary made grits for breakfast, and we sat and talked about what had happened. Both of them were very much affected by the loss but were determined to rebound. I gave them a piece of advice. Hillary, I said, had to become "Hillary Clinton" and not "Hillary Rodham," as she had been known up until that point. It might have been acceptable in places like Manhattan or Washington, D.C., for a wife to keep her maiden name, but in Arkansas at that time it was off-putting to the average voter. They took that advice and made a number of other adjustments of their own, and Clinton recaptured the statehouse in the next election.

I was very acutely aware that my constant traveling was helping to shape a childhood for my daughter very different from the one I had known. This nagged at me. There were no Sunday morning walks to church, no drives to the countryside to visit relatives, no Southern sense of community—things that stand out in my memory, helping me create (as many of us do about our childhoods) a version of a golden age.

We did have our own rituals, though. I made sure to limit the weekends I was away so that I would not miss going to the Couples Club, a group formed by upwardly mobile blacks who had joined the very new exodus of the black middle class to the suburbs. The club meetings were held at different homes throughout the bedroom communities north of the city—Yonkers, Mt. Vernon, Scarsdale, Hartsdale. We would not have been accepted en masse into area country clubs, even if we had desired it, so we fashioned our own social world and were very happy in it. There were games, good food, conversation. Shirley, always very sociable, loved these gatherings. I tried hard to be home for that as often as possible. We also vacationed in Martha's Vineyard every August.

In a very real sense, the Urban League became a part of our family life. Sometimes Shirley and Vickee accompanied me on trips, either together or individually. They would come to the annual Urban League conferences, meet new people, and renew friendships made in the previous years. Shirley's role during those years was like that of the wife of a CEO. She was a full partner in my career. Like most men of my generation, I saw providing for my family as a primary duty. I marvel at today's fathers. Even those in so-called high-powered positions often take an active role in the day-to-day operations of family life—something with which I seldom dealt. I was free to concentrate on my work because Shirley made sure that life at home ran smoothly, so I never had to concern myself with that.

Then Shirley was also a wonderful hostess. Her natural warmth put everyone at ease, and I got the great benefit of that: Not only was I the head of the Urban League, but I also had a beautiful and gracious wife. From our days in Atlanta, we entertained in our home a great deal, an important part of building a career. That is one thing I don't think blacks in professional life do enough. We can't always be guests, we have to be the hosts or hostesses, too. The event doesn't have to be really fancy—all that is really required is good food and good conversation.

With all this, one could still say I was not home enough. The drive to work, strong in me since childhood, merged so completely with the conception of myself as "the provider" that it's hard to say where one part began and the other part left off. I was driven to succeed because I always wanted success and because I had a family, and very crucially, a disabled wife for whom I wanted to provide in the best way I knew how.

While all families have struggles, the presence of a disability in one member alters that dynamic, forcing the family to respond not only to ordinary life crises but also to the vagaries of a special force beyond its control. Shirley, Vickee, and I had to look at the world in a different way, attending to details and working out problems that other families—which could take for granted the health of all their members—would never confront.

Very early on, Shirley and I decided to handle things by not letting her illness be distracting to our lives. While we could not ignore reality, we simply tried our best to live a normal life within our own context. In order to do that, we understood that we would always have to have a steady support system. Back in Atlanta, we had housekeepers to do the things that Shirley could not do. It was also clear in Atlanta that Shirley could never hold a regular job again—a real blow to her because she loved being a social worker.

We set ourselves to taking care of things as they came along. When we traveled, if we had to get a wheelchair, we got it. If she needed to be lifted up a flight of stairs, we got her lifted up the flight of stairs. When she needed to go to the hospital, we went, accepting it as just a regular part of our lives, because it was. Angst was pointless and wasted too much energy. Our minds were very much as one in that belief.

In many ways, coming to New York was a great help to us because, even in those days, the state and the city had more services for disabled people than any other area of the country. There was a car service that ran out of Manhattan whose drivers were off-duty police officers, firefighters, and the like—very dependable individuals.

We could book a driver who would come to our home, pick up Shirley, and bring her into the city for a day's recreation or to meet with me, and then we would come home together.

Things are so different today for the disabled. The disability movement, which borrowed very heavily from the principles of the civil rights movement, has started the work of opening the world to those with special needs. Sidewalks and building entrances with ramps, lifts for wheelchairs, accommodations in workplaces—Shirley missed all these things that we have now come to take so much for granted. But in her time, she was always very game, and made the most of life that she could.

One of the main reasons we chose to move to the suburbs was that Shirley felt more comfortable driving there. The car was a tremendous source of independence for her (she was all over Westchester County) because she could get around on her own and take Vickee and her friends wherever they needed to go. There is no doubt that this evidence of self-sufficiency preserved her spirit.

Shirley had a great sense of humor about life and could tell jokes and make comments—sometimes even mildly off-color ones—in a very Southern ladylike fashion. Most of all, she could find fun in the most awkward situations. Not long after we got to New York, we went to our first black-tie dinner at the Colony Club on Park Avenue, a place we would come to know fairly well as time went by.

We arrived and rode up alone in the elevator to the second floor, where the dinners were always held, listening to the buzz of cocktail conversation as we ascended. The door opened, and it was as if the conductor had stopped the orchestra from playing. Talking ceased, and the people (all of them white) turned to look at us. The silence was embarrassing as we made our way across the floor very slowly, because that was the only way Shirley could walk.

So we walked, Shirley holding onto me tightly with her left arm, her cane clasped firmly in her right hand. When were about halfway to the safe harbor of our table, which seemed yet another mile away, Shirley looked up at me, smiled, and said, "Do you think I should walk more slowly so that we can really enjoy this?"

CHAPTER 12

AT THE HELM

HENRY FORD II WAS NOT HAPPY. It was November 1971 and the National Urban League was hosting its annual Equal Opportunity Day Dinner. Some 2,000 supporters attended this always festive celebration. That year, we had more CEOs on the dais than ever, because so many corporations wanted to show respect for Whitney Young and his leadership. This was, I thought, the perfect place to deliver a message that was long overdue. The time had come for the corporations of America to demonstrate a real commitment to bringing blacks into full participation in society by integrating their own boards of directors. Addressing the corporate titans specifically, I said it was wonderful to see them there, but it was not enough for them to come to our dinners. It was not enough for them to give money. If they were serious about equal opportunity, they could set the tone for the rest of the country by extending this ideal to the boardroom.

Ford, who for some reason always called me "Virgil," was listening to this and, apparently, fuming. Some time after the dinner he complained to McGeorge Bundy, the president of the Ford Foundation, and Katharine Graham, the chairman and publisher of the

Washington Post, "What's wrong with Virgil Jordan? He can't tell me who should be on my board."

Ford had gotten along very well with Whitney Young, and he was extremely generous to the Urban League, customarily giving $100,000 a year personally, over and above what we received from the Ford Motor Company in charitable donations. After my speech, Ford decided not to make his usual gift. One hundred thousand dollars was too much money to forgo without some effort, so I went to Detroit to see him about it. First things came first.

"You know, Mr. Ford," I said, "if there's something you don't like about what I do or say, you don't have to call Kay Graham or Mac Bundy. You should call me. There's no need to deal with me indirectly. I'm always open to conversation."

"I'll do whatever I want," he said.

"I understand that. But I want you to know that we can talk."

We did not get very far in the rest of our conversation. The Ford Motor Company made its usual donation, but Henry Ford II did not. He would eventually relent, but at that moment, Ford was unhappy with me because he felt I was not enough like Whitney. That was one of the problems that black institutions faced with regard to their white donors, who tended to give to the individual who was the head of the institution, not to the institution itself. That worked well as long as they liked the person in charge. If they got angry at their favorite, they would pull back their support and the black school or charity would suffer. In contrast, when they gave to white institutions, it was the institution that mattered. I have often said that if a dog were made the president of Yale, Yale would still get its money. This attitude had to change, and the most reliable way to make sure it changed was to increase the number of black people on company boards and in the higher echelons of corporate enterprises.

My time at the United Negro College Fund taught me the importance of having a good working relationship with corporate America. In fact, it exposed me to an aspect of life that I had not thought about very much. I knew about the important role that government plays in all our lives, just as any average citizen would. I knew about foundations because they had been critical in supporting the organizations for which I had worked. But the College Fund was my first serious exposure to corporate life, and the Urban League continued and broadened my relationships with that world because I worked very closely with many of its leaders.

At the outset, I fully understood the need for corporate leadership. William Simms, the legendary Urban League fund-raiser, had impressed upon me the importance of getting corporate executives involved. There were a number of corporate titans on the board of trustees. Among them was Edgar Bronfman, the chairman and CEO of Seagram, who introduced me to Gil Fitzhugh, the chairman of Metropolitan Life. Fitzhugh became my first corporate chairman. A Princeton graduate, Gil was quite conservative politically, but he had had a good relationship with Whitney and was a big supporter of the League. We traveled around the country together raising money.

Gil and I took our first trip to Akron, Ohio. We were to fly into Cleveland, and I got to the airport ahead of him. While I was arranging myself in the first-class cabin, Gil got on, said hello, and took his place in coach. That was an uneasy moment, a bit of unexpected irony. Gil had his own way of running his company, and I, the hard-worn traveler, had my own way of managing this critical aspect of my job. I didn't move, and he didn't either. Many trips followed that one: Detroit, Houston, Dallas—city after city, lunch after lunch. We worked well together. His conservatism and my liberalism never came into conflict where the Urban League was concerned. We even socialized together, going to the opera with our wives, and to each others' homes for dinner.

In talking with Gil and observing his work, I came to see that if I wanted to raise a serious amount of funds for the League, I would have to increase my presence and involvement in corporate America. This was a plan that Whitney had started, and I wanted to extend it as far as it could go. The time was ripe for doing that. One of the ripple effects of the civil rights movement was that some white institutions and corporations, though not nearly enough, wanted to be seen as doing their part to integrate American society.

The first real breakthrough came in the 1960s when Whitney Young and Dr. Vivian Henderson, the president of Clark College in Atlanta, were elected to the board of trustees of the Rockefeller Foundation and the Ford Foundation, respectively. There was, by no means, a stampede following this—by the early 1970s, you could count the number of blacks on the board of directors at Fortune 500 companies on two hands, which was why I had made my speech about it—but the doors were opening for a few: William T. Coleman, Jr., at IBM; Jewel LaFontant at Pantry Pride; Barbara Scott Prieskel at the Jewel Companies; Rev. Leon Sullivan at General Motors; Franklin Thomas at First National City Bank; Clifford Wharton at the Ford Motor Company; and Thomas Woods at Chase Manhattan Bank.

In 1972, John Brooks, the chairman of Celanese Corporation, a major chemical company, called and asked if he could meet with me. He came to my office and said, "I think you ought to put your money where your mouth is."

"What do you mean?"

"You're talking about blacks on boards of directors. Why don't you come on the board at Celanese?"

John had been in the audience when I talked about the lack of a black presence in corporate boardrooms. This was his way of responding.

Not everyone at the Urban League was supportive of this turn in my career. When I told Jim Linen, the Urban League's president, that I had been invited onto the Celanese board of directors and asked what he thought he replied, "Well, Whitney didn't do it."

That was not a sufficient reason. Whitney, to my knowledge, had not been asked to be on a corporate board because, I believe, things had not moved to the point that he would be. Had he not died in 1971, there is no question that he would have been tapped for such positions. I really saw moving in this direction as a good idea, for me and for the League. From my personal standpoint, there was the attraction of learning the workings of and participating in an important part of American life, one that I had increasingly come to see as crucial to almost all aspects of our society and those abroad. As a matter of policy, why shouldn't blacks be at the table? Why should we just be the beneficiaries of corporate largesse but not have a say in how that largesse would be distributed? If members of corporate America could be on our boards, why couldn't we be on theirs?

From the Urban League's standpoint, my participation would widen the network of people from whom to draw support. Those relationships would be even deeper because they would be based upon personal interactions, not just scripted presentations before an assembled group. By that time, one thing was clear to me: Personal relationships make all the difference in the world. My progress through life had taught me that. So many of the opportunities I'd had up until that point were the results of my being seen and known at the right time by the right individuals. All I had to do was to work as hard as I could to vindicate their faith in me. There was no reason my personal experiences along these lines could not be transferred to the Urban League. The potential benefits far outweighed any potential burdens—which Jim never really laid out—so it seemed unwise to miss the opportunity. To his credit, once I told him I wanted to do it, Jim was very supportive.

Not long after I was asked onto the Celanese board, I was asked to join the board of directors of Marine Midland Bank. The next day brought an offer to join the Bankers Trust board of directors. The thought of joining three corporate boards at once, two of them banking boards, was overwhelming. Not knowing what to do, I called David Rockefeller, told him the situation, and asked for his advice. Without missing a beat, he said, "There's only one choice. It's Bankers Trust."

I asked why.

David explained. "Because it's a national bank with an international banking practice. If you go on a bank board, you ought to go on one that's international. You'll learn more that way."

I thought it appropriate to run this by John Brooks. I said, "John, I have this choice."

"What do you mean, you have this choice?"

I said, "I've been asked onto the boards of Marine Midland and Bankers Trust. I cannot do both."

John said, "You don't have a choice. It's Bankers Trust."

"Why do you say that?" I asked, half expecting him to repeat David Rockefeller's advice.

"How do you think you got nominated to be on the Bankers Trust board? I'm on the board. I nominated you."

In the whirlwind of those three days, I hadn't gotten around to reading the annual reports or proxy statements of either bank. As we talked, I flipped through the Bankers Trust materials and saw John's name.

"I proposed you. You really should do it," John said. So I did.

I remember my first meeting as a member of the Celanese board, at the company's offices in Rockefeller Center. I walked into a dark, mahogany-paneled room and sat down at a long table with my fellow directors. In front of me was a leather-bound black book with my name emblazoned in gold. I'd been in boardrooms before, as a servant with my mother and later as a fund-raiser—but never in this capacity. Flummoxed for a moment as to what to do, I remembered what my mother taught me. She said that if I were to go to an event, a dinner for example, and didn't know what to do—which fork or glass to use—I was to watch the hostess and do whatever she did. There was no "hostess" here, so my fellow directors would have to do.

I looked around. All these white men (there were no women, and I was the only black) immediately opened their books and took out a white envelope that had been placed in the left corner. I took out mine. They ripped open the envelope. I ripped open my own. They pulled out and counted four crisp one-hundred-dollar bills and put the money in their pockets. I did the same.

At that precise moment, when I should have felt happy, I was seized by a sinking feeling as the thought came to me, "We can never catch up." I almost mouthed the words under my breath. Of course I meant black people. Men like the ones who surrounded me that day had been sitting at tables such as that, or their equivalent, for two hundred years. This ritual, which they thought nothing of, was a stark reminder of the financial gap, the gap in status—all the gaps— that existed between their people and my own. As far as we had come, we had so far to go. Once again, at a moment of triumph in my life, there was bitter with the sweet.

Although the very slow inclusion of blacks into corporate board-rooms was an important step in the culture, it would be a mistake to see it as anything more than a side effect of the civil rights move-ment. This was not equal to ensuring the right to vote, ending de jure segregation, and outlawing employment discrimination. Blacks in general were unaffected by the fact that a handful of black people were becoming corporate directors. The primary beneficiaries of this phenomenon were the white corporate directors themselves. Having a black presence in the boardroom was, quite simply, an education for them. Many of those men had never in their lives come into any serious contact with black people, other than the ones who cleaned their houses.

It was a fascinating experience. Even though I was the ultimate outsider, in terms of my color, I found that some directors enlisted me, either unwittingly or deliberately, in their skirmishes against other "outsiders." The first time this happened was at a sharehold-ers' meeting early in my tenure as a director at one company. In those days, the directors sat on a stage before the shareholders. One of my fellow directors leaned over to me and said, "Vernon, this is about a four-and-half-hour meeting we're into now. Have you no-ticed something?"

"No. What?"

"The only shareholders out there raising hell are those god-damned Jews."

I sat for a moment and didn't say anything. Then I touched him hard enough on the shoulder to make him turn and really look at me and said, "No shit." At that precise moment, he turned beet red and leaned back in his chair. During the course of that four-hour meet-ing, he had forgotten that the composition of the board had changed. In his mind, the board was still made up of WASPs who had gone to elite private schools and Ivy League colleges. So it was nothing out of the ordinary to lean over to the guy sitting next to him and say what he said. "No shit" were the last words I ever said to him about that issue. He got the message.

There were the comments as well. "Vernon, thank God," one corporate director said to me. "At least I can say Merry Christmas to you." Another director swore that there would never be a Jewish chairman of the company, only to be proven wrong not long after his oath. I found if I let people know where I stood right away, that I was offended by comments like that, they found other bases for conversation. This was more a feature of the 1970s. Since then, the culture of the boardroom and society at large has moved to the point that people really do try to think carefully about what they say. Some lament that fact, complaining about "political correctness." I do not. There is nothing wrong with feeling compelled to act in a civil manner toward fellow human beings.

As my experiences with Celanese and Bankers Trust foretold, once I started going on boards, I began to receive offers from other companies as well. When I approached Peter McCullough, the CEO of Xerox, about succeeding Gil Fitzhugh as corporate chairman of the National Urban League, he made a deal with me: "I'll be your corporate chairman if you come on the Xerox board." I agreed.

To the extent that corporate America was looking to have blacks as directors, I had an advantage. First, I knew key figures in corporations from my fund-raising activities; and second, my early membership on boards served as a validation for the latecomers seeking to integrate their own. I was a known quantity, no small thing for the corporate culture, which has a deep aversion to surprises of any kind. By the end of the 1970s, I was on about ten boards of directors.

Not all directors were happy about the push to integrate. In one case, a director voted against my membership, taking the position that it would be bad for the company to be out in front on the question of having black directors. The time was not right, he said. He didn't carry the day; I was elected. In the spring, there was a huge fight about whether a potentially embarrassing fact should be disclosed in a proxy statement. I argued in favor of disclosure, and the man who had voted against me chimed in on my side. As the only lawyers in the room, we knew that disclosure was the right answer, though we eventually lost. That shared struggle and defeat was the start of our friendship. At the end of the year he sent me a bottle of

Jack Daniels and a note. He didn't say he was sorry for voting against me. Instead he simply wrote, "It's wonderful to have you as a fellow director."

There was some grumbling among members of the black community who wondered if I could be a civil rights leader and a member of corporate America at the same time. As far as I knew, these comments were made by people who were outside the Urban League, and there was only so much attention I was going to pay to that. As a leader with a constituency, I had to keep my eye on what concerned my constituency. Never once, at any conference or general assembly of the Urban League, did I hear anyone say, "Jordan, you cannot do that. You have to get off the corporate boards if you want to represent us." It never happened. The reason it did not happen is that there was, in fact, no inherent conflict. It was all a matter of how I handled myself.

I was on two different tracks. I had a public advocacy role which everyone understood, and I tried not to spare anyone—not a succession of presidents, Nixon, Ford, Carter, and Reagan, all of whom I criticized strongly and publicly as required, and not members of corporate America.

In the late 1970s, I went to Boca Raton, Florida, to give a speech before the New York Savings Association. We had done a lot of work at the Urban League on the lackluster role that savings-and-loan institutions were playing in the black community. As part of their charters, they were required to reinvest funds in the communities where they made money. Instead, they were taking money earned in Brooklyn, for example, and investing in retirement communities (hence Boca Raton as a conference locale), where they could get a better return on their investment. This did nothing, of course, for the communities and neighborhoods that could have benefited from the infusion of cash. I was going to go to Boca Raton to say that this practice was wrong. The speech, as requested, was sent in advance.

When I arrived at the airport, the driver said, "Mr. Jordan, I've been asked to tell you that there are some people who are going to be at the conference who want to see you. I'm supposed to take you to them. They're in a room on another floor of your hotel." I was led into a room full of bankers who knew what I planned to say.

One of them said, "You can't say that."

"Is it true?" I asked.

They conceded that in some cases it was, but they still didn't want me to say it.

I said, "Well, that being the case, I can just go back to the airport, get on the plane and release this to the *New York Times*."

"No, no. We don't want you to do that."

Two of the more liberal bankers, who had been friends of Whitney's, pleaded for me to change my speech, telling me that speechwriters were readily available to help me make any needed changes.

I repeated my vow to leave.

"No. That would be embarrassing," he said. It certainly would have been that, drawing more negative attention than if I simply gave the speech. So I proceeded as planned. And the *New York Times* covered my speech anyway.

Just as I suspected and wanted, serving on corporate boards not only helped me network for the League but also helped teach me how to run the organization. The companies on whose boards I sat had market capitalizations of millions of dollars and could have a board meeting in two to three hours. The Urban League board meetings lasted a day and half. The lawyer in me had already gone to work on the written presentations of my staff, who spoke and wrote in the somewhat elliptical language of social workers. "Get to the point," I would say. "Say it as clearly as possible in as few words as possible." Now it was time to overhaul the process by which the board itself worked. We redid the agenda book and whittled things down so that we could have shorter meetings.

As much as I wanted to import the corporate model into the League, there were limits. Unlike a corporate board, we had to answer to constituents at our meetings. That took time. Also, in that very youth-oriented era, there was a requirement that 30 percent of the board had to be under thirty years old, a noble idea but somewhat problematic in its execution. Too much of our time was given over to listening to members of this contingent mau-mauing the white establishment. Under the circumstances we could not, and should not have, completely mirrored our corporate counterparts. Still, I did aim for some degree of corporate efficiency in handling our business.

Having learned so much from attending the American Management Association training program, I thought that the local executive staff would also benefit from a similar experience. We took a grant from the Henry Luce Foundation to run our own executive training program at our New York headquarters. We had the executives practice making speeches, and we taught them how to do presentations before potential donors and how to write proposals. It was a new day. At every phase of the process, donors and potential recipients were becoming much more sophisticated. We couldn't expect to get by any longer just saying, "Give us money because we're colored." We had to have a program and present a rationale for why the United Way or any other entity should fund our projects.

Similarly, if we wanted to firmly establish the Urban League as a civil rights organization, we also had to develop and maintain a recognizable and steady presence in the national community—to let the country know what we were doing as a body, instead of just having me comment on various issues of the day. I had learned from my time at the Southern Regional Council and at the VEP the importance of doing research and issuing reports on areas of interest to one's organization. In its heyday, members of the media, scholars, and politicians viewed the VEP as the place to go to gather information about the political situation for blacks in the South. We had carved out a niche and enhanced our reputation in the process.

Research was also a great Urban League tradition. Under the leadership of Dr. Robert Hill, the director of research, we inaugurated an annual report called *The State of Black America*, which gave statistics and other information about such issues as black health, education, and employment. Every year, to great fanfare, we held a press conference to announce and disseminate our findings. This really took hold and has become a much-anticipated and still relied upon presentation of the condition of black life in the United States. Most gratifying of all was to see the trickle-down effect of the report. As happened with the VEP, journalists, scholars, and politicians used it as a source for their discussions of race in a variety of ways. This is what we most wanted to achieve: to have others see the Urban League as a resource, the foremost repository of important information about black people.

We also added voting rights, my perennial concern, to the league's agenda. Our Voter Education Citizenship Participation Program was a mini-version of the VEP, with the aim of increasing black participation in electoral politics. This, in particular, was a real departure for the League, bringing it squarely into the political realm. As a not-for-profit entity, we could not jeopardize our tax-exempt status by getting directly involved with politics. The fact is, however, that since 1964, the overwhelming odds are that a newly registered black voter is likely a newly registered Democrat. In doing registration drives among League constituents, we were indirectly (and completely legally) having an impact on the fortunes of the two political parties.

There was some opposition to this among traditionalists, who thought I was taking the organization way too far afield. But it was never true that the new political angle and the traditional mission of the Urban League were mutually exclusive. And even as we broadened the League's agenda, our social-services activities continued. Money from foundations and from the government came in to allow us to do that. No one could say that we were neglecting the League's core constituency.

From my perspective, the times demanded that black organizations work on as many fronts as possible, as creatively as possible. I was somewhat frantic about this. Things were slipping, I felt, and forces were at work to declare the civil rights movement over, the most pressing legal battles having been won. Many in white America seemed bored with black people and their problems and were being offered too few reasons that those problems should still concern them.

The growing cynicism within some segments of the black community troubled me deeply. There were those who hinted, or argued outright, that interracial cooperation to achieve black equality was passé. The signs that whites were disengaging from the struggle and the very real need to assert black identity in a positive way fed this sentiment. I understood that; but for one who takes his pragmatism straight up, the notion that blacks could achieve equality in America without interracial cooperation struck me as simplistic and dangerous. While it made sense to pay close attention to the terms of that engagement, there was no doubt in my mind that we had to engage. The National Urban League was, for me, one of the perfect places to do that. I had a platform, and I wanted to use it to continue the work of the civil rights movement in the form that I had always known it: blacks working in tandem with enlightened, or even struggling-to-be-enlightened, whites.

Not all of my efforts at innovation succeeded. After casting about for a way to get more young potential donors into the Urban League, I settled on the idea of having an annual event called the "Party at the Plaza." The idea was to invite a big-name celebrity to entertain, which would draw in young people, particularly young whites, who knew little of the league. Our first celebrity was Roberta Flack. It was a great success.

One year, Nancy Wilson performed, and she was just spectacular—when she started to sing. This was an era when the political atmosphere was really charged. Everyone had an opinion, and felt moved to give it, about the war, Nixon, race relations, the ecology (as it was called in those days)—about everything. I was in the audience listening to Nancy sing in her inimitable way and talking with some of the guests when I noticed she was not singing any more. I looked toward the stage to see our guest performer talking to the audience about race relations and the meaning of the Urban League. That was fine enough, I thought, between songs. The monologue, however, went on and on.

Finally I went up near the stage and said, "We really want to hear you sing. That's what everyone is here for—to hear you sing."

Nancy's heart was very much in the right place, but she was not too happy about my interruption. She did start singing again, and the evening was a great success.

After a while, we decided that the "Party at the Plaza" with a celebrity headliner was simply too complicated and distracting for us. "Simplicity" became our watchword: Get a good local band, dance, eat, and raise the funds.

I FOUND A LIFELONG FRIEND during those years in New York: Franklin Thomas, the head of the Bedford-Stuyvesant Corporation, which had been started by Robert F. Kennedy to promote community development in that economically distressed Brooklyn neighborhood. We were introduced by Mitchell "Mike" Sviridoff, a Ford Foundation executive who had funded some of Frank's Bed-Stuy projects. Mike knew me because the VEP had been partially funded by Ford. He thought that Frank and I should know each other. From our very first meeting, as Frank has put it, "it was as though we had been separated at birth and were now reconnected in some way." We have been true brothers in every sense of the word.

Despite having grown up in different regions of the country, with different cultural backgrounds—Frank is of West Indian origin—the parallels in our childhood experiences and in our professional careers were uncanny. Both of us had strong mothers who told us we could do whatever we wanted in life. We had both gone to white colleges, Frank to Columbia, and had the experience of being in the extreme minority at a white institution. At the same time, we are different enough in our personalities—Frank is more quiet and reserved—to complement each other.

In Frank, I found someone roughly my age in whom I could confide and discuss my concerns and aspirations without the slightest feeling of risk that my confidences would be shared. Everyone should have at least one relationship like that, and it may just be one because such a thing is rare—particularly among men, in my experience. That had been a problem for most of my life; my high-school buddies who were my friends so long as I had no dreams different than their own, the friend to whom I had rushed to show the letter offering me the position as head of the United Negro College Fund because I thought, foolishly as it turned out, that he would be happy for me. My hopes were dashed by all of them. That has never happened with Frank. Throughout the many good things that have happened to me and the many good things that have happened to him (including his successful tenure as president of the Ford Foundation in the 1980s and 1990s), we have always rejoiced unequivocally at news of each other's good fortune and have been supportive in times of trouble.

Frank was particularly helpful as a sounding board for me throughout the 1970s because we were going through similar experiences. We straddled the black and white worlds in the same peculiar fashion. Frank answered to a board of trustees composed of leading lights in the corporate world, along with Ethel Kennedy, who had taken her husband's place after his assassination, and a group of grassroots community activists, including Al Vann and Sonny Carson, who would later become famous in New York City for his radical politics. My Urban League board was similarly constituted: The establishment mingled with the activists. Both of us knew about the problems of trying to bridge those two worlds and satisfy competing constituencies.

Along with our day jobs, Frank and I were branching out into other areas where we were in the extreme minority, including joining corporate boards. We talked of our difficulties and successes over long dinners and drinks—sometimes slightly amazed at our circumstances.

Frank and I were an odd pair for New York City. From the very beginning, we posed something of a challenge to the black establishment there, which didn't quite know what to make of us. We are physically similar: large men—six foot four, over 200 pounds—with dark complexions. We were both working firmly within the black community and, at the same time, interacting with great ease at the highest level with members of the white power structure in corporate America. Both of us were outsiders, me from Atlanta, Frank from Brooklyn—which, it may surprise non–New Yorkers to know, made him an "outsider" to the black leadership from Manhattan. We defied all conventional wisdom about how to be black and succeed in New York City. Not only were we doing well, but we were also breaking new barriers. More than outright hostility, there was a curiosity about us. How had this happened?

In days of old, when people observed a phenomenon they didn't understand, they pronounced it the work of the Devil. A bit of that feeling was at work in the response to Frank and me in the 1970s, attaching itself much more to me than to Frank. The reasoning went something like this: "If you are going these places, doing these things, getting these things, you must have made some sort of evil bargain. That's the only way it could happen."

This was superstition pure and simple. There was no bargain, nothing mysterious about how my life was unfolding. In the 1960s, I was brought along by the forces that put voting rights at the heart of the struggle for black advancement. I took jobs that trained me to deal with that and also put me in the view of others who could judge my capabilities and point me toward additional opportunities.

The same thing happened in the 1970s, only this time the economic development of the black community was at center stage. That could come through increases in black businesses, greater participation in the corporate community—a myriad of ways. Being in New York City as the head of the Urban League, which did a great amount of fund-raising in the corporate community at a time when that community was opening itself to black people, was another case of my being in the right place at the right time. And when a man from my home state, Jimmy Carter, whom I had known for a number of years, was elected president of the United States in 1976, I suddenly had connections to the White House in a very public way that I wouldn't have had if Gerald Ford had been elected. That certainly was not in my control, but it was an event that helped shape the trajectory of my career.

In the beginning, I had only a vague sense of being viewed as an outsider. My status would soon become clear as I charted my own course on various issues. One in particular stands out. In the mid-1970s, long-simmering tensions between blacks and Jews came to a boil after several very high-profile events. Andrew Young, the Carter administration's ambassador to the United Nations, got into trouble when he met with a low-level member of the Palestine Liberation Organization. Official U.S. policy at the time forbade any government contact with the PLO until it renounced its call for the destruction of Israel. Young was forced to resign after a hailstorm of criticism from some members of Jewish organizations and other supporters of the Jewish state.

Many black people saw Andy's appointment as ambassador to the UN as a true sign of racial progress. His removal from that office, at the behest of members of the Jewish community, was taken in some quarters as confirmation of the suspicion that Jewish Americans were not the friends of blacks they presented themselves to be—that there had always been an undercurrent of paternalism that revealed itself during the flap over Andy's interaction with the PLO.

Around the same time, Jesse Jackson led a delegation to the Middle East to meet with the chairman of the PLO, Yasser Arafat. A photograph of Jesse embracing Arafat appeared in newspapers and magazines across the country and set the tone for black-Jewish relations, fairly or unfairly, for years to come.

Tensions ran so high that a group of blacks convened a meeting in Manhattan to discuss the unfolding events and to suggest a plan of action. The group met at the headquarters of the NAACP, announcing in advance that only black people could attend. I thought that was unfair and unjust. White people such as the prominent attorney Joseph Rauh, who had given so much of their time and energy to the civil rights movement, were frozen out. This was not the civil rights leadership I knew. It was against every principle that the movement held dear. The media, of course, was all over this, especially the statement the group issued, calling for a black "Declaration of Independence"—not from working with Jewish groups altogether but from what they considered the undue influence of those groups. I couldn't go along with that.

Not long afterward, I made a speech at the Catholic Charities convention in Kansas City in which I countered their statement by saying that blacks and Jews did not need a Declaration of Independence. We needed a "Declaration of Interdependence." I meant it. It was heartbreaking to see two peoples with a history of oppression on these shores, and in other countries, tearing apart a coalition that offered hope for the transformation of American society. Certainly there were tensions between blacks and Jews, issues to be resolved—

working cross-culturally is never easy. Still, the potential rewards were so great they more than made up for any of the problems we were having. I wanted to be on record saying that we should not destroy our chances to reap those benefits.

If I was viewed suspiciously before, this made me even more of a pariah to some. People telephoned to offer their support in private. They would not do so publicly, afraid of being seen breaking ranks in front of the white community. I understood. Every group under siege feels that its members have a duty to stick close together. But if one firmly believes the group is marching in the wrong direction—indeed, marching toward a cliff—it is also a duty to speak out, or at least to sound a cautionary note. That's what I wanted to accomplish in my talk at the Catholic Charities, to remind both groups of what we had in common, what we could teach the world together, and how we should not throw that away over differences that could be worked out if we talked to each other openly and honestly, with mutual respect.

That totally escaped my critics. Breaking ranks was my sin, and they wanted me to atone. There was actually a meeting to discuss what to do about me, at the office of my old mentor and friend, Kenneth Clark, who was also extremely upset about my comments. On a Saturday afternoon, I got a telephone call from Roger Wilkins, the nephew of Roy Wilkins. Roger and I were friends, so I was not surprised to receive a call. When I discovered what it was about, I was stunned. Roger explained that he was with a group that wanted to talk to me about what I had been saying about the recent controversies between blacks and Jews. The purpose of the call was to invite me to come before those assembled at Ken's office to explain myself. I declined.

We just had a fundamental disagreement about the proper course for black leadership to set. This was not about whether blacks have the right to speak out on foreign policy. Of course we do. It just struck me that this had nothing to do with foreign policy, and everything to do with the frictions on the domestic front between blacks and Jews. If I was correct, then those problems should have been addressed specifically and head-on without dragging in the Palestinians as a weapon to fight a battle they had no real interest in or power to affect. Why the Palestinians? Why not the Cypriots? Why not the Basque separatists? The answer was clear: Those groups had no enemies that the people at Ken's office, and others of similar views, wanted to tick off. The fundamental concerns about black-Jewish relations may have been legitimate, but this was not the right way to meet them, I thought.

I was also very concerned about Jesse Jackson's overtures to Yasser Arafat. I have known Jesse since 1960, when he came to Atlanta to speak at the Omega Psi Phi Achievement Banquet at the Hilton Hotel. He was then, as he is now, a very dynamic speaker who captured the room. Over the years we have worked together, and just like preachers visiting each other's churches, we would speak on each other's turf. I spoke to his organization, People United to Save Humanity (PUSH); he'd speak to the Urban League. Sometimes when Jesse introduced me, he would say, "Vernon Jordan ought to be president of the United States." I always had the feeling he thought he should be president one day, too. I was right.

In response to press questions about Jesse's trip and his views on the Arab-Israeli conflict, I simply stated that Jesse did not speak for all black people. He did not, and neither did I. I have often said that when black civil rights marchers crossed the Edmund Pettus Bridge, there should have been no expectation that we would come out on the other side thinking alike and acting alike. The task for us was to figure how to disagree—even sharply—while keeping the lines of communication open.

For a time, this controversy played in the newspapers as if there were a big rift between the two of us. There was not. We just disagreed. When I stopped in Chicago to visit Jesse on my way home from giving the Catholic Charities speech, *Newsweek* ran a story saying that "Jordan and Jackson patch up their differences," as if we had been at war and had lately come to the peace table to sign an armistice agreement. It was never like that.

From that time on, it was clear that an image was forming about me in the public consciousness. Until that time of crisis, I had floated along on the goodwill of those who ardently supported me and those whom I hadn't yet offended. After this period, feelings about me definitely hardened. There was a clear demarcation between those who supported my approach to the role I was playing and those who simply could not stand it.

The tenor of the times helped shape my public image. I was the leader of an organization considered moderate both in its goals and in its manner of achieving those goals, at a time when strident rhetoric and radical posturing were the flavors of the day. The well-known faddishness of the 1970s tended to mute good common sense on many subjects—political activism, clothing, hairstyles. Who alive during that time has not looked at pictures from that era and wondered, "What was I thinking?"

A lot of what went on was essentially a form of political theater: making extreme comments, advocating utopian programs that had no chance of coming to fruition, all for the purpose of making the audience feel good for that moment and making the proponent seem progressive and ahead of his or her time. When the moment passed, as all moments do, there was nothing concrete, nothing lasting left to show for it—no program, no action, no end result—nothing but words and the memory of a good show. That was not what I wanted for the Urban League. Every action, word, and program had to lead to a productive result. Anything else would have been a waste of time.

I remember very vividly sitting at a meeting in New York with a group discussing the idea of supporting a Malcolm X University in North Carolina. The school recruited black students from Duke, North Carolina A&T, the University of North Carolina, and other schools to come to Malcolm X University, where they followed a curriculum that was, in substance, an extended black studies program. There was talk of getting Ford Foundation funding.

I listened as long as I could and then asked a question I already knew the answer to: "Would any of you be willing to take your kids out of Duke University and put them in Malcolm X University?"

The room erupted. "Oh, that's not fair! That's not the point!"

It was fair, and it was precisely the point. These people clearly wanted to be identified in the public mind as radical and, in the words of the day, "right on." To me, this was a sideshow with other people's children as bit players. What was real and substantive in the world was what they wanted for their children and for their own lives. Why pretend otherwise for public consumption?

Throughout the years, I have seen firsthand this type of public-private distinction at work. On many occasions, individuals who have issued harsh public denunciations of me personally, or of my stewardship of the Urban League, have approached me in private for help with their various ventures, personal and professional. In this way they get to keep intact their public images as radical actors, while seeking in private what is really important to them—usually something completely bourgeois and pedestrian.

This double dealing might be considered harmless and, at times, a little humorous. It is, however, a serious problem because it hinders frank and honest discussion of what really matters to us, where we actually are, and where we want to go in the world. Members of the public (and I am particularly concerned about young black people) too often fall for the posturing and take it as evidence of real political commitment or, even worse, effective political action. And it is all an illusion—more about individual personality quirks than a program for political advancement.

To be honest, we all bear some responsibility for the way we are perceived. It is possible—and very likely—that at least part of the problem I had, particularly with members of the black leadership in New York, lay in my personality. My inclination always is to be friendly and cordial—joking, flirting, doing whatever I can to smooth things along. At the same time, I have never been one for indiscriminately sharing my innermost thoughts and feelings. I always had the sense that people wanted me to do that—that they wanted to hear me complain about the problems I faced on my job or talk (or cry) openly about Shirley's illness. But that is not my way—either because of my upbringing or because I was hardwired by my DNA not to do that.

This trait came through very clearly in the late 1970s at a gathering of the leadership of the civil rights movement in America in a suite at the Waldorf-Astoria. There was much singing and praying. At one point, someone said, "We need to get closer together, closer to God—lay our burdens on the table before one another." It was a quintessential 1970s moment, very "touchy-feely"—an encounter group with an element of Christian-based "witnessing" thrown into the mix.

One by one, people began to talk about their difficulties, some even crying. When my turn came, I said, "You know, I don't believe in this process. I have nothing to say."

Everyone jumped on me at that point, "Jordan, you just don't want to cooperate with anybody. You're selfish!"

I was definitely in the doghouse, but this was not my way. "It won't work," I said. And it didn't.

THE ELECTION OF JIMMY CARTER to the presidency of the United States in 1976 profoundly affected my career at the Urban League. Carter had come out of nowhere (a famous headline of the day read, "Jimmy Who?") to beat a large field in the Democratic primaries. Then he went on to squeak out a victory over President Gerald Ford with the aid of a near-solid block of black support—in the South, almost 98 percent. He would not have won that region, or the presidency, without that astonishing support from black people.

Everyone was curious about Carter, and members of the media were looking for anyone who had a clue about who he was and where he might take the country. Because both he and I were from Georgia and people knew that we were well acquainted with each other, from the very beginning members of the media sought me out to talk about the man from Plains.

After the cocktail party in Atlanta in 1969, where Carter had announced his run for governor and I my bid for Congress, we had kept in touch off and on. Unlike me, Carter had gone ahead with his plans to run, and he was elected governor of Georgia in 1970.

Carter was always very receptive to the Urban League, and he came to speak to us on a number of occasions, the first time at a black executive exchange program meeting we were having in Atlanta. Even then, black people responded to him with great enthusiasm.

In 1973, my corporate chairman, Peter McCullough, and I were to take a trip to Atlanta to attend a fund-raising event. I called Carter, who was also serving as the chairman of the Democratic Campaign Committee, and told him I wanted to stop by and introduce him to Peter, who was not only the CEO of Xerox but also the treasurer of the Democratic Party. Carter suggested that we come to the governor's mansion, have dinner, and spend the night.

We accepted his invitation. This was something of a homecoming to me because the governor's mansion sat on the very same property owned by Robert F. Maddox when I had chauffeured for him twenty years earlier. I knew the place very well. As we drove up, I couldn't help reflecting on how much my life had changed since those days.

Carter met us as we got out of the limousine, his usual casual self, in polo shirt and slacks. I was a little taken aback by that. This was the era before the casual look reached into every aspect of American life. Peter and I were our usual more formal selves in dark-blue business suits. Rosalynn Carter was away for the evening, and we had dinner with Carter's daughter, Amy, and his son, Jack, and his wife.

After dinner, Carter, Peter, and I went into the library and talked politics. Carter told us in no uncertain terms that he was going to be the next president of the United States, explaining how it was going to happen. Peter and I were surprised by this, especially by Carter's vehemence. We talked on, and Peter was the first to retire. Carter and I continued the conversation until I got too sleepy to go on.

"Well, Governor, I'm going to bed," I said.

Carter walked me to my room—actually came into my room—telling me how he was going to make his successful run to the White House.

I was about to drop, so finally I said, "Listen, you won't be president for three reasons. Number one, no one knows you. Number two, you won't be in office when you're running. And number three, you're a Southerner."

He said, "I am going to be president."

What I told Carter that night was no different than what others had been saying to him. But it did not matter. He was certain.

The next morning, Peter and I had breakfast at my mother's

house, and we talked about what appeared to us to be Carter's bizarre notion. "This country is not going to elect anybody named Jimmy Carter," Peter predicted.

After breakfast, I took Peter to Martin Luther King, Jr.'s grave site. He had never been there. We stood a while, taking things in, and finally I said, "Peter, we have to go."

Peter asked, "Vernon, do you think Martin would mind if I left a prayer?"

"Of course not."

At that point, Peter McCullough, a devout Catholic, knelt and prayed at Martin's grave. This CEO of a major company, who lived a life so far away from King's, cared enough and understood sufficiently what King had done that he wanted to kneel and pray. I was never more happy or proud to have him on our side.

J IMMY CARTER AND I continued our contacts and kept up very friendly relations. We gave the Morehouse College commencement addresses together in 1975. In 1976, I had several of the candidates for president—Carter, Lloyd Bentsen, Morris Udall, Fred Harris— come to the Urban League to talk to the staff. Carter was particularly wonderful in the small groups, and my staff loved him. At another point in the campaign, he came by my house in Westchester County, and we had good Southern-fried chicken. As a tax-exempt entity, the Urban League could not endorse a political candidate, but it became generally known that I, personally, was a Carter supporter.

There was only one moment of friction between us during the campaign. At a stop in Philadelphia, Carter made a very clumsy attempt to appeal to working-class white ethnic voters. Seeking to allay their fears about integration, Carter expressed understanding of their desire to maintain the "ethnic purity" of their neighborhoods. This very famous gaffe had Carter, who is no racist, sounding like someone from the Third Reich. The press hammered him. I called him myself, expressed my dismay, and told him that he should apologize. He was reluctant to do that because he knew that his words were simply ill chosen and that he didn't adhere to the interpretation others were placing on them. But in politics, where perception is truly more important than reality, what he knew in his heart did not matter. Carter apologized, and he weathered the storm. Of course, he did that and more: He was elected the thirty-ninth president of the United States.

The Thursday after the election, I was in a hotel putting on my tuxedo, getting ready for an Urban League dinner. The phone rang and a voice said, "This is a call from President-elect Jimmy Carter."

When Carter came on, I said, "Mr. President-elect, congratulations. It was a great victory."

He said, "Vernon, do you remember that night in the mansion when you gave me reasons why I would not be elected president?"

"Yes, I remember," I said.

"I'm calling to tell you that I am the president-elect of the United States."

Carter had never wavered in his faith in himself. At the same time, he had not forgotten that others had doubted him.

President Carter's people went to work to set up their administration, and I was asked to serve on a committee designed to help with hiring staff. Once that word got out, I started to get mail from all over the country from people who wanted to come to Washington to work. When the time came to discuss the staffing of the White House, I wanted to make sure that black people were being considered. I immediately suggested to the president that he hire Richard Hatcher, at the time the mayor of Gary, Indiana, and a rising star in American politics.

"You should bring him into the White House," I said. "I think he could really help you."

Carter declined and expressed his preference for Bunny Mitchell, a black woman who had worked on his campaign. I offered that Mitchell was a good person but said she did not know anyone, no one knew her, and, therefore, she would not be able to help him. He needed someone prominent in the black community. Carter had run as an "outsider" and had filled his White House staff with what came to be know as the "Georgia Mafia," men who had served him with fierce loyalty during his governorship. Now he had to have some people around him who had relationships that could be of help when things went bad, as they inevitably do from time to time.

President Carter responded that Hatcher had not "come out" for him until late in the campaign. I said, "Mr. President, no one came out for you early on except Andy [Young], Daddy King, and Coretta [King]. So you can't hold that against Dick Hatcher. You need Hatcher's help." I was very high on Hatcher and wanted him to leave Indiana, transform his considerable skills, and take them to another plateau, preferably on the national stage.

Carter was adamant about hiring Mitchell. Although I thought it was every bit the mistake it turned out to be, I wanted to make the best of the situation. I went to the White House to see Mitchell and told her frankly that I had advised the president that she was the wrong person for the job. "But he's the president, not me," I said, "and he says you're his person. So I'd like to make a suggestion. First, I suggest you allow me to give you a dinner in your honor at any restaurant you want, in Washington or New York. We can invite all the black leadership to come meet you." This was important because she was supposed to be the liaison to the black community and no one knew her.

Mitchell said, "I don't have time to do that."

I pressed on. "Well, I also suggest you meet Louie Martin. Spend a day with him talking about your job and about working around the president. You could learn a lot from him. He's a great political leader, a wise man. He's been around forever and he knows all the ins and outs. I'll let him know you're calling."

"Who is Louie Martin?" she said. It was like talking to a stone wall. I gave up.

Because we had known each other so long, I had access to the Carter White House beyond what would have been normal for the leader of the Urban League, or any other organization like it. This turned out to be another aspect of the very different turn the League was taking at the time. Just as I was trying to tilt our axis toward greater political involvement, I had a literal friend in the highest political office in the land—once again, a strange confluence of circumstances.

There was great promise in the air. Black people felt a great sense of power from knowing that their votes were the key ingredient to electing the new president of the United States. The promise of the Voting Rights Act was on full display in this exercise of political muscle. Carter was, in every sense, "our president." We had delivered, and now was the time for the beneficiaries of our show of faith to return the favor.

But it wasn't happening. As I observed the administration in that first half year, it seemed to me that President Carter had forgotten how he had gotten elected. It was almost as if the black community did not exist. This was not only my perception. There was much grumbling to me about it by other black leaders and members of the general community, though no one would say it aloud. I suppose that at some level, people wanted to give the new president a chance. But situations have a way of getting out of hand when they are left unmanaged. My fear was that if we didn't set matters straight at the very beginning, it would only get worse. Someone had to say something, and do it soon.

I began to send signals to members of the administration that they were not moving forward on the issues of principal interest to blacks. "Remember who brought you to this ball," I said. Nothing seemed to move them.

We had invited President Carter to address the next National Urban League Conference, to be held in Washington that year. I, along with members of my staff, decided this was perfect place and time to make our feelings known. My speech, the keynote address, was a truly corporate effort. Every senior staff member reviewed it in advance, and we sat around a big conference table, discussing nuances, changing emphases and language, in a very animated way. We all had the sense that this was going to be a turning point for us. We would be viewed, and would view ourselves, in a different light. Although I had been very critical of President Nixon when warranted, this was different. Carter was really our man. Black people had given their best to him, and it is always more difficult to say hard words about those closest to us.

On July 24, 1977, I opened the Sixty-Seventh Annual Urban

League Conference with a blistering attack on the Carter administration's record to date. The basic thrust of my indictment was that while the new administration had devoted a good deal of time to formulating a new energy policy, defense policy, and foreign policy, no new domestic policy was in sight. In those first six months, it had given virtually no attention to the goal of full employment, to revamping the welfare system, or to health care, urban renewal, and affirmative action.

Patience may sometimes be a virtue, but in this circumstance it would have been destructive. Our forbearance on issues of concern to us would have ratified the apparent assumption that other issues were, in fact, vastly more important. The tasks that any new management team sets itself to at the start of its tenure says very loudly what it deems most important. In political terms, had the administration moved swiftly on these matters, it would have served as a great example to the country as a whole about the nation's priorities.

This is not to suggest that providing for the defense of the United States, ensuring our access to energy, and setting a firm course in foreign policy were not important to black people. But there were other major problems that should have been on the table as soon as President Carter walked into office—not the following year, or the year after that.

The response to my speech was staggering. Sunday night is usually a slow news night, but this was a jolt. What gave the story such resonance in the media was that the president and I had been seen only as friends. The speech could be played as the great falling out. Carter addressed the conference the next day and defended his record as best he could. The two of us appeared on the front page of many newspapers the following morning, seated next to each other, arms folded, staring grimly in opposite directions.

The tension continued throughout that week, as columnists and others commented on my charges and the president's response. At one point, Carter, who was in a cold fury about all of this, called me a demagogue. He later called to apologize. I told him I accepted but he needed to do that in public, which he did after a fashion.

Not all of my colleagues were happy with what I had done, giving a speech that sounded more like the NAACP than the Urban League. The traditionalists were riled, and once again they had the chance to ask, "What the hell is Jordan up to?" Dr. Francis Kornegay, the executive director of the Detroit Urban League for many years, was among those most upset. "That," he said fixing a hard gaze on me, "was not an Urban League speech."

I stood my ground, insisting that, no matter how painful, the words had to be said. This was an exercise in leadership, doing something I believed was right, even though I knew not everyone would agree with me. I had been at the Urban League for six years. It was Whitney's goal, and I continued the pursuit, to firmly fix the League's place in the galaxy of civil rights organizations. I am a great believer in concerted efforts; each person or group using their abilities, contributing what they can, to move things forward. In 1977, the League was in the position to agitate in its own way on behalf of some items on the black agenda. It would have been a waste if we had let the moment pass.

Having engaged the administration in so public a fashion, I knew matters could not be left hanging. Simply venting frustration or posturing was not the point. There had to be some form of follow-through. I had been thinking about it for a long time. To concentrate our power and efforts, I proposed that the heads of all the major black organizations should meet on a regular basis, to plot strategy and to press our case in a coordinated fashion. There was power in numbers. I had access to the White House, but it hadn't made as much difference as I wanted. If we went as a group, on occasion, things might be different. So I proposed the Black Leadership Forum to bring together all the heads of black organizations toward this end. Over the course of Carter's term in office, we met with him several times and, in the main, had constructive discussions.

As for President Carter and me, over the years we have worked our way back to some equilibrium (toward the end of his presidency he had me to the White House for a social visit), but our relationship has never really been the same. Carter clearly thought I had betrayed him. What bothered him most was that I had gone public about our differences. "You could have told me that yourself," he said. I explained to him that that was not the way it worked. This was not about Jimmy Carter, the man. It was about Jimmy Carter, the president. The president had very publicly relegated black issues to the back burner, after blacks had placed near total faith in him—one columnist had even referred to the black voting block for Carter as "mindless." A similarly public expression of outrage was more than warranted. I had not betrayed him. I was keeping faith with my obligations to represent my constituents and what I thought were their aims, interests, and aspirations.

Despite the certainty about what I had done, I experienced a huge letdown after the speech. That evening, there was a party in my suite, and the place was filled with people talking about what had happened and what was going to happen. I walked around in something of a fog, with a drink in my hand, wishing everyone would disappear. I wanted so much to be alone. Bernice Powell, a member of my staff who had been watching me move through the crowd, said, "You're the loneliest man in this room." She was right.

CHAPTER 13

ENDURANCE

IN 1980, AMERICA WAS AT A CROSSROADS. A crucial presidential election was on the horizon, and blacks were terrified at the prospect of the Republican candidate, Ronald Reagan, defeating Jimmy Carter and rolling back many of the gains we had made in the previous two decades. That was pretty much Reagan's stated goal, wrapped in language about states' rights and traditional values. He signaled this by beginning his campaign in Philadelphia, Mississippi, the site of the 1964 killings of three young civil rights workers, Andrew Goodman, Michael Schwerner, and James Chaney.

Alarmingly, it was Reagan's retrograde (at the time I said "racist") posture on issues of concern to black people that seemed to be the source of his appeal to large segments of American society. The ardent embrace of Reaganism seemed a rejection of us. My preference, of course, was to see Jimmy Carter re-elected. There was no doubt in my mind that he would be better for the country, and he was a good friend to the Urban League. With Carter in the White House, our contracts with the government would remain secure, and we could continue our work at a high level. Reagan had taken aim at government–private sector cooperation, such as our efforts to provide job training for the unemployed. Nevertheless, pragmatist that I am, I was fully prepared to do my best to work with Ronald Reagan, if he were elected, though I knew that that would pose a real challenge.

This was my state of mind when I went to Fort Wayne, Indiana, on May 29, 1980, to address the Fort Wayne Urban League's annual Equal Opportunity Dinner at the Marriott Hotel. It was a big event, and about a thousand people turned out. By all accounts, it was a great success. After my speech, I stood around greeting people, and then, as I always did, I went to my room and called Shirley to tell her how things had gone.

There is always something of a letdown after giving a speech. It is truly work, both physically and emotionally. Afterward, I often feel drained and restless at the same time. On this particular night, it was getting late, but I knew that sleep would be impossible. I went out and wandered around the hotel a bit, talking to several people who had been at the dinner. Eventually I ended up with a group of Urban Leaguers in the hotel bar, among them a member of the local board, Martha Coleman. When I mentioned that I had not eaten, which I seldom did at those events, she invited me to her house for a snack and coffee, and I went.

Later I would be asked whether that was not a risky thing to have done. She is a white woman. I am a black man. I was married; she was not. None of those facts raised a "risk" even remotely related to what happened later that night. After any terrible event, it is possible to work one's way back to the conclusion that it could have been avoided "if only." The nature of my life was such that I did not process leaving with Martha Coleman as a specific risk.

I lived a life very different from most people, traveling from place to place, being the center of attention—flattery and praise one moment, being left totally alone the next. There was very little glamour in this. Instead, it was just one of the demands, a grueling one, of my job. After speeches, there were often parties in my hotel suite with people I barely knew but had to talk to. I met Urban League members and sometimes went to their homes or to local restaurants with them after events—it could be one person, it could be ten. They could be black. They could be white.

I rode around countless towns with men and women assigned to be my hosts for the day, and I know people viewed things differently when they saw me with a woman rather than with a man. In the culture in which I lived, associating with people—male, female, black or white—on the spur of the moment was part of the routine. That's the way things were.

I was scheduled to fly to Houston the following morning, and that was on my mind as Ms. Coleman drove me back to my hotel. While we were on the road, some white teenagers passed us screaming epithets. They continued on, and I thought nothing of the episode. This was Indiana. It was all very familiar to me. I had driven around the state as a college student—by myself or with friends, black and white, and was always comfortable doing so.

Instead of dropping me off at the front of the hotel, Ms. Coleman took me around to the side entrance, closer to where my room was. As I was getting out of the car, a bullet fired from a 30-06 hunting rifle tore into my back. I didn't hear the gunshot, but the impact lifted me into the air, and I had a sensation of floating—unreal, as if I were in a dream. And then I was on the ground.

One of my first thoughts was that I had to get back to my room and go to bed, so I could make my flight to Houston. I remember thinking, "This has to be over; I've got to be somewhere tomorrow"—a crazy notion under the circumstances. But when I began to feel blood soaking my shirt, I knew I would not be catching that plane to Texas.

The pain was indescribable, brutal beyond all measure. I had often heard that human beings shut down in the face of overwhelming pain. I did not. I remained wide awake, and I could feel the blood running out of my body. "This is it for me," I thought. "My life is over." I then heard in my mind my mother's voice saying, "Son, if you trust Him, He will take care of you." Those were the words she would write to me at the close of every letter. Hearing them was one thing; believing was another.

In the rooms above, people came to their windows, but no one would come down. I assumed they were afraid that the shooter was still out there and that they could be targets, too, if they were to come out into the open to help me. So I lay there alone on the pavement, all the while with a vivid sense that people were watching me from above.

Then there was a wonderful sound—a siren. I heard it in the distance and tracked its progress as the ambulance eventually rolled up near me with its lights flashing. To this day, I always have a buoyant reaction to hearing a siren. Others may take it as a negative sign: that someone is hurting. But to me, a siren means that someone is going to get help. The paramedics put me on the stretcher, and I talked to them all the way to the hospital. In all the uncertainty, with all the mixed-up thoughts, I was sure of one thing: I knew I could not go to sleep. Doing that would surely be the end of me.

When I got to Parkview Hospital, I told the emergency room attendant to safeguard the money in my pocket. I had come from a Celanese board meeting earlier in the day, and I was carrying about $1,400 in cash. I asked them to call John Jacob, my deputy at the Urban League, in whom I had great confidence, thinking it better that he break the news to Shirley than to have a stranger from the hospital call her in the middle of the night. Over my protests, the orderlies then began to rip open my Brooks Brothers suit to get me ready for surgery. I do not remember much of anything after that.

Dr. Robert Stovall, a member of the board of the Fort Wayne Urban League, had been at the dinner that evening, and when he heard about what had happened, he rushed to the hospital. Apparently, there was a debate about who would operate on me. Stovall was insistent that Dr. Jeffrey Towles operate, rather than the surgeon on duty. The doctor on duty was white, Towles was black. But race did not figure into Stovall's consideration; He simply knew that Towles was the better surgeon. When he called Towles, Towles said, "I'm not on call. It's not my turn."

Stovall was having none of it. "This is Vernon Jordan," he said. "You have to operate on him."

Towles was an interesting story himself. He had grown up in a small town in West Virginia, the son of a single mother who was a cleaning lady. One of the places where she worked was a doctor's office. Having no babysitter, she often took her little boy with her to work. While she cleaned the doctor's office, Towles would go through the medical books, and he became fascinated by the diagrams and pictures. These experiences eventually led him to medical school.

The first operation—there would be five altogether within a sixteen-day period—lasted four hours. A 30-06 is designed to take down a large mammal and is most commonly used to hunt deer. The ammunition exploded upon impact, creating a wound the size of a man's fist and sending bullet fragments throughout my body. Dr. Towles told me quite candidly later that at first he did not think he could help me. He said he thought he had seen everything during his residency in the emergency room of Detroit General Hospital, "but I had never seen anything like you. By my calculations you were not supposed to make it. All I knew was that I was supposed to do the best that I could do." And he did.

Despite all their efforts, my doctors were unable to remove every fragment. Even with that, I had to count myself lucky: Had the bullet entered one quarter-inch to the left, it would have severed my spine, bringing instant death or paralysis for life. Before hitting me, the bullet had ricocheted off a fence. Without that slight alteration in trajectory, there would have been a clean hit, and that would probably have been the end.

My initial doubts about surviving disappeared almost as soon as I woke up after my first operation. I suppose the shock and sense of personal helplessness in the moments after being shot had left no room for the possibility that others might know what to do and be able to help. Thankfully, that was not true. My doctors at Parkview Hospital went to work immediately and efficiently. My anesthesiologist, like Dr. Towles, was a black physician. I was adamant about noting that fact once I started to give interviews. Those two men saved my life, and I was very proud that they were black.

Shirley, Vickee, and my mother arrived right away, all shocked and afraid. When given the news, Shirley had initially believed that I was dead and that our friends were simply trying to spare her feelings. So, as bad as things actually were, she arrived at my side having lived through believing that they were much worse. She appeared steady and calm and told me that I was a "champ," and I thought the same about her because I knew she was unnerved at the sight of me hooked up to so many monitors and devices.

Under the circumstances, I could not interact with my mother and my wife too much, but seeing them and feeling their support lifted me up. They made me feel even more strongly that I would survive. Frank Thomas learned about the shooting while he was about to start his vacation, getting the message as he arrived at the front desk of his hotel to check in. He turned right around, booked a flight, and flew to Fort Wayne. His presence, as always, was a deep comfort.

During the course of my stay in Parkview, others came—President Carter, Senator Edward Kennedy, Wiley Branton, Reverend Joseph Lowery, Andrew Young, Weldon Rougeau, Reverend Otis Moss, Richard Hatcher, and Jesse Jackson. Members of my staff came, including Enid Baird and Don Thomas, my general counsel. Enid walked into my hospital room, and as soon as we saw one another, we wept. The doctors and nurses were doing everything they could to keep me alive, and my friends were doing all they could to keep my spirits up, too.

The media coverage was intense, as news organizations converged on the scene. We had, in fact, just entered the world of twenty-four-hour news coverage. The Atlanta-based all-news channel, CNN, had come on the air three days after my shooting, and a report on my condition was the first news item that ran on the network. By 1980, America was far too used to the idea of violence against those considered leaders on the national scene, and many thought that the shooting was part of a conspiracy. Newspaper articles explored the possibility; some members of the black community promoted the idea. Given our recent history, there was good reason to have been concerned. In the end, the truth would turn out to be more banal, though no less evil.

Although I was in no position to follow what was going on outside my hospital room, I do know that Reverend Jesse Jackson had held press conferences at the Marriott and at the courthouse in Fort Wayne. He had planned to have one at the hospital, too, but my mother intervened. I am told that she said, "Jesse, there is only one issue here, and that is whether Vernon Junior is going to live or die.

So we don't need any more press conferences. What I want you to do is go back to Chicago, now."

Everything was ready to go; the press was waiting. But Jesse, who I think can stand up to any force in the universe except black maternal power, said, "Yes, Mama Jordan," and that was it. There was no press conference.

Although Jesse is a controversial figure to many Americans, that time he spent with me in Fort Wayne fixed forever my personal opinion of him. He came to support me when I most needed it. At the end of the day, he is a Southern man and a preacher. While I was in the hospital, he called Shirley nearly every morning as a way of supporting her and Vickee. I will always remember his friendship at that dark hour in my life.

WHEN THE DOCTORS AT PARKVIEW had done all they could do for me, I was transferred to New York Hospital in Manhattan. The staff at Parkview had kept me from dying, but the hospital was not as well equipped as the large hospitals in New York City. I had developed a persistent low-grade fever, and the doctors in Fort Wayne could not figure out why. This was a serious concern, and there was some talk about sending me to the Mayo Clinic or to a hospital in Chicago. But there was only one place I wanted to go, and that was home to New York.

I was flown there by military medical transport, arranged by President Carter at the request of Louis Martin. I was accompanied to New York by my personal physicians, Dr. Adrian Edwards and Dr. LaSalle LeFall, both graduates of the Howard University Medical School. It was my first day outside of the hospital, and I saw the whole world anew. Certain familiar sites, no matter how mundane, brought on a feeling of exhilaration. I remember telling someone as the ambulance came upon the sign for the Triborough Bridge into Manhattan, "I never thought I'd see that sign again."

My arrival at New York Hospital began the second phase of the fight to get back on my feet. In the end, I would spend eighty-eight days there, on top of the ten days spent in Parkview. That is what it took, and I did not fight it, resolving early on to do whatever the doctors and nurses told me to do. When you are sick like that, you just have to turn over your body and almost your mind to the doctors. Perfect submission was the plan, and I followed that prescription to the letter, so badly did I want to walk out of there fully recovered and ready to get on with my life again.

I got extraordinary care at New York Hospital, especially from my surgeon, Dr. Thomas Shires, who operated on me three times and surely saved my life as much as Dr. Towles had in Fort Wayne. Dr. Shires was the head of surgery at New York Hospital and seventeen years earlier had been the surgeon who operated on Governor John Connally of Texas when he was wounded in Dallas on November 22, 1963. He would later become president of the American College of Surgeons.

It did not take my doctors long at all to figure out why I was running a fever. Unlike Parkview, New York Hospital had the latest diagnostic equipment, and a CAT scan quickly located an area of infection in my back. One of my doctors took a long needle, stuck it in my back, and drained about a quart of what looked like stale orange juice from the area. The low-grade fever disappeared almost immediately. That mystery solved, I was free to concentrate on healing.

My surroundings were as comfortable as any hospital room could be. I was in the suite that the Shah of Iran had used on his final trip to America to receive treatment for cancer. The mail poured in, and when able, I occupied myself by reading it and directing Enid to respond to many of the letters.

My family came on a daily basis, and Frank Thomas was there just about every day as well. Frank would come into the room and grasp my hands as if he were giving some of his strength to me, and he was. Reverend Gardner Taylor, the dean of black preachers and pastor of Concord Baptist Church, came often with counsel and prayer. Reverend Taylor has been present at every major moment of my life since that time, and he is still my friend and mentor. Hardly a week goes by that we do not speak with one another. It was his belief that I had been spared for a reason and that I had to discover for myself what that was.

For the most part, my days were taken up with recuperation and seemingly endless medical procedures. There are rituals to hospital life—patients on the floor come and go, doctors make rounds at certain times, nurses have set shifts—and some of the people who cross your path you get along with better than others. Rose Fiorelli, who worked the morning shift, was my favorite. As time passed, I became worried about one feature of my day: the early-morning shot of morphine given to get me ready for the doctors' examination of my midsection. It worried me that I looked forward to the shot with so much eagerness. One morning I told Rose, "I'm not going to take this anymore."

Rose was very skeptical and suggested I talk with the doctor, who reminded me of how painful it would be once they started to manipulate my insides without benefit of morphine. I was adamant. So every morning I held the guardrails on my hospital bed in a vise grip while my doctors worked as quickly and thoroughly as they could.

Even before I stopped taking the morphine, though, I learned that being in a hospital is not like spending time on a beach. A friend extolled and then brought me a biography of Winston Churchill. I got through exactly one chapter. I had simply no energy for high concentration. Light, inconsequential fare attracted me. I watched television and became, for the first time, a Yankees fan as I cheered on Reggie Jackson, who was having a great season that year. Pete Rozelle, the commissioner of the National Football League, and Martin Davis, the head of Paramount Studios, sent over and set up a special video receiver so that I could watch tapes of movies and football games. Even though I had just been shot, I fell back into watching my favorite type of movie—Westerns—comforted by their simplicity: a hero, a villain, several good fistfights, and a pretty girl who is won by the hero in the end.

The exception to my focus on pure entertainment was the attention I paid to the tapes sent to me by Dr. Howard Thurman. From that day at DePauw back in 1953 when my family and I heard him preach, he had been one of my heroes. Over the years he crossed my mind often, and not long after I came to the Urban League, I decided to give him a call. When I introduced myself, Dr. Thurman asked, "What took you so long?" After that we would see each other periodically. I remember one long evening—an entire evening lasting until dawn in fact—spent talking to him about life and what he had learned. Thurman is seen by some as a mystic, but I found him firmly grounded, a repository of great wisdom.

The television and my visitors were my links to the outside world. As the summer drew to a close and we moved closer to the presidential election, I paid more attention to the coverage, talking back to the screen when warranted, wishing desperately to be a part of things. The candidates came by. President Carter visited me again. Ronald Reagan, of whom I had been very critical and would be again, also came to wish me well, neither of us dreaming that less than a year later, he too would be the target of violence and that I would visit him in the hospital in Washington in the spring of 1981.

When I went to see Reagan that time, he was his usual wry self. He grabbed my hand, smiled, and said, "This is a switch," and then, "It sure hurts getting shot."

"It hurts like hell," I replied. We talked a while and then I promised that I would see him again when he was back at work.

Despite all the hard words I had had for him, it was as if Reagan and I had entered some strange brotherhood because we had both been through something that, mercifully, the vast majority of people will never know. I would have much the same experience with Governor George Wallace, who had survived being shot in 1972. God knows, Wallace and I were on the opposite side of the fence about almost every issue, except maybe where the sun rises and sets. But his had been among the first telegrams I received after being shot, because he knew so well the pain and the struggle that was ahead of me.

In 1983, Wallace came to a speech I gave in Montgomery, Alabama at the George Washington Carver High School. It was an event honoring E. D. Nixon's fifty years in the civil rights movement. Nixon had been one of A. Philip Randolph's Pullman porters and president of the Montgomery NAACP and had been intimately involved in the Montgomery bus boycott in 1955.

Wallace was there in his wheelchair. When I greeted him afterward, he insisted I lean down and hug him, which I did. As he sat back in his chair, he said, "You know, I think about you a lot. I hear you play tennis. You got shot worse than I was, but I got hit in a worse place, and so I'm in this chair. You don't know what I would give to be able to stand up and make a speech."

This was the man who had stood symbolically in the doorway to protest the admission of black students into the University of Alabama. He had started his political life as a moderate, but after getting nowhere with that, he made himself over into a rabid segregationist and rose to become the most powerful figure in his state. What I saw before me that day was a man transformed by tragedy, and I thought again of how lucky I was.

THERE WAS A MEDICAL SIDE to the story and there was the legal side. The FBI, under the leadership of William Webster, launched an investigation, sending agents to Fort Wayne to work with local officials. The investigators proceeded under a federal statute, 18 U.S.C. Section 245, which had been enacted to prevent the harassment of blacks as they exercised such basic rights as voting, serving on juries, or using public accommodations. I was using a public accommodation, a hotel, which triggered federal involvement in what otherwise would have been a matter of state criminal law. Of course, none of this was on my mind as I lay in the hospital preparing myself for operation after operation, struggling to go the distance.

FBI agents visited me twice when I was hospitalized, once in Fort Wayne and once in New York. In Fort Wayne, they asked me to take a lie-detector test. I said, "Wait a minute, I'm the one who's hooked up to all these IVs, and you want me to take a lie-detector test? I'm the one who got shot. You need to go talk to somebody else."

They were trying to figure out a motive for the shooting. Was my assailant a jealous lover, perhaps, enraged at the sight of me with Martha Coleman? As far as I was concerned, I had told them my story. Someone had shot me, and I was not in the position to tell them why. I refused to take the test.

In New York, they tried a different tack. Agents came to my hospital bed and said, "We would like to hypnotize you." My response was, "You know, I do not have control over my body, and I am not about to lease my mind to the FBI." After they left, I got on the telephone with Bill Webster and said, "There is no way I'm going to do this. What is this all about?" He explained that this, too, was part of the investigation. Perhaps I might remember a face or an event that would give clues as to what happened and why.

Again, I refused. It was not my goal to be difficult or to make the agents' job harder. In my view, I was the victim. Why should I take a lie-detector test? As to hypnosis, I was lying in a hospital bed attached to IVs, not in control of my body, on a schedule dictated by others. I was not joking. Under the circumstances, I really did not want to turn my mind over to the FBI, if that was even possible. That was the end of my personal participation in the investigation.

As the days went by, and no suspect was arrested and thoughts of a wider conspiracy abated, the focus of discussion about the shooting began to shift slightly. I was only vaguely aware of this at first, because my mind was so totally focused on recovery. The fact that I had been shot in the company of a white woman emerged as point of concern—if not controversy—within some quarters of the black community. Somehow, I had become a traitor to the black race, and to all black women in particular. This became one more item on the bill of indictment being drawn up by those critical of my stewardship of the Urban League.

Ethel Payne, the longtime columnist for the black newspaper the *Chicago Defender*, who was known as "the first lady of the black press," put it all out in the open. She said flatly that black women would (and should) reject me after Fort Wayne because they now knew who I really was, and what I really valued. In her view, no self-respecting black woman would ever again have anything to do with me.

As deeply hurtful as her comments were—the most important people in my life, my daughter, my wife, and my mother, were black women—I knew that this was just insane. It was nevertheless an issue I had to deal with when I began to give interviews after leaving the hospital. Very often I had the feeling that some people wanted me to apologize. In my view, there was nothing to apologize for. Whatever anyone else wanted to think about the matter, I had just been shot with a deer rifle and had experienced pain that no human being should ever endure. Nothing I had done, nothing that others imagined I had done, could justify that. I nearly lost my life; my wife almost lost a husband; my daughter, a father; my mother, a son. In what world could my association with a white woman be talked about on an equal basis with that? There were even hints that somehow I had it coming to me. To my mind, those who believed that were every bit as sick and cruel as the person who shot me.

Over the years, I have come to know very well the nature of celebrity in this country—how it removes one from the species just a bit. The media, with the acquiescence of modern First Amendment law, turns famous people into the equivalent of cartoon characters who can have anvils fall on them, be flattened like pancakes, and then in the next frame pop right back into shape. In today's world, fame—perhaps even more than money—is seen as the engine for rejuvenation, the balm that supposedly heals all wounds. The most awful words can be uttered, the harshest uninformed judgments rendered, in a way that people would never want applied to themselves or their loved ones. But it is okay when the object of this negativity is well known.

Even Shirley was forced to address this question in newspaper articles of the time. She was often asked, "How did it feel to know that your husband was out with a white woman?" or other variations of the question, which she responded to openly and generously. She got some of this from her friends in that "I'm only raising this because I care so much about you" manner that is, of course, actually very hostile. Why would a real friend want to make another friend feel bad, especially in the midst of a serious life crisis? Through it all, we persevered.

I HAD HOPED TO LEAVE New York Hospital in August, to attend the Urban League's Seventieth Annual Conference. My doctors absolutely insisted that I preserve my strength and save the heroics for later. On the night of the traditional keynote address, which was the high moment of every conference for me and which I always looked forward to giving, I was alone in my hospital room. Judy Ney, the wife of Ed Ney (the chairman of Young & Rubicam and chairman of the conference), was thoughtful enough to remember me in this lonely and depressing moment, and I shall never forget her kindness. She visited me during the time John Jacob eloquently delivered the keynote address in my stead.

A few weeks later, when I was told that I was ready to be discharged from the hospital, I called Howard Thurman to give him the good news.

He said, "The Lord's going to be very happy to hear that."

"He's going to be happy? Why do you say that?"

"Because he's sick and tired," Thurman said, "of hearing me talk to him about you three times a day."

For eighty-eight days, the seventeenth floor of New York Hospital had been my world. But for the occasional foray onto the roof or a walk to another floor to get exercise, I stayed within its boundaries. I wanted to go home, but I had been living in a sheltered environment, almost a cocoon, that was very comforting in its predictability and security. As the time to leave grew near, I felt some small apprehension. Among other things, my weight had dropped from about 225 pounds to about 170 pounds, and none of my old clothes fit.

Rose, my favorite nurse, came home with me that day, September 4, to help ease my reintroduction to the world outside. By this time, my family and I had moved from Hartsdale to an apartment in Manhattan. Rose helped me get situated, and then I walked her to the elevator. One of us pressed the button, and we stood for a moment saying our good-byes. The elevator arrived, and tears welled up in our eyes. It had been a long haul for both of us and now it was really over. We hugged each other tight, and as the elevator door opened, my ill-fitting trousers fell down around my ankles.

Fortunately, the only passenger on the elevator was the attendant, who got a full view of this moment and, true to his profession, said nothing. But we could only laugh. After all that had happened, there I was in the hallway, embracing a woman—a white one at that—with my pants down.

Returning home was not unlike coming back from Fort Wayne to New York and noting the landmarks along the way with a sense of wonder. Easing back into the routine of being self-sufficient brought on a sense of euphoria about the commonplace, and each small thing I was able to do for myself became a milestone. For nearly three months, the nurses at the hospital had bathed me. The first time I stepped into my shower alone at home I felt like crying. It represented such a victory—I was alive and moving under my own steam.

From my perspective, work is always the best answer to feelings of apprehension, and so I made arrangements to get back to the Urban League as quickly as possible. Foremost in my mind was the problem of my weight. I was down fifty-five pounds and was very self-conscious about the way I looked, which I thought was horrible. My skin sagged, my face was gaunt, none of my clothes fit. As anxious as I was to see everyone at the Urban League, I wasn't too anxious to be seen.

And then, quite frankly, there was a question in the back of my mind about how I would be received. My conscious mind knew that I had the support of my staff, which had shown as much over the months of my convalescence. The Urban League had lost no support during my ordeal; in fact, contributions had actually increased. There was really no concrete reason to have been concerned. Despite this, I had the nagging feeling that somehow this was different. I looked different. I had been through a lot, and as crazy as I thought it was, even the suggestion that I had become persona non grata to black women disturbed me.

Before I had left the hospital, my tailor had come to see me, and he measured me for a double-breasted blue blazer and gray flannel trousers so that at least I would not have to worry about how I looked. We set a press conference for September 10, my first day back on the job. My staff greeted me with great warmth, and when I got through the press conference with no problem, I knew I would soon be able to work my way back into things.

Not long afterward, I attended the Ebony Fashion Fair, sponsored by the National Urban League Guild—my first meeting before a group of black women. I was to say a few words, nothing major. After the poisonous sentiments that had been unleashed into the atmosphere over the previous months, I wondered just a little how they would receive me. When Molly Moon, president of the guild and a trustee of the Urban League, concluded her introduction by saying, "Our leader is back," and the audience broke into sustained applause and a standing ovation, I had my answer. That meant so much to me. As I walked across the stage, I thought to myself, "Where are you, Ethel Payne?"

G RADUALLY, MY LIFE BEGAN to take on its familiar shape. The main difference was that I now had increased security when I made public appearances. This was both good and bad. On the one hand, the security did make me feel safer. On the other hand, having it sent the signal that I was the kind of person whom others want to hurt— I was an announced target. That my assailant was still at large contributed to the thought that I needed security. There was little I could do about it. It was seen as a public-safety issue, and whatever personal qualms I had were outweighed by the interest in preserving public order.

My first major speech was at Tuskegee University at the beginning of October, honoring a commitment I had made long before Fort Wayne to help the school celebrate its one-hundredth anniversary. I was on the board of directors of the J. C. Penney Company, and I arrived in Montgomery, Alabama, on the J. C Penney corporate jet. I came down the steps to find several police cars parked on the tarmac. They were there to escort me to Tuskegee, and so we went, caravan-style, down the highway to the school and my first post–Fort Wayne speech.

The heavy security continued. Not long after the Tuskegee speech, I traveled to Mobile, Alabama. When the plane landed, the pilot came on the public-address system and said, "Will Mr. Vernon Jordan please come forward, and will everybody else please keep their seats?"

The door opened and I looked out onto a huge security detail. There were six motorcycle cops surrounding our limousine, and one police car that led the motorcade. We all took our places and started off on our way to the hotel, not stopping at red lights or stop signs. When we got there, I saw on the marquee the words, in very big letters, "WELCOME VERNON JORDAN." That was not a comforting sight.

The chief of the security detail accompanied me to my room. As we walked, I said, "You know, I don't like all this. Can't we do something about it?"

He looked at me and said, "It doesn't matter. I like it!"

This wasn't just a mania of the South. During this period, I traveled to a small town in Ohio, and I was met by the now-familiar contingent of police officers who took me to my hotel. When I travel, I want to get to my room, close the door, and be left alone. Two of these officers followed me into my room, sat down, and one turned on the television set. I said to myself, "This has got to stop."

At an event in Riverside, California, cops were just everywhere. They were all white, very large, and in the fashion of California law enforcement, absolutely no-nonsense. They were supposed to protect me, but I was scared of them. After the speech, I told the League's regional director, Henry Talbert, "I'm not staying in the hotel tonight with these cops." We figured out a way to give them the slip. While they were looking for me, I was on the freeway to Los Angeles.

It all got to be too much. The last straw was in the spring of 1981 when I was leaving a Penney board meeting on my way down Sixth Avenue to go over to the University Club. The mayor of New York, Edward Koch, had very graciously provided me with security from within the police department. Two New York City plainclothes officers were my bodyguards that day, wonderful guys both. They were following me as we walked east on Fifty-fourth Street, when suddenly a car screamed to a halt right there in the middle of the street. Three detectives jumped out of the car with their guns pulled and said to my security detail, "Put your hands up, now!"

The detectives had recognized me and thought that the officers were stalking me and were about to attack. I was being protected from my protectors. This was just insane. Over the course of the next months, protection by the NYPD ended quietly. I shall always remember and thank them.

ABOUT A YEAR AFTER MY SHOOTING, the authorities arrested Joseph Paul Franklin and charged him with a violation of my civil rights. The state of Indiana declined to prosecute Franklin, saying there was not enough evidence to prove beyond a reasonable doubt that he had shot me, but the federal government moved forward with its case. I was not much involved in the legal proceedings surrounding Franklin. That was for law enforcement to deal with. It was enough for me to tackle my health problems and get back in shape for the Urban League without playing sleuth or following the trial on a daily basis.

I did go to South Bend, Indiana, to testify at Franklin's trial, although there was not much for me to add, because I had not seen who shot me. For the most part, I was there to establish for the record my activities and whereabouts during the evening. In the end, however, Franklin was acquitted. Section 245 was a very weak basis on which to have proceeded because the prosecution had to show that I had been shot because my attacker was trying to prevent me from using a public accommodation. That was never the issue. I was shot because I was black and in the company of a white woman. Afterward, several of the jurors said as much. They believed Franklin had shot me because of race, but the statute required more.

Franklin's acquittal or conviction was not my issue. I was well, back home, back at work, playing tennis, living my life. I took my cue from scripture: "Forgetting those things which are behind and reaching forth unto those things which are before, I press towards the mark." It was useless for me to be embroiled in Franklin's fate.

Later, Franklin was tried and convicted for the murder of two black men who were out jogging with two white women. While he was in prison, Franklin confessed that he had, in fact, shot me. There was some skepticism about this at first. Serial killers have been known to confess to well-known crimes, in an effort to appear more evil and deadly than they are. But Franklin had lots of information about the case and filled in holes in a way that suggested he could have been my assailant.

Franklin explained to the authorities how I came to be his target. He had, at first, thought to kill Jesse Jackson and had gone to Chicago to seek Jesse out. Jesse was not in Illinois at the time, so Franklin left. While driving through Indiana, he heard that I was going to be speaking in Fort Wayne. He went there, found out where I was staying, and lay in wait for me in a grassy area just beyond the parking lot outside of my room.

Franklin, who was on death row awaiting execution as of August 2001, was an avowed racist who believed that the mixing of races was abhorrent. So, in the end, there was no conspiracy, grand or small—just a corrosive belief in white supremacy that led to a hate crime.

A few years after all this, William Webster called me.

"Mr. Director, good morning," I said.

"Vengeance is mine, saith the Lord," he intoned.

"Bill, are you feeling all right?"

He explained, "I want to report to you that last night in the Marion prison, Joseph Paul Franklin was stabbed thirty-eight times."

"What happened?"

"Well, when he got to prison, he became buddies with this black guy. The black guy gained Franklin's confidence, and then asked him, 'Did you shoot Vernon Jordan?' Franklin said, 'Yeah, I shot him.' A few nights later, a group of black prisoners cornered him and stabbed him. They had knives made out of tin cans. They weren't trying to kill him; they just wanted to hurt him. So they stabbed him in the arms and thighs."

"You're kidding."

"No," Webster said. "They're putting him by himself from now on."

That was really my last extended thought about Joseph Paul Franklin.

AFTER THE SHOOTING, the trial, and the acquittal, many of the people around me expressed great interest in my state of mind, and it was my judgment that I should talk to someone about the impact of what had happened to me. The doctors at New York Hospital had raised the issue of psychotherapy with me, as they do with all patients who have experienced trauma, and once out of the hospital, I decided to give it a try. So, for a time, about six months, I went to a psychiatrist.

The whole process was strange from beginning to end. And it was, frankly, a little discomfiting to be seen going to the therapist's office with all the day-to-day personnel of the building—superintendents, elevator attendants, and doormen—knowing why I was there. That was not the right response, of course. People who need help should seek it. But I was the head of a major organization, and I prided myself on my ability to be in control. Anything that suggested otherwise was not welcome.

With that said, my own therapy sessions were not particularly helpful. I did not then, and I do not now, feel I had any specific anger about what had happened in Fort Wayne. I recall the subject coming up in a conversation with Gardner Taylor over lunch one day. He said, "Vernon, I want to ask you something."

"What is it?"

"Do you dream about being shot?"

"No."

"Are you bitter and angry about it?"

"No."

"Are you afraid?"

"No."

"If what you're telling me is true," Gardner said, "then something is wrong with you. And I say that as a Christian preacher."

I related this conversation to my doctor. He said, "I agree with the preacher."

I said, "Listen, if after coming to you I am dreaming about this, and bitter and angry about it, there's going to be another shooting. I'm going to shoot you."

Both Gardner and my doctor thought, in the jargon of psychology, that I was in "denial." Perhaps. All I know for certain is that my whole existence during that year was given over to walking away from that experience as healthy and as whole as I could be. There was no energy to spare on anything—any emotion—that was not going to help me do that.

I wanted to know what, if any, impact the shooting might have on the rest of my life and what the signs would be that I was not adjusting sufficiently. These issues were not getting addressed, at least not to my satisfaction. Instead, the doctor wanted to go back to my early childhood years and talk about my relationship with my mother and father (had they mistreated me?) and my siblings. What, I wondered, did that have to do with the hole in my back?

Too many of our discussions seemed to grow out of the doctor's obsessions and fears rather than my own. So when he got better, I stopped going.

I HAVE OFTEN BEEN ASKED whether the shooting and aftermath changed me in any way. I always answer no, although some of my friends insist otherwise. After my talk at Tuskegee, which marked my return to the public sphere, I spoke to my friend Louis Martin about how things had gone. Louie would later recall that our conversation that time was very different from others we had had after one or another of my speeches. He said that before I was shot, I would report to him about the politics of the speech and how people responded to it. This time, he noticed that I seemed especially enamored of the choir. I told him every song they sang and quoted from hymns. He took this as my having developed an interest in "the broader meaning of life." Gardner Taylor has said similar things—that since the shooting I have expressed a more spiritual approach to life than I did before.

I remain unconvinced—I think I was spiritual before then. But we never see ourselves as others see us. The one thing I am certain of is that having lived the experience, I preferred to close that chapter and concentrate instead on Reverend Taylor's belief that I had been spared for a reason. It was for me to discover, in the quiet of my own mind, just exactly what that reason was.

CHAPTER 14

AMERICAN DREAM, AMERICAN REALITY

HERE WERE SOME MISCONCEPTIONS about why I decided to leave the Urban League. When I announced in September 1981 that I was leaving, only a year after having been shot, many people assumed that my health had forced me from the field, that I had not fully recovered from my wounds. Others thought I was afraid—getting shot had made me skittish about the business of being a civil rights leader out in the open for all to see.

Neither explanation was true. As for my health, I was in pretty good shape for a man my age. Tennis was still my game (I hadn't yet taken up golf seriously), and I was on the court at least three times a week. If I had been frightened, I would never have come back to the League at all. It would have been a very simple matter to have left the hospital and said that I was quitting to regain my health, to spend time with my family, and to stop and smell the roses. I was hurt seriously enough for there to have been an easy out had I wanted to take it. No one would have blamed me.

The fact is, the events in Fort Wayne interrupted a process of psychological—and then actual—disengagement from the League that was already in its initial stages. I had made it very clear when I took the job in 1971 that ten years was my limit, a huge commitment for me, given my job history up until that time. As my tenth anniversary approached, it became increasingly clear that my original judgment about how long to stay was correct. I had grown weary of the routine: the endless travel, giving the same speech—or variations—night after night, the same issues and problems arising to be solved over and over. It was like 1969 at the VEP, when I had reached the limit of my creativity in that particular job. Of course I could have changed my plan and carried on, going through the motions. That did not seem right for me personally, nor was it fair to the League. It was in the best interests of the organization to have someone come in who was fresh and ready to fight.

And we did have a fight on our hands. To my great disappointment, Jimmy Carter had not been re-elected in 1980, and the Reagan landslide had changed the atmosphere in Washington and throughout the country. But we had to carry on. "If we survived Nixon," I said at the time, "we can survive Reagan." From the very beginning I thought it important to keep open the lines of communication to the new administration—I attended Reagan's inauguration and the festivities after it, and I was even asked to suggest some language for his Inaugural Address, which I did. (Though he didn't dwell on the point, Reagan did pledge in his speech to support "equal opportunity for all Americans, with no barriers born of bigotry or discrimination.") Still, I spent a good part of my time after his election denouncing his policies as racist.

There was just a different sensibility at work during the Reagan years. William T. Coleman, Jr., who had served as Gerald Ford's secretary of transportation, called this to my attention as we returned from Clarence Mitchell's funeral in Baltimore. Mitchell had been one of the giants of the civil rights movement, presiding over the NAACP's Washington bureau and known on Capitol Hill as "the 101st Senator," and we all felt his loss deeply. Coleman pointed out to me an item in that morning's *Washington Post*—the list of guests who had attended a state dinner at the White House the previous evening for President François Mitterand of France. "Look at this," he said. "They are all white." I looked and found that he was exactly right. So I called up Gail Burt, who was the social director at the White House and said, "Ms. Burt, my name is Vernon Jordan. I'm calling to ask you a question."

"Okay," she said.

"Couldn't you all find any black people for the state dinner last night?" I said, "Let me tell you something. In 1981, you cannot have a state dinner and not have any black people. You just cannot do that."

She didn't know what to say, but our conversation got back to Nancy Reagan, who vowed that it would never happen again. She wasn't too happy with my criticism, but, to my knowledge, it never did happen again. Blacks were just not on the Reagan administration's radar screen—socially, politically, or economically. That was pretty evident without black leadership making the point, but we kept saying it to keep up the pressure in every way we could. As much as I enjoyed being in the fray, behind the scenes and in public, this was the time, I really believed, for new voices to be heard and new approaches taken.

Other things were on my mind as well. I wanted very much to take care of my family in the best way my skills allowed, particularly to provide for Shirley in a manner that compensated, if only in a small way, for the unfairness that fate had dealt her. Money does not buy happiness, but it does allow us to do some of the things we want in life, and it also brings a measure of security. Anyone who has lived with serious illness knows that not having to worry about finances makes life just that much easier, and I was determined to make sure that even as we enjoyed some of the good things in life, there was never cause for concern about our financial status.

While I knew it was time to leave, the final decision to make the break was not easy. My supporters would be disappointed and would think I was abandoning them in the middle of what we all perceived was a crisis. Once again, I was faced with the choice of answering my own private call or doing what I knew others expected me to do—and either choice was worthy. I talked with Shirley and with my mother. Both were predictably supportive of my doing what I thought best for myself. I also talked with my closest friends and reached out to others whose wisdom I admired, like the distinguished historian John Hope Franklin, to get their views on the matter.

The real question was—what to do next? It is easier to leave if you have some definite place you want to go, and that place was not fixed in my mind at first. I had to figure that out among the choices that were open to me. Should I go to work for a corporation? Did I want to practice law? And what about moving back to Atlanta? Shirley and I had left there only because of my positions at the College Fund and the Urban League. Once the reasons for having come north were over, should we go home?

Things were a bit complicated because there was no real model of an "ex-civil rights leader" for me to follow. What does one do after having served in that role? The fact was that a number of people who had been leaders in the movement, well known and not, had been killed. Sadly, we never got to see what my friend and colleague Medgar Evers would have gone on to do, had he been allowed to live a normal life span and experience the United States of the 1970s and beyond—a world with opportunities that were nonexistent at his death in 1963. In the case of the previous leaders of the Urban League, the answer was clear: They died in office or retired. With de facto life tenure, the issue of what to do afterward never arose.

There were other obvious choices, none of which appealed to me. I could run for office, like my contemporaries John Lewis and Andy Young. But I had closed that door back in 1969 when I decided not to run for Congress. Working in the public sector was not a real option. I had never wanted to do that.

As I thought of my position, I chafed a little at the idea that my role in life was going to be limited to what was expected of a person in my position—that I was to either stay put forever, go into politics, or work for the government in some capacity. My yearning grew, in part, out of the experiences I'd had during the 1970s. Having spent a good amount of time in the corporate world and having seen up close the kinds of people involved in it, I instinctively compared myself and measured the skills I believed I possessed against those of the men and women I observed. To be blunt, I did not believe they had any "thing" that I did not have.

What I had done in my life was take away certain skills and knowledge from every job and outside activity and apply them in each new arena in which I played. Working in the law with Mr. Hollowell, fund-raising, making speeches, conducting negotiations, managing people and situations—these were things I had spent two decades doing. Why couldn't those skills be parlayed into a position for me in the private sector?

The work of the lawyers and corporate executives who were volunteering with the College Fund and the Urban League had always interested me. I heard them talk about their deals, transactions, and cases. My membership on corporate boards was an even more direct window into this world. Put simply, I wanted to be a part of it—a real part of it. Just as some want to be artists and others want to teach or be surgeons, I decided that I wanted to practice law in a private law firm with corporate clients.

As I thought of it, I asked myself, "What has all this been for, if someone in my position could not, if he wanted, make the transition from the not-for-profit world into the corporate world?" White people did this kind of thing all the time, and no one thought anything about it. It was the accepted prerogative of white people, particularly white men, to establish themselves in one field and then go into another. Success was their calling card. Once they had that identity, they could go almost anywhere they wanted.

My whole life had been geared toward saying that the horizons of black Americans should be as unlimited as those of whites. I had a law degree, the same contacts, and the same skills (if not more extensive ones) as many whites who went from the public or not-for-profit sectors into the private sector without comment and with great ease. Why shouldn't I try this?

THAT SOME CIVIL RIGHTS LEADERS tended to stay in their positions forever was, in part, a function of the limited opportunities open to them had they wanted to leave. Certainly, some of them would have continued on their paths no matter what. But by the 1970s and 1980s, the world had changed enough so that the leader of a black organization could get a job in corporate America if he or she wanted. So, much as in the mid-1960s when I was driving my father-in-law crazy by jumping from job to job, seizing opportunities as I found them, I saw an open door that I wanted to go through for a host of reasons, among them my own personality and my family situation. I began to take steps to go through it.

In 1979, a year before Fort Wayne, I had quietly begun to put out feelers to people who might be able to help. Walter Wriston, the CEO of Citibank, was one of the first people I spoke to about my plans. He introduced me to people at Shearman & Sterling, a large and very well established law firm in New York. We had a number of serious conversations about my joining the firm. Later on, I spoke to Cyrus Vance, who had been secretary of state in the Carter administration, about his firm, Simpson, Thacher & Bartlett, and had similar discussions.

I also approached Morris Abram, a partner at Paul, Weiss, Rifkind, Wharton & Garrison, another New York firm. We had known each other since the late 1960s, socializing on many occasions. Morris had been the chairman of the board of the United Negro College Fund during my time there, and I had received my first honorary degree from Brandeis University shortly after his retirement as president. Morris had been lead counsel in the case that had ended the county-unit system in Georgia; he had defended civil rights workers in Americus, Georgia; and he was extremely well known and generally well respected in civil rights circles. That would change during the 1980s, when he was made the chairman of the U.S. Civil Rights Commission under Ronald Reagan and launched an all-out attack on affirmative action.

At a breakfast in 1979, I put everything on the table to my friend Morris. It had been almost ten years since I had come to the Urban League, and I was ready to move on. The idea of going into the private sector, more specifically into a law firm, appealed to me. "Would you," I asked, "be willing to approach your partners about taking me on as a partner?"

Morris thought for moment and said, "Well, I'm sorry. That wouldn't be possible."

"Why not?"

"Because we don't bring in laterals," he said, meaning that the firm only made partners from the associates who had worked their way up at Paul, Weiss.

That was not true. And more important, Morris knew that I knew it was not true. Suddenly thrust onto unsteady terrain, I said, "You were a lateral. Ramsey Clark was a lateral. Ted Sorensen was a lateral. Arthur Goldberg was, too."

"That's different," he said flatly.

There have been very few times when I can honestly say that I was thunderstruck by anything another person said to me. This was one of them. I sat looking at Morris Abram, seeing him clearly for the first time. Up until that second, I would have argued to anyone in the world that he was my very good friend, which was exactly why I had approached him. Now, he appeared alien—unrecognizable.

In that moment, I felt some embarrassment at having so overestimated my worth to Morris. Had I ever truly known him? In the immediate aftermath of our discussion, I replayed in my mind all of our interactions over the years to see if I could recall anything—a word, glance, a deed—that could have tipped me off to this. But nothing specific came to mind.

I have never been certain whether Morris was just making a commonsense judgment about what his partners would have accepted in 1979 or whether he had his own problems with the idea. Either way, the fact that he was unwilling to even consider going to bat for me with his colleagues was searing and took a bit of the wind out of my sails about venturing into new horizons.

That's different. He may as well have added, "You're black."

Morris, of course, would never accept that view and would, most likely retreat, as he did during his years as the embattled head of the Civil Rights Commission, into talk about "merit." Which raises the question: What constitutes merit? Who gets to decide what ingredients go into the mix to make up what is often a very subjective judgment of a person's capabilities? These questions were (and are) critical, given the role merit plays in maintaining the status quo. People in power, in any field or society, have a vested interest in believing that whatever qualities they may have are what it takes to be a person in power.

In my view, the civil rights movement had rendered a negative judgment on the status quo in America. There was no way to finish the work of the movement without questioning the basic assumptions that led to defining "merit" as those experiences possessed by a narrow class of white men, which automatically threw almost everyone outside the magic circle into the category of the presumptively unqualified.

There was no doubt in my mind that I was qualified to do the work of a partner in a law firm. I certainly knew that I could pay my own way. The years of fund-raising and networking, my experiences and contacts in the corporate world and in government would make it possible for me to bring in clients—to be a "rainmaker"—and to serve those clients well. My career profile may not have been the same as that of the whites who made lateral moves into partnerships at big firms, but it was equivalent. What has happened in my career in the years since my talk with Morris Abram has more than borne that out.

Some might read the story of Morris Abram and Vernon Jordan, wrongly, as a parable of black-Jewish relations in America. Here was a Jewish man, Abram, who had aligned himself very publicly with blacks, arguing for equal opportunity, championing their causes, heading up an institution that benefited blacks, saying the right things, all the while making himself a pariah among elements in society who hated both Jews and blacks. But when the time came for him to apply those ideals in the place where he lived, so to speak—his primary job, with his real colleagues—all of that went by the wayside.

Morris Abram had apparently put the work of the civil rights movement in one category and the work of the corporate professional world in another. It was possible for the inhabitants of corporate America to handle the affairs of the black civil rights world, but the inhabitants of the civil rights world could not handle the affairs of white corporate America. In the end, we blacks were "the other," who had to be helped along, who had to be protected from certain depredations, but always "the other" and never true equals.

Abram's response to me that day was exactly in line with what segments of the black community had been saying during that era about blacks and Jews. But what happened next in my life shows the fallacy of imputing Abram's problem, whatever it was, to the Jewish community as a whole. In early 1980, Peter McCullough happened to mention to Robert Strauss, our fellow member on the Xerox board and the former chairman of the Democratic National Committee, that I was going to be in the job market and wanted to come to a law firm.

Strauss was a founding partner of the Dallas-based law firm Akin, Gump, Strauss, Hauer & Feld and was one of the "wise men" of Washington whose counsel has been sought by presidents of both parties. Strauss is Jewish, and he could not have expressed more enthusiasm for having me come on board. At one of our meetings, he said, "Vernon, come over here in the corner. I want to talk to you about something."

I said, "Bob, the last time I went in a corner with you I almost lost my 501(c)3 status." At one point during the Carter campaign in 1976, Bob, who was trying to do everything he could for his man, had asked me to endorse Carter as an individual, and not on behalf of the Urban League, which could not take a formal position on political contests, lest it lose its all-important tax-exempt status. It was a daring thought, but I declined. And I do know that had I said yes, even if there had been no serious fallout from it, Strauss would never have asked me to be his partner, because that would have been a tip-off as to the quality of my mind. Strauss made his pitch to me, and I listened. He knew of my overtures to Paul, Weiss, and said in effect, "Oh, you don't want to do that anyway."

To his credit, and my eternal gratitude, Robert Strauss looked at me and saw that I had the potential to contribute to his firm, even as I transformed myself. He truly valued who I was and took seriously what I had accomplished up until then, and he knew that those skills could be put to a different use in the service of Akin, Gump. By this time I was an experienced corporate director, sitting on several boards. Between all that and my work at the College Fund and the Urban League, I knew and was on a first-name basis with nearly all the major players in corporate America. Strauss was aware of this and thought my relationships could be an asset, especially for a Dallas-based firm with an expanding Washington, D.C. practice.

It was vision and character that set Robert Strauss apart from Morris Abram on this question. He was flexible enough, his mind subtle enough, to see where and how I could fit in. Most important, he didn't demand 100-percent up-front assurances that it would all work out immediately. Too often when blacks are considered for positions in white institutions, the tendency is to focus on the potential downside instead of evidence of possible good outcomes. Even today, in a corporate world more open to blacks than ever, all one has to do is compare the range of schools attended by white associates and partners in major law firms to those attended by black associates and partners, the vast majority of whom must come from the top four or five law schools in the country even to be considered for employment.

Strauss was willing to accept an element of risk, which one is more likely to do with a person one considers an equal. "We'll carry you for a while until you figure all of this out," he said. "Then you'll carry us for a lot longer." His attitude is still all too rare for whites in the private sector. I was greatly impressed with Strauss and took his overtures very much to heart.

THE FALL AND WINTER OF 1980–1981, after I came out of the hospital, were taken up with getting back into my role at the Urban League. Although Shirley and I had grown comfortable in New York, I had an instinctive feeling that Washington would be better for me. The New York firms were very structured, divided into specialized departments. Usually, if you were at one of the big firms, you were in the antitrust group, or the labor group, or the real estate group. You were labeled a mergers-and-acquisitions lawyer or a trusts-and-estates lawyer. It was clear to me that in my situation, given the limits of my experience in the practice of corporate law, I could do better if I were not so structured. The practice had to be tailored around my strengths, which called for a more entrepreneurial and creative approach. I had to be a generalist.

With this in my mind, coupled with Strauss's enthusiasm, by the end of spring I was all but sure that I was going to be a partner at Akin, Gump. My trip to the firm's headquarters in Dallas sealed things for me.

The firm hosted a dinner for me at The Mansion. Jack Hauer, another named partner who was a very well known and respected litigator around town, was the lead host. When we were down to the brandy and cigars, Jack said, "I'd like to ask you a question."

"Sure," I replied.

"You write a column for the *Dallas Times Herald*," he said, referring to the weekly syndicated column, called "To Be Equal," that I published in my capacity as president of the Urban League.

"Yeah."

He said, "It comes out every Wednesday."

"Yeah."

"Well, I want you to know that I read that crap you write every Wednesday, and every Wednesday it makes me want to regurgitate. Having said that, I have two things I want to say to you. The first is that I hope you're going to decide to become my law partner. And when you do become my law partner, I hope you won't stop believing that crap you believe."

I knew then that Akin, Gump was where I wanted to work. Jack's Southern honesty won me right over. Northern whites tend to be secretive about their true racial views, which can lead you astray as you think they are on your side when they really are not. I knew where Jack stood, and at the same time, he was big enough to let me be myself, so long as that self was a good and productive member of his firm.

In the years that followed, I went to Dallas each year to speak to the firm's summer associates, except for a period when I boycotted the event until they hired more blacks for the summer program.

When more black associates began to show up, I went back. Jack insisted on introducing me at these events and would sit and listen to me every time. He became one of my biggest supporters within the firm and without. When I gave a lecture in 1984 at the University of Dallas, Jack and his wife, Mary Lou, were right there in the front row. He came up to me afterward and said, "You know what my problem is with you?"

"What's that, Jack?"

"The more I listen to you, the more I begin to believe that crap you believe."

That spring I made a deal to become a partner at Akin, Gump. It was the best kept secret in town and at the firm. Once again, pretty late in life—I was forty-five—I gained a new career and another mentor in Bob Strauss. On September 9, 1981, there was a public announcement that I was leaving the Urban League for the practice of law at Akin, Gump, Strauss, Hauer & Feld.

THE ANNOUNCEMENT OF MY pending departure from the Urban League came one day after the death of Roy Wilkins. Although Roy had retired from the NAACP, members of the press love a good hook, and they immediately linked Roy's death to my leaving, saying that both events signaled a passing of the torch in the civil rights movement. That did not adequately describe the situation. The torch had been passed before that, and not from one individual to the next but from one generation to another. It was now in the hands of a generation of black Americans who were, for the first time, entering colleges, professional schools, and graduate schools in record numbers. These men and women were able to vote, run for office, and get jobs without fear of blatant discrimination, and they had a greater chance to participate in American life than ever before.

Roy's life and passing were significant to the country because he had had such a hand in making possible the existence of that new generation, one that would set the tone for all generations to follow, each building upon the victories of the previous one. In that respect, the spirit and contributions of Roy Wilkins will live forever.

News of my departure for the private sector drew support and praise from many members of the League, who saw my signing on with Akin, Gump as an accomplishment that reflected well on the Urban League: One of their own was going on to something prestigious, partly on the strength of what he had learned while at the organization. It was all to the good.

There were also some negative comments, though not a lot of that reached my ears, from people who took the view that I had done good, and now all I wanted was to do well. This sentiment came from blacks and whites, to some extent egged on by the media. During my last appearance on the Sunday talk show *Meet the Press* as head of the Urban League, Robert Abernathy of NBC News asked me about my resignation. He said, "So, you're leaving the Urban League to go and make money," as if in the United States of America there was something wrong with that. I responded evenly, in the way viewers have come to expect from those types of shows. I didn't say what I really wanted to say to him, particularly after I'd had the chance to think about the assumptions lying just below the surface of his comment.

Didn't he have a job that paid him, presumably, very well? If he decided he needed more money to take care of his family in the manner of upper-class white men—the way their wives expect them to— it would be his right to change jobs to do that. No one would ever question it seriously. In fact, he would be applauded for it.

If Abernathy decided he had come to the end of the road at NBC and that he wanted to take on other professional challenges, I'm sure he would have been incredulous at anyone's sneering at that very personal judgment. The only difference between him and me was that he was a white man and lived with the expectation of being free to make choices. My skin is black and, therefore, my choices in life were to be limited.

Since the time of my *Meet the Press* interview, the black presence in corporate America has greatly increased. So to a large extent, people are now used to the idea that blacks do other things besides teaching school, preaching, practicing social work, medicine, dentistry, and working for themselves or in government jobs. Even with that, the attitude expressed in the *Meet the Press* interview is alive and well, most annoyingly among some white people who can say the most amazing (and utterly revealing) things to black people, thinking they are entitled to because their hearts are in the right place.

The head of a major foundation once came to me for help in finding a black businessperson to join his board of trustees. I sent him to see a young black executive of a major corporation who I was convinced was on his way up. He went to the executive's office at the top of a New York skyscraper with a panoramic view of the Statue of Liberty and New York harbor, and they had their talk.

Immediately afterward, I got a telephone call from the black executive. "What is the matter with this man you sent over to see me?" he said.

"What happened?"

"We were talking and he asked me, 'What are you doing sitting here in this big office with this great view? Why aren't you in Mississippi helping your people?'"

I flashed back almost twenty years to *Meet the Press*. The two questions were really the same, borne of the same prejudice. Why was I trying to move out of my "place," and why was this black executive already out of his "place"? No white executive would ever be challenged about his decision to be in that job and not devoting his life to leading marches, or working in a soup kitchen or, for that matter, dancing in a Broadway show. It would be assumed and accepted that he was doing what he wanted to do and had the right to do. That is what it means to be white in America, hence the saying, "I'm free, white, and over twenty-one!" We have yet to get to the point that black people are allowed the same unfettered freedom.

As I saw it, back when I left the Urban League, my going to a law firm was a personal decision that in no way signaled a lack of commitment to the progress of black people. As the head of a major black organization, I had been a general in the movement, and now I would be a foot soldier, a private citizen doing what he could within the context of that different role. It is a fact that all blacks who are doing good and honest work—whether for the government, for law firms, for corporations, for newspapers, or as poets and priests—are contributing to the advancement of the black race. Some people, black and white, disagree with that notion, taking the view that only certain jobs or professions can be considered "in the public interest" or in the interests of black people. I do not agree.

For twenty years, I had been on a mission, part of a movement designed to bring black people into full citizenship. What did that mean, if not that blacks on an individual basis would be free to chart their own courses in life—to figure out for themselves what role they were best suited to play, given their talents, interests, and personal responsibilities.

For most of our history, the ideal of "community" drove the black model for leadership and group participation. Blacks were enslaved as a community, we were disenfranchised as a community, we had been terrorized as a community. We responded to all these assaults as a community—a noble and necessary reaction. Community solidarity in the face of oppression makes sense. But what does it mean, particularly when the black community in America is becoming more diverse by the moment—economically, geographically, linguistically, even in terms of religious practice? How can we ignore individual striving and impulse in such a world?

One way—a bad way—is through attempted coercion. All too often, the idea of solidarity is presented as a requirement (on pain of being labeled a traitor) that all blacks must think alike, act alike, and choose from the same narrow set of acceptable aspirations. Strangely enough, those aspirations have often been defined by white people like the NBC correspondent and the head of the foundation who did not think blacks should be business executives without feeling guilty about it (whites who think they know what is best for blacks), and by active white racists who don't believe blacks should have anything at all. Think of black kids who have now characterized wanting to learn to read and do well in school as "acting white." Or think of the idea that some subjects or professions are for whites only. All this works to keep white supremacy right on track: Blacks are supposed to go only a few places, whereas whites are supposed to go anywhere they want.

I admire the story of Ruth Simmons, the president of Brown University, the first black woman to hold that position, who was once asked by an interviewer why she got a Ph.D. in French literature. Her reply was perfect. "Because everything in the world belongs to me," she said. She knew that such a question would never have been asked of a middle-class white woman with the same unspoken implication: This is not for you! Why should anyone suggest that she could not go wherever her mind and talent would take her?

I agree wholeheartedly with Simmons; everything in the world belongs to black people, and there is much in this world. We cannot all lead marches or be the head of a black organization our whole life long. There are 30 million black people in America, and there is a role and function (perhaps even several over the course of a lifetime) for each of us. Someone has to be and wants very much to be the accountant. Another wants to do mergers and acquisitions and has a talent for that. Still another wants to be a lawyer for a while, then switches gears and becomes a writer. That is what the movement I had devoted a good part of my life to was all about: working for the chance to allow these and other things to happen, to remove barriers and let black people listen to that voice inside that tells them what their honorable life's pursuit should be. No black movement worth its salt would ever attempt to still that voice.

I left the Urban League and started at Akin, Gump in January 1982, in their new Washington office. Bob Strauss was right. There were things for me to figure out at the very beginning. Clients did not just magically fly into my office window, and there were early frustrations. It took a little time, but with the support of Strauss and my other partners, I found a comfortable place for myself. We have done very well together over the years.

CHAPTER 15

FAMILY MATTERS

AFTER I ACCEPTED the partnership at Akin, Gump, Shirley and I decided initially that we would keep our primary residence in New York and that I would commute to Washington during the week. A few years earlier, we had moved from our home in the suburbs to live in Manhattan. Vickee's graduation from high school had removed a serious rationale for staying in Westchester, and so we left. This was something of a trade-off for Shirley. Moving into the city meant that she had to give up driving, but it freed her to enjoy the convenience, excitement, and, above all else, the shopping that only Manhattan has to offer. Shirley grew to love Manhattan and the life she was able to build for herself there. It had truly become our home.

But with my new position, we now had a stake in Washington, and to make travel between the two cities easy for Shirley, I bought a van specially outfitted for her. It had a ramp that allowed us to push her wheelchair up to the van's entrance, where it was an easy matter for her to slide into a chair already on board. We installed a captain's table, and Shirley and her girlfriends played bridge as they rode around town or on trips back and forth to D.C. Her drivers took her anywhere she wanted to go.

Multiple sclerosis is a disease of the brain. During its course, the coverings of the nerves are gradually destroyed. MS can affect any part of the brain, and as a result, the disease takes different turns in different individuals—some experience problems with their eyes, others with their motor skills, or a combination of symptoms can result. To complicate things further, there are times when the symptoms are more severe than others. It is, in a sense, unpredictable. During some periods, with no discernible trigger, Shirley was able to walk just using a cane. Then, inevitably, her condition would deteriorate. In the 1970s, the intervals of relatively free movement grew shorter and shorter, until Shirley generally became confined to a wheelchair.

Through all of this, Shirley remained upbeat about life. This is not to say that there were not difficult moments. Chronic illness is not easy, but she dealt with it by keeping active, and there was much in our lives indeed. When I was at the Urban League she attended our annual conventions and hosted lunches for the Ladies Auxiliary, becoming a well-known figure on her motorized scooter greeting everyone. She also became a spokeswoman for research into the causes and possible cures for MS, writing articles and putting a human face on the problem.

Just as the previous twenty years had transformed my life, they had transformed Shirley's as well. She too was something of a pioneer. As I became involved with more corporate boards and eventually moved into corporate America myself, a good amount of our socializing—for business and for pleasure—was done in all-white, or almost all-white, settings. Shirley was thrust into positions that few black women had ever experienced, just as I was going places where few black men had ever gone.

She had to learn how to deal with (or politely not deal with) being taken as a spokeswoman for the race at dinner parties where we might be the only blacks in attendance. This was quite a journey for a woman who had started life in the segregated South. I had something of an advantage because from a very early age I had the chance to observe white people in social settings during my mother's parties and because I had gone off to a white college. Even without this, Shirley was a natural, and she handled herself with great aplomb through every variation in my career that was, in a real sense, a variation in her own.

She was very conscious of her public role, and she wanted to do the best she could, understanding that appearance counts. This realization provided a very happy coincidence with another of Shirley's lifelong passions: buying clothes. The wife of the head of the Urban League, of the corporate director, of the partner in a law firm, has to dress well. And Shirley threw herself into the effort with an enthusiasm that, at times, made my head spin.

The saleswomen in stores all around Manhattan knew her very well. Until late in her life, when the medicine she took caused her weight to fluctuate, she was a perfect size eight. She would go into stores and try on the latest fashions, which always fit her very well. When combined with her beautiful skin, she made a stunning appearance. Sometimes she managed to leave without buying anything. More often she did not.

This became a running joke in our family. Whenever I came home from a trip, I always took Shirley and Vickee out to dinner. Shirley would come out wearing some outfit I had never seen.

"Is that new?" I would ask, knowing the answer.

"This? No," Shirley would reply, knowing I knew better.

"I've never seen it before."

"Oh, you have. You just don't remember," she'd say, or "I've had it a while. I just haven't worn it."

Vickee, who loved to shop with her mother, was in on it as well. They managed to keep some of their shopping excursions secret, the two women of the house ganging up on the lone male. Sometimes the solidarity would break when Vickee, in the grip of some teen rage at her mother, would tattle on Shirley, "Daddy! Mommy's been shopping again!"

My serving on corporate boards added another dimension to Shirley's life. Traveling on board business, I was able to take her all over the world, in her wheelchair, doing things together that we would never have been able to do otherwise. My colleagues were just fabulous to us. On one trip to Brazil for Xerox, we were on a sight-seeing tour, and all the spouses took turns pushing Shirley's wheelchair. Later at dinner, Peter McCullough, who was supposed to be in the receiving line as the chairman of the company, refused to take his place until Shirley got up the stairs and could join the assembly.

On a trip to Williamsburg, Virginia, for the Rockefeller Foundation, Elaine Wolfensohn, the wife of James Wolfensohn (who is now the president of the World Bank), wheeled Shirley around and made her feel right at home. Elaine had a friend back in London with multiple sclerosis, so she understood Shirley's predicament very well.

There were other moments on trips throughout the world that we could scarcely have dreamed of when we were a young couple just starting out, hoping our check to the diaper service didn't bounce. Once, in Holland, we were to have dinner in a castle. All the corporate directors and their spouses were set to go there by bus, which posed a problem for Shirley. So they gave us a car to make things easier, while everyone else traveled as planned. We went along and made it to the castle ahead of the others. The bridge was down, and as we drove across the moat, with the banners flying, all the trumpets on the ramparts and on the bridge began to blow—the perfect entrance, I thought, for the two of us. Not bad for two black kids from Atlanta, Georgia.

We went everywhere until about 1983, when long-distance travel became too difficult for Shirley. After that, our socializing was mainly close to home. In December 1985, as we did every year, we went to the Christmas celebration hosted by the Boulé, a black fraternal organization. Social events like this were at once happy and sad because there was dancing. One of the many cruel aspects of MS is that it took dancing away from Shirley. Despite her limitations, she was very much the socialite and would not have missed those occasions for the world, even though it was a stark reminder of what she could no longer do.

That holiday season of 1985, Shirley busied herself even more than usual getting everything ready for Christmas, with every package wrapped well before the middle of December. It was almost as if she knew that the time of her departure was at hand.

The call came to me in Washington that Shirley had been taken to the hospital. Periodic hospital visits had become fairly common for her, so I did not immediately think she was seriously ill. I arrived in New York to find that things were much worse than I thought: Shirley had gone into cardiac arrest. Two weeks later, on December 27, she died.

Multiple sclerosis is not itself a fatal disease, but people sometimes die from complications that arise from it. We knew that Shirley had contracted an illness that had to be managed for the rest of our lives, which I thought—hoped—would be a long time. Instead, our life together, our marriage, was cut short. Marriage is a mystery, occasionally to the people who are in it, but at all times to those outside the partnership. The shared struggles, triumphs, hopes, tragedies, and vulnerabilities create a unique culture of two—a bond. The death of a spouse, an involuntary rupture, is a trauma that every couple determined to go the distance knows one of them will inevitably experience. Shirley was only forty-eight years old. There is not much to be said, except that my sense of loss was immense, too large to take in or to adequately describe.

Gardner Taylor gave Shirley's eulogy and spoke of her good humor, her strength, and her perseverance in the face of all that life had thrown her way. I thought back to that day so many years earlier, when I had talked to my mother, telling her the hard news about Shirley's illness. I had felt so keenly the unfairness of life, sharper and more piercing than anything I had ever known. The truth, of course, is that I was just an innocent then. I really did not know the half of it.

Twenty-seven years had passed since I had promised Shirley behind Founders Library at Howard University that if she married me, I would be somebody one day. As low as I felt at that moment, I felt some small satisfaction knowing that she believed I had kept my promise.

My mother was traveling in Europe when all this unfolded and was unable to make it back in time for the funeral. She felt bad about this, as though she had let me down in my time of need, which, of course, she had not. When she arrived, she actually had to find me, as I was wandering around Manhattan aimlessly, needing to get myself to some point of equilibrium.

In the weeks that followed, one thing was clear: With Shirley gone, there was no point in remaining in New York. We had come to the city together, as I advanced in a profession that she had watched me begin and then end. From the law student hero-worshiping the civil rights attorneys who visited Howard Law School, to her young husband making $35 a week in the civil rights law firm, to the middle-aged corporate lawyer making considerably more, Shirley had seen and been part of the arc of my life. The root having been pulled, there was no reason for me to stay. I sold our apartment and moved permanently to Washington.

In November 1986, I married Ann Dibble Cook, then a professor at the University of Chicago and director of social services at the University of Chicago Medical Center. Ann had been reared in Tuskegee, Alabama, where her father was a prominent physician, and was educated at Northfield, Vassar, and the University of Chicago. We were married in a small family ceremony, in the home that I had purchased in Washington. Our marriage brought together our two families, and my friend Reverend Gardner Taylor performed the ceremony in the presence of all of our children. It was a happy time and a new beginning.

THAT MY MOTHER WAS TRAVELING when Shirley died was not a surprise. In the twilight of her years, she committed herself to seeing the world. Actually, she had gotten the travel bug much earlier. When I took my first trip overseas to Israel in 1967, she and Shirley met me in London when I was on my way back home. She loved being overseas and by the 1980s was really in the position to do that pretty much at will. My brother Windsor had joined her in the business, and he took care of things while she was away. Through Henderson Travel, one of the oldest black travel agencies in the country, she signed on for package tours with groups or planned vacations with friends.

Then there was the social club she started with a group of women in Atlanta. They christened themselves "The Fourteen New Yorkers," although not one of them was from New York, and I don't know how many of them besides Mama had ever been to that city. I suppose they were hoping to sound sophisticated. Going to dinner and socializing at one another's homes were their principal activities.

Of course, the St. Paul AME Church remained at the core of her existence. It was her rock, providing her with a sense of community and purpose beyond her catering business. She went each Sunday, as she had done for six decades. She was also a trustee of the church and was very much involved in everything that went on there. One of her proudest moments was when she received St. Paul's Mother of the Year award in 1984.

Mama kept up with me, too. No one felt more deeply about all that had happened since I left home to go to college. Every turn of my career was noted and memorialized in the clippings she kept and shared with her friends. During my time as the head of the Urban League, she was a fixture at our conferences and was well known among the members. When I talked to her about leaving the Urban League, she was characteristically supportive. As much as she relished the role I played there, she understood about moving on and making changes.

My life as a corporate director gave her other opportunities to see what she and my father had wrought. She loved coming to shareholder meetings of the various companies where I was a director and was very proud to see me operating in that milieu. During times when Shirley was too sick to travel, Mama would be my date at the corporate dinners, basking in the attention she received and no doubt marveling at the road she had traveled, too. The dinner at an American Express annual meeting in Atlanta, at the very old and exclusive Piedmont Driving Club, was a special treat. That place had once been off-limits to blacks, except in a serving capacity, and there we were—very much at ease, knowing that our presence was a repudiation of the insult of exclusion.

On a personal level, it was a nice change of pace for her, as a caterer, to sit and be served by others. Even then, my mother could not help notice the way things proceeded, how the food compared to hers, how the waiters and bartenders conducted themselves. She got to see her business from another vantage point, and she enjoyed the view.

In 1987, I was a director at RJR Nabisco, and we were on the verge of doing a multi-billion-dollar deal, one of the largest in history. I was in Atlanta for the meeting. Afterward, I stopped off at my mother's business. I walked in to find her decorating a wedding cake. In 1958, she had gone to the Wilton School of Cake Decorating in Chicago so that when she catered weddings she wouldn't have to buy the cake from another company. She was very good at it. I said, "Mama, you can't tell anybody this, but I've just come back from a meeting where we've agreed to sell the company for twenty-five billion dollars. It's a very, very big deal."

She kept working, squeezing the tubes, at first with no expression. Then she flashed a smile that was just pure joy, and started to laugh softly, all the while continuing to work. She didn't say a word.

I chuckled a little myself and asked, "What are you laughing about?"

"I'm laughing because I'm so happy that my Vernon Junior is involved in a business deal worth twenty-five billion dollars," she replied, and kept decorating her cake.

I'LL MEET YOU IN WINSTON-SALEM." It was my mother on the line. I always told her when I was going to get an honorary degree or deliver a commencement address. At first I only invited her to events if they were in or near Georgia, thinking she would have little interest in going too far away. I was wrong. I soon found out she would go almost anywhere. Even when I did not ask, she would invite herself. "I've got my ticket," she'd say. I loved having her come, and it was amusing to have her announce that she was meeting me at some far-off venue (or show up there) just to listen to me make a speech.

She came to hear me once at Friendship Baptist Church in Atlanta, where the woman introducing me had apparently been given an unabridged version of my résumé. After giving the general information about me, instead of just noting that I had received a number of honorary degrees, she started to read through the entire list. The minister, seeing where this was headed, intervened, making a joke of it. "We'll never get out of here if you do that. So sit down," he said, and she did.

When the talk was over, I took my mother to Morrison's Cafeteria, a place she loved, for lunch. "Their vegetables are always fresh," she said, ever the cook judging the food. As we walked in, I said, "Mama, did you hear that lady? She was going to stand there and read out all twenty-three of my honorary degrees."

"It would've been just fine with me," my mother said, without cracking a smile. She didn't care how long it took. She wanted to hear them all read aloud.

In the summer of 1978, I received an honorary degree from Princeton University on a Tuesday, one from Harvard University on a Thursday and one from Dartmouth College the following Monday. My mother attended each commencement. The following Tuesday morning we were standing at LaGuardia Airport as she prepared to go home.

She said to me, "You know, I'm really very pleased. But I'm not surprised, because it's what I expected. I am so pleased that if the Lord called me right now, I'd take the wings of a dove and fly away and be at rest."

Here was a woman who had put so much into preparing me for life without ever knowing exactly how it would turn out. She "expected" it, she said. But what exactly did she expect? The roles I was playing did not exist for people like me back when she brought me home from Grady Hospital to the University Homes housing project in the middle of the Great Depression. We were not from a family or race that could expect any specific result from our efforts. Neither she nor I had been born in a time when it was reasonable to even dream that all that had happened to me could happen. And yet it had. I suppose what my mother expected all along was just that good things would come to us if we moved with faith. With a lot of determined effort and faith, good things would happen. "If you trust Him, He will take care of you." She really believed that.

ALTHOUGH IT IS BETTER THAN THE ALTERNATIVE, watching your parents grow old, which I did during the 1980s, is very hard. The once seemingly invincible people begin to show physical weaknesses. Things they could do with ease, like driving a car or cooking for themselves, gradually become more difficult until the parent-child roles are reversed and they become the objects of late-night worry and concern.

Because my mother and father were divorced, my relationship with them during the final period of their lives proceeded on two different tracks. My father had remarried not long after he and my mother were divorced, and quite frankly, I had never been overly fond of his second wife. There was no hostility between us, but it made keeping a connection to him more difficult than if he had been single or, of course, if my parents had remained together.

Despite that, I always felt close to my father. Although he was extremely proud of my accomplishments and boasted to others about them, he was not one for flying all over the country to watch me do things, as my mother was. Instead, I saw him whenever I came home to Atlanta. He loved to pick me up at the airport, until his driving skills began to deteriorate.

When he retired from his job in the U.S. Army Post Office in 1977, he took the word "retirement" literally and spent most of his days watching ball games on television and keeping up with sports. He was very content to do that.

My father's wife died before he did, which was a very great trauma for him. We didn't know it at the time, but he was gravely ill, too ill in fact to attend his wife's funeral. That was when we realized how serious things were. It turned out that he had lung cancer, and he did not have long to live.

I gave the eulogy at my father's funeral in 1987, and spoke of his basic goodness and decency, of how he had been a calm and steady presence throughout my childhood. The role of "father" may be more difficult to define than that of "mother," and it is hard for some men to know how to do it, even though it is, perhaps, the most important role a man can play, shepherding children into adulthood, giving them the benefits of your experiences. I really believe, under our circumstances in this country, that black children need the support of strong fathers as well as mothers. I was lucky to have had a father who believed that as well, and I tried to say that day how grateful I was for that.

As for my mother, her retirement from the catering business in 1990, when she was eighty-three years old, was the end of an era. By that time, she had become a much beloved figure in Atlanta. She served on the Georgia Commission on Aging. She won many awards and was an item in the Atlanta newspapers.

For some people, the end of their working days really becomes the end of their lives. I think that held true for my mother to a great degree. She was never really the same after she stopped working, which she really did not want to do. Failing eyesight and other health problems made continuing in her very arduous trade difficult. In many ways, the different responses of my father and mother to retirement were very much in keeping with their way of going through life. My father left his job and never really looked back. It had not been as much a part of his identity as my mother's work had been for her. For my mother, the loss of the daily routine was also the loss of what had sparked her existence for over five decades.

I worried about her driving. The Atlanta she had first encountered as a young woman, and that I had known growing up, was long gone. Now there were six-lane highways, endless traffic jams, a soaring crime rate. Life was much more complicated, and I worried about her living alone. Windsor kept a vigilant eye on her, but she was always independent and wanted to be in control.

We went along in this way until a series of, at first, small strokes, and then one very serious one incapacitated her. She lost the ability to talk and could only use her hands for communication. Of course she needed around-the-clock care. So she went to live in Wesley Woods, a nursing home near the campus of Emory University.

It hurt immensely to see my mother unable to do things for herself. This woman who had been so dynamic, a literal force of nature, now lay virtually still on her bed, perceiving the outside world but unable to say with words what she was thinking.

Sometimes words were not needed. When Vickee (by this time married, with two children) visited, she would put her sons Jordan and Brodie on my mother's bed. Mama knew exactly who they were, and what they were to her, and that made her very happy. She would touch them lovingly and her quick breathing conveyed the power of her love and sense of connection to them. She knew her life was winding down and that these boys were her own living projections into the future.

Besides the difficulty of watching her physical decline, I knew that I was about to lose my greatest friend and principal counselor throughout life. Speaking with her about what I was going to do next or how to respond in a crisis was such an integral part of my existence that I dreaded the prospect of days when I could not do that. The last time I consulted my mother about a major decision was in 1992. I was serving as the chairman of the transition team for President-elect Bill Clinton, the first, and to date only, time a black person has served in that capacity.

I had to decide whether I wanted to be a part of the new administration myself. Working in government had never appealed to me, but these circumstances were special. I was acutely aware that my blackness created some expectations about my serving in the cabinet. As far as we have come, many blacks still thrill at the sound of "the first" one of our own to hold this position or that position—and rightly so.

In the end, that was not enough for me. Early on, I told the president-elect that I did not want to serve in his cabinet. I flew down to Little Rock to tell him that face-to-face. There were two reasons: First, I was very proud to serve as the transition chairman, and I thought I could do a better job if it was clear that I was not in contention for any position. Second, I had done pro bono work for the first twenty years of my career, and I was not prepared to do that again. For me, going to work in government would be in essence working pro bono.

My thoughts on this matter were firm, but I was also very mindful of that fact that I was speaking not merely to the president-elect of the United States but, just as important, to a man who had been my friend for many years. There was no way for me to know where my decision might take our friendship. Later, I would find that it strengthened our bond because instead of being in the official cabinet, I was very much in the "kitchen cabinet," and thus able to give the president advice unclouded by other considerations.

I was fortunate, in addition to advising the president, to continue in advisory roles to corporations, foundations, nonprofit organizations, and the civil rights movement. In the twenty years since leaving the National Urban League, I have discovered that I can play a valuable role on the outside, one that is just as necessary as the roles played by those within an organization or government. By moving from "active status" to "emeritus status," I became a resource, a person for other people to call upon to evaluate a situation and give unbiased and honest advice. This was not a role that I chose to assume, but it came to me naturally, because I knew about so many different worlds: organizing, fund-raising, corporate governance, national politics. My various experiences had allowed me to become, to many people—white, black, old, young—a confidant, one who acts with discretion and is able, when needed, to help others view their situations in a different light. I enjoy this role, and I am grateful to have been able to play it.

AFTER I LEFT LITTLE ROCK, I flew to Atlanta to see my mother. The die had been cast, but I needed some affirmation from her that I had done the right thing. One of my greatest frustrations was that although she knew I was heading the transition and understood the historic nature of that, she could not participate in it with me, as she had done in every other phase of my life.

As always on these visits, I held her hand as I caught her up on everything that was going on in my life. I said I had gone to Little Rock and told the president-elect that I would not serve in his Cabinet. I said I thought I had done the right thing. At that moment, her hands grasped mine excitedly, and I immediately recognized her signal for happiness.

Until the very end, my mother was in my corner. As much as I relied on her for support, thinking she would have the answer, she trusted my judgment about my course in life every bit as much as I valued her counsel. I think she believed she had taught me well. I left her that day very acutely aware that our time together on earth was coming to a close. Later that year, she slipped into a coma, from which she never awoke.

Although I am not certain I strictly believe in life after death (Reverend Gardner Taylor and I have discussed this often), I do feel that my mother and father are still with me in some fashion. In their own way, they had each stood up against a society that sought to crush or ridicule my dreams, and I learned from them not to be discouraged by people like Robert F. Maddox and his mocking incantation, "Vernon can read." Their lives stick in my mind as examples of the true genius of black Americans—making do with what you have against seemingly insurmountable odds, pressing forward always, and passing on a sense of optimism and faith to the next generation. Whatever good that I am, have done, or will do, I owe to their influence. The rest is all on me.

EPILOGUE

IN THE WINTER OF 2001 I received news that I had been chosen by the NAACP to receive its highest honor: the Spingarn Medal. The award is named after Joel E. Spingarn, who was the chairman of the NAACP board of directors in 1914. Since 1915, it has been given to "the man or woman of African descent and American citizenship who shall have made the highest achievement during the preceding year or years in any honorable field of human endeavor." Eighty-six other distinguished Americans had been given the medal before me: men and women such as W.E.B. Du Bois, George Washington Carver, Mary MacLeod Bethune, my friend Medgar Evers (posthumously), my boss and mentor Roy Wilkins, and so many others who made outstanding contributions to America and, indeed, the world.

The honor meant everything to me, not only because the NAACP chose to place me in such illustrious company, but because it closed a circle in my life. I thought back to the beginning of my professional career in 1960, working in association with the NAACP through Mr. Hollowell's office, and to 1961, when I became part of the NAACP family proper as the organization's Georgia field director. I looked it up. In those years, the poet Langston Hughes and my friend and mentor the psychologist Kenneth Clark received the Spingarn Medal. The thought that forty years later I would join them on the list of recipients was both humbling and gratifying almost beyond description. But I had to have words. The award would be presented at the NAACP's Ninety-Second Convention in New Orleans in July 2001. That ceremony would mark the last official act of the convention.

Recipients of the Spingarn Medal are allowed to choose the person who will formally present it to them. For me, one name rose quickly above all others: Reverend Gardner Taylor. Reverend Taylor has been present at the most significant moments (both sad and joyous) of my life. He performed the eulogy for Shirley, and he married me to Ann. He officiated at Vickee and Barry's wedding, and he christened two of our grandchildren, Jordan and Dwight. No one else was better suited to the task of standing with me at the apex of my career.

As I began to think seriously about what I wanted to say, I realized that it was most important to acknowledge that I had not come alone to the place where I could receive the Spingarn Medal. I thought of my mother, my strong, determined, driven, and always loving mother. How she would have loved this! Of course she would have said, "I expected it," but her joy would have been unlimited. My father, who took me to the NAACP Emancipation Day celebrations, how he would have loved it, too! They had pushed, shoved, pulled, and loved me to the point that put me on the road to New Orleans.

The first twenty-seven years of my professional life had been shared with Shirley, who gave me great love, support, humor, and, most important of all, Vickee, the apple of my eye. They were my family, my world, during those early days with Mr. Hollowell, Ms. Hurley, and the NAACP. Both of them saw me through every one of my varied incarnations as a soldier in the civil rights movement. Certainly, part of the medal belonged to them.

When multiple sclerosis took Shirley away, I was blessed to marry Ann, who in addition to bringing great love, strength, discipline, culture, and guidance into my life, brought her wonderful children, Mercer, Toni, and Janice. They have in turn brought spouses into our family, Cindy, Dwight, and Richard, and their own children, giving Ann and me a total of eight grandchildren. They have all shared in and enriched my life immensely.

I saw this as a time to remember my civil rights family as well. I wanted to call the names of my former bosses, mentors, friends—recalling their support, the times we had seen, the memories we had shared. But I thought it important not simply to go to New Orleans to tell war stories. My message had to be about the past and about the future.

I thought of all we had accomplished just in my lifetime. When I was a young man, aching to play a role on the public stage, there were too few models of leadership for me to follow. A preacher, a teacher, perhaps a lawyer—these were the main avenues open to people with dreams like mine. Had I been born in 1960, when my professional life began, so many more roads would be open to me today. There are so many more ways now to make a contribution to the uplift of black people. Since the 1960s, we have created five new leadership classes within the black community. A Vernon Jordan born in 1960 could be a member of the newly created class of black elected officials. That class did not exist before the civil rights movement. He could become a part of a corporation, as an executive, manager, member of the board of directors. If corporate life held no attraction, he could lead one of the many community-based organizations that work at the grassroots level within the black community. Another option would be to head up a traditionally white institution—a foundation, university, or health-care organization. Finally, if a forty-one-year-old Vernon Jordan wanted to work for himself, he could join the new class of black entrepreneurs who are running businesses far more varied than the mom-and-pop stores that have traditionally served a primarily black clientele.

All this came to mind as I pondered how to put together an appropriate message to deliver. The phrase "Look what we have wrought" came to mind. There is a tendency these days to focus on what we have not yet accomplished without pausing to think of how much we have accomplished thus far. It is important not to lose sight of our victories. It is only moral to pause and reflect on what our brains, blood, sweat, tears, tired feet, and beat-up heads—the sacrificed lives of our loved ones—have bought for the generations to come.

What I most wanted to say out loud, though, is that we are a great people. Black people have done wonderful things for this country (saved its soul, in fact), and we have been an example to the world in the process. That should never be forgotten, even as we continue to press ahead, in our many and varied ways, toward our future. If we did so much when we had so little, think of what we can do now that we have so much more. That was the message I most wanted to convey.

That evening in New Orleans was everything I hoped it would be. There, surrounded by my family and friends, by colleagues whom I'd known from the movement, and by the spirit of those no longer with me, I said what I wanted to say, and felt at peace.

ACKNOWLEDGMENTS

FOR A VERY LONG TIME I had given some thought to writing about my experiences growing up, linking them to my days in the civil rights movement. After many fits and starts, how to do it crystallized one Saturday afternoon in June 1997 in Washington, D.C.

I stopped in at Politics and Prose, a bookstore on Connecticut Avenue. While browsing in the biography section, I saw a blue book titled *Thomas Jefferson and Sally Hemings: An American Controversy* by Annette Gordon-Reed. I pulled it off the shelf and stood there, and read the book's preface. I knew immediately that I had found the person I wanted to help me write my own book.

The following Monday morning I called New York Law School, where Annette is a professor, and left a message on her answering machine. I introduced myself and asked her if she would give me a call, which she did that afternoon.

After telling her that I was impressed with her work, I said, "I have something I want to say to you. One, I am a devotee of Thomas Jefferson. Two, I am in love with Sally Hemings." We had a good laugh about that. We arranged to meet in New York City, where I told Annette that I wanted to write my memoirs and that I wanted her to help me do it. She said yes to the idea, and we have been partners and friends ever since. This book is a reflection of that fact. I thank Annette Gordon-Reed for agreeing to travel with me on my journey.

This book bears the stamp of the Perseus Books Group, of which PublicAffairs is a member. Frank Pearl, my friend and the chairman of Perseus, has my heartfelt gratitude for introducing me to Peter

Osnos, the publisher and CEO of PublicAffairs, where I was allowed and encouraged to write the book I wanted to write—the one I felt most needed to be written. Peter deserves credit for needling and prodding us to give more when we thought we had given all, thus contributing to the book's final incarnation. Paul Golob, our editor, brought his fine mind, gentle manner, and good humor to the enterprise. Working with one author is tough; working with two at a time is even tougher. Paul's patience, diligence, and keen eye for detail, improved the quality of our work. We owe him a great deal. David Patterson, Paul's assistant, was on the case whenever we needed him, providing critical help in getting the project finished when it needed to be finished. Publicity director Gene Taft and marketing manager Nina D'Amario were also especially helpful to me in bringing this project to completion.

I could not have written this book without the indispensable help of my two executive assistants, Gayle Laughlin in Washington and Jeannie Sotomayor in New York. They have been loyal and patient and have earned my deepest gratitude.

Although these are my memoirs, others offered help in putting this work together: my daughter, Vickee Jordan Adams; Griffin Bell; Leslie Dunbar; John Hope Franklin; T. Herman Graves; Jesse Hill; Richard Holbrooke; Donald Hollowell; my brother, Windsor Jordan; Herman Russell; Reverend Gardner C. Taylor; Frank Thomas; and Judge Horace Ward. We are very grateful for all their assistance.

Finally, this book was written by two people with families to whom we are greatly attached. Our work could not have been completed without the support of Annette's husband, Robert Reed, and the forbearance of their children, Susan and Gordon. I also want to thank my wife, Ann, for putting up with my moods as I waded through the uncharted waters of writing a book. We hope we have done all our friends and family members proud.

INDEX

PublicAffairs is a new nonfiction publishing house and a tribute to the standards, values, and flair of three persons who have served as mentors to countless reporters, writers, editors, and book people of all kinds, including me.

I. F. Stone, proprietor of *I. F. Stone's Weekly*, combined a commitment to the First Amendment with entrepreneurial zeal and reporting skill and became one of the great independent journalists in American history. At the age of eighty, Izzy published *The Trial of Socrates*, which was a national bestseller. He wrote the book after he taught himself ancient Greek.

Benjamin C. Bradlee was for nearly thirty years the charismatic editorial leader of *The Washington Post*. It was Ben who gave the *Post* the range and courage to pursue such historic issues as Watergate. He supported his reporters with a tenacity that made them fearless, and it is no accident that so many became authors of influential, best-selling books.

Robert L. Bernstein, the chief executive of Random House for more than a quarter century, guided one of the nation's premier publishing houses. Bob was personally responsible for many books of political dissent and argument that challenged tyranny around the globe. He is also the founder and was the longtime chair of Human Rights Watch, one of the most respected human rights organizations in the world.

·　　·　　·

For fifty years, the banner of Public Affairs Press was carried by its owner Morris B. Schnapper, who published Gandhi, Nasser, Toynbee, Truman, and about 1,500 other authors. In 1983 Schnapper was described by *The Washington Post* as "a redoubtable gadfly." His legacy will endure in the books to come.

Peter Osnos, *Publisher*